Official
Cambridge
Exam
Preparation

COMPLETE

Key
for Schools

Teacher's Book

A2

WITH
DOWNLOADABLE
RESOURCE PACK

Rod Fricker

Cambridge University Press
www.cambridge.org/elt

Cambridge Assessment English
www.cambridgeenglish.org

Information on this title: www.cambridge.org/9781108539418
© Cambridge University Press and UCLES 2019

First published 2019
20 19 18 17 16 15 14 13 12 11 10 9 8 7 6 5 4 3 2 1

Printed in Great Britain by CPI Group (UK) Ltd, Croydon CRO 4YY
A catalogue record for this publication is available from the British Library
ISBN 978-1-108-53941-8 Teacher's Book with Downloadable Resource Pack

Contents

CAMBRIDGE

Official Cambridge Exam Preparation

DEAR TEACHERS

I'm delighted that you've chosen our official preparation materials to prepare for a Cambridge English Qualification.

We take great pride in the fact that our materials draw on the expertise of a whole team of writers, teachers, assessors and exam experts. These are materials that you can really trust.

Our preparation materials are unique in many ways:

- They combine the skills and knowledge of the teams at Cambridge Assessment English, who create the tests, and the teams at Cambridge University Press, who create the English Language Teaching materials.

- They draw upon the experience of millions of previous exam candidates – where they succeed and where they have difficulties. We target exercises and activities precisely at these areas so that you can actively 'learn' from previous test takers' mistakes.

- Every single task in our materials has been carefully checked to be an accurate reflection of what test takers find in the test.

In addition, we listen to what you tell us at every stage of the development process. This allows us to design the most user-friendly courses, practice tests and supplementary training. We create materials using in-depth knowledge, research and practical understanding. Prepare for Cambridge English Qualifications with confidence in the knowledge that you have the best materials available to support you on your way to success.

We wish you the very best on your journey with us.

With kind regards,

Pamela Baxter
Director
Cambridge Exams Publishing

PS. If you have any feedback at all on our support materials for exams, please write to us at cambridgeexams@cambridge.org

The Complete Exam Journey

The unique exam journey in *Complete Key for Schools* allows learners to build their confidence and develop their skills as they progress through each unit, ensuring they are ready on exam day. Along the journey there are ...

Full reading, listening, writing and speaking exam tasks in every unit with step by step preparation exercises to ensure students have the skills necessary to understand and do the exam task.

Exam advice boxes with up-to-date tips which are placed before every exam task in every unit, so students can apply the tips as they do the task.

Opportunities to fine tune and practise each exam task, confident in the knowledge that the materials are checked by the same team who writes the exams.

Extra practice sections for writing and speaking exam tasks at the back of the book with preparation exercises and model exam tasks for students to follow.

Exercises targeting common A2 Key problem areas, using data from the Cambridge Learner Corpus, so students can overcome language areas of difficulty in time for the exam.

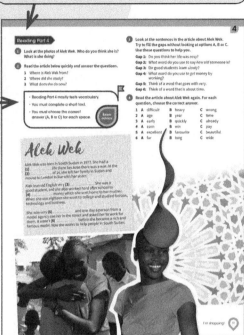

Student's Book overview

All *Key for Schools* full listening, reading, speaking and writing exam tasks have topics specifically chosen for teenagers.

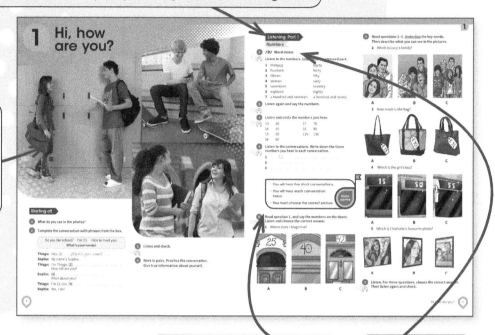

Eye-catching images in the *Starting off* section at the beginning of each unit get students interested in the unit topic.

Brightly designed *Exam advice* boxes precede all exam tasks in every unit.

Relevant pronunciation points clearly link to input language.

Clearly flagged, brightly designed grammar rules boxes explain the key grammar points.

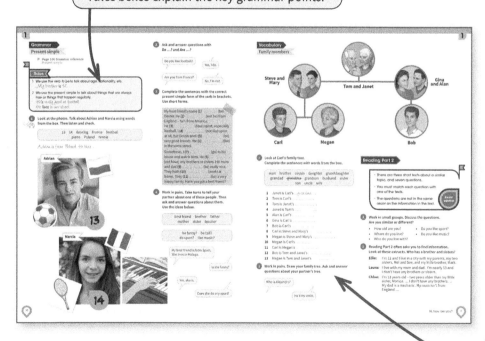

Communicative speaking activities encourage topic discussion.

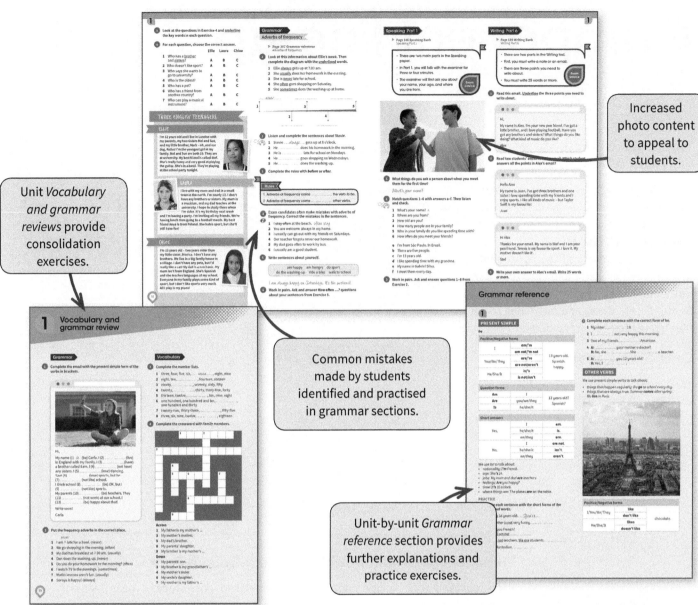

Unit *Vocabulary and grammar reviews* provide consolidation exercises.

Common mistakes made by students identified and practised in grammar sections.

Unit-by-unit *Grammar reference* section provides further explanations and practice exercises.

Increased photo content to appeal to students.

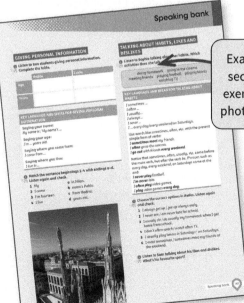

Exam task *Speaking bank* section includes practice exercises, useful language, photos and model answers.

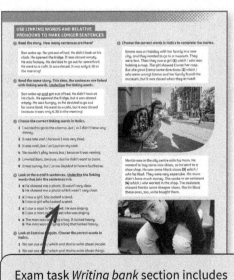

Extra grammar and vocabulary exercises for students organised by topic and language area can be found online.

Exam task *Writing bank* section includes useful language, practice exercises and model exam answers.

Component line-up

Workbook without answers with Audio Download

The activities in the Workbook consolidate the language presented in the Student's Book. It also includes extra exam practice with exam advice boxes.

12 pages of Vocabulary Extra consolidate topic vocabulary taught in each unit in the Student's Book.

Students can access and download the audio files using the code in the book.

Online Workbook

The Online Workbook is a digital version of the print Workbook and allows you to track your students' progress, highlighting areas of strength and weakness for ongoing performance improvement.

Teacher's Book with Downloadable Resource Pack

The Teacher's Book includes step-by-step activities for each stage of the lesson, with answer keys, background information, extra activities and photocopiable audioscripts. It also includes unit target vocabulary word lists with two vocabulary practice activities per unit. The Teacher's Book also provides access to:

- **The Class Audio**
- **Extra teacher photocopiable resources**
- **Speaking videos**

Test Generators

The test generator allows teachers to build their own tests for each unit, term and end-of-year assessment. They are available at two levels: standard and plus.

Presentation Plus

Presentation Plus is easy-to-use, interactive classroom presentation software that helps you deliver effective and engaging lessons. It includes the Student's Book and Workbook content.

A2 Key for Schools content and overview

Part/Timing	Content	Exam focus
1 **Reading and Writing** **1 hour**	**Part 1:** Discrete three-option multiple choice questions on six short texts. **Part 2:** Matching. There are three short texts with seven items. Candidates are asked to decide which text an item refers to. **Part 3:** Three-option multiple choice. Candidates read a text and are asked to choose the correct answer from five multiple-choice questions. **Part 4:** Three-option multiple-choice cloze. A text is followed by six questions. Candidates select the correct word from each question to complete the text. **Part 5:** Open cloze. Candidates complete gaps in one or two short texts. **Part 6:** Writing – short message **Part 7:** Writing – story	**Part 1:** Candidates focus on overall understanding of emails, notices and messages. **Part 2:** Candidates read for specific information and detailed comprehension. **Part 3:** Candidates read for detailed understanding and main ideas. **Part 4:** Candidates read and identify the appropriate word. **Part 5:** Candidates read and identify the appropriate word with the focus on grammar. **Part 6:** Candidates write a communicative note or email of at least 25 words. **Part 7:** Candidates write a narrative of at least 35 words describing the people, events and locations that are shown in three pictures.
2 **Listening** **approximately 30 minutes**	**Part 1:** Five short dialogues with three-option multiple-choice questions with pictures. **Part 2:** Longer dialogue. Five gaps to fill with words or numbers. **Part 3:** Longer informal dialogue with five three-option multiple-choice items. **Part 4:** Five three-option multiple choice questions on five short dialogues or monologues. **Part 5:** Matching. There is a longer informal dialogue. Candidates match five items with eight options.	**Part 1:** Candidates are expected to listen and identify key information. **Part 2:** Candidates are expected to identify and write down key information. **Part 3:** Candidates listen to identify specific information, feelings and opinions. **Part 4:** Candidates listen to identify the main idea, message, gist, topic or point. **Part 5:** Candidates listen to identify specific information.
3 **Speaking** **8–10 minutes per pair of candidates**	**Part 1 Phase 1:** Each candidate interacts with the interlocutor, giving factual information of a personal nature. **Part 1 Phase 2:** A topic-based interview where the interlocutor asks each candidate two questions about their daily life. **Part 2 Phase 1:** A discussion based on topic-based artwork prompts. Candidates discuss the objects and activities in the artwork with each other. **Part 2 Phase 2:** The interlocutor leads follow-up discussion on same topic as Phase 1. Each candidate is asked two questions.	Part 1: Candidates focus on interactional and social language. **Part 2:** Candidates focus on organising a larger unit of discourse.

1 Hi, how are you?

Answers
2   Nice to meet you.
3   I'm 13.
4   Do you like school?

Topic: families and personal information

Listening Part 1: discrete 3-option multiple-choice: listening to identify specific information

Reading and Writing Part 2: matching: reading for specific information and detailed comprehension

Speaking Part 1, Phase 1: individual personal questions: focus on interactional and social language

Reading and Writing Part 6: short message: writing a communicative note or email of 25 words +

Grammar: present simple; adverbs of frequency

Vocabulary: numbers; family members

Pronunciation: word stress in numbers

Starting off SB page 8

Lead-in
Before students open their books, write some simple verbs on the board, e.g. *like, go, have.* Ask students: *What kind of words are these?* Elicit or tell students they are verbs. Put students into small groups and ask them to think of as many verbs as they can in one minute. Elicit ideas and write these on the board. Mime one verb that can be easily shown, e.g. *sleep, eat* and then ask students to do the same for other verbs.

 The students stay in the same groups as for the lead-in. Choose an object from one of the photos and write the word on the board, e.g. *boy.* Set a time limit of one minute for students to do the same. Elicit the words. Ask students: *Where are the people in picture 1?* (at school); *What are they doing?* (they are talking). Do the same for the other two photos. Drill the present continuous forms without explaining the grammar.

 Allow students to work in pairs. Set a time limit of one minute for students to read the dialogue and think about the correct words. Elicit ideas but don't give the correct answers yet.

 Students can change any wrong answers on the second listening. Elicit the answers. Ask students what the two people's names are (Sophie and Thiago) and elicit the correct photo and how they know (1 – it shows a boy and girl).

Track 2
Thiago: Hey. What's your name?
Sophie: My name's Sophie.
Thiago: I'm Thiago. Nice to meet you. How old are you?
Sophie: I'm 13. What about you?
Thiago: I'm 13, too. Do you like school?
Sophie: Yes, I do!

4   Tell one student in the pair to close their books. The student with their book open asks the questions. The other student answers. They then swap roles. Monitor and help students where necessary. Invite pairs to ask and answer the questions for the class.

Listening Part 1 SB page 9
Numbers
/P/ Word stress

Lead-in
Tell the class they are going to try to count to twenty. Students can say a number when they want but only one person can speak at a time. No one can say more than one number at a time. Someone must speak in two seconds or less. Start by saying the number *one.* If no one speaks for two seconds, tell them they lost and try again. Every time two students speak at the same time, they have to start again. This should work a few times before students work out a system so that they don't speak at the same time.

1   Elicit someone's age and write it in words on the board, e.g. *fourTEEN.* Model and drill the number showing the stress. When students have listened to the recording, write *FORty* on the board. Drill both numbers several times to practise the difference.

Answers

2	four<u>teen</u>	<u>for</u>ty
3	fif<u>teen</u>	<u>fif</u>ty
4	six<u>teen</u>	<u>six</u>ty
5	seven<u>teen</u>	<u>seven</u>ty
6	eigh<u>teen</u>	<u>eigh</u>ty
7	a hundred and nine<u>teen</u>	a hundred and <u>nine</u>ty

Track 3

1 thirteen thirty
2 fourteen forty
3 fifteen fifty
4 sixteen sixty
5 seventeen seventy
6 eighteen eighty
7 a hundred and nineteen, a hundred and ninety

2 Pause the recording after each pair of numbers so that students can repeat them both with the correct stress. Drill the whole class and then in small groups, pairs and individually.

3 Tell students that, this time, they are only going to hear one number from each pair. When they have listened once, allow them to compare their answers in pairs. Play the recording again, pausing after each number to elicit the answer and drill the word.

Answers

13 14 50 60 17 80 119

Track 4

thirteen
fourteen
fifty
sixty
seventeen
eighty
a hundred and nineteen

4 Look at the instructions with students. Ask: *How many numbers will you hear in each conversation?* (three). Play the recording twice then elicit the numbers. Ask: *How old is the girl in conversation 1?* (16). *Where does the boy's uncle live?* (19). *How tall is the boy?* (170 cm).

Answers

1 15, 16, 12
2 90, 19, 13
3 163, 170, 20

Track 5

1

Woman: How old are you? Are you fifteen?
Girl: No, I'm sixteen, and my brother is twelve.

2

Boy: I live at number 90, Moore Street, and my uncle lives at number 19. Where do you live?
Girl: Number 13, Bank Street.

3

Girl: I'm one hundred and sixty-three centimetres tall.
Boy: I'm one hundred and seventy centimetres. That's 20 centimetres shorter than my dad.

Listening part 1 (short conversations)

Look at the information with the class. Tell students that there will always be three pictures in the question. They should read each question carefully and look at the three choices to prepare themselves for what they are about to hear. Tell students that this task often tests times, prices, days of the week and other numbers. Look at the sets of pictures and ask what they show: 1 numbers (on doors) 2 families 3 prices 4 bus numbers 5 photos.

Exam advice

5 Tell students that, in the exam, they will hear each option but only one will answer the question. Tell students to listen for the correct answer and also try to hear what the other two options refer to (A Stevie's house C in the question).

Answer

B

Track 6

1

Narrator: Choose the correct answer. Where does Thiago live?
Girl: There's a boy called Thiago in our class. He lives in our street.
Man: Really? In the blue house? Number 42?
Girl: No, Number 40. And my other friend, Stevie, lives at number 25.
Man: It's great that you have friends in the street.

6 Look at the first question with students and elicit the key words. (Lucy's family). Elicit why this is important – we may hear about someone else's family. Give students one minute to agree on the key words in the other questions and why they are important (3 – we may hear the price of something else; 4 We may hear the number of someone else's bus; 5 We may hear about a photo of Charlotte's she doesn't like).

Read through the exam advice again. Even if they think they are correct when they hear it the first time, they should listen carefully the second time to check their answer.

7 Allow students to compare their answers in pairs after they have listened once. Don't elicit the answers yet. When students have listened a second time, elicit the correct answers and how students found the answer (e.g. 2 C She has a brother and a sister – five people altogether; 3 A It's a special price for today; 4 A I think my bus is the 15; 5 A That's the best one. It's me and my best friend).

> **Answers**
> 2 C 3 A 4 A 5 A

Track 7
Narrator: For these questions, choose the correct answer.
2
Narrator: Which is Lucy's family?
Man: So, can you tell me about your family, Lucy.
Girl: Yes, of course. There's me, my mum and my dad. We live in a house in a village.
Man: Have you got any brothers or sisters?
Girl: Yes, I've got one brother and one sister. There are five of us.

3
Narrator: How much is the bag?
Boy: Excuse me, how much is this bag? Is it £30?
Girl: I don't think so. Let me look. Ah, yes – today it's £13.
Boy: It's a beautiful bag. Oh, but look here. It says here it's £31!
Girl: I know, but today it's on offer.

4
Narrator: Which is the girl's bus?
Girl: Are you catching the bus home?
Boy: Yes. Look, that's my bus , over there.
Girl: Is it the number 50?
Boy: No, that's not the one I need. My bus is the 55.
Girl: Oh, yes. Well, I think my bus is the 15! See you tomorrow!

5
Narrator: Which is Charlotte's favourite photo?
Boy: I like this photo. Is that your dad?
Girl: Yes, it is. But I don't like the photo at all. Look at this one. What do you think?
Boy: Hmm – I don't like it. You don't look happy. This one's nice!
Girl: Yes! That's the best one. It's me and my best friend!

> **Extension idea**
> Make one copy of the audioscript for each pair. The students find information which shows that the other two options are wrong, e.g. 1 *The man asks about number 42 but it is wrong: another boy, Stevie, lives at number 25.* Elicit the answer.

▶ **Workbook page 4**

Grammar SB page 10
Present simple

> **Lead-in**
> Write on the board on separate lines: *I'm; I'm not; I like; I don't like.*
>
> Students work in pairs. They think of different ways of completing the sentence prompts. Monitor and help where necessary. When they have finished, put the pairs together in groups of four. They share their information to find out how they are the same or different. Elicit sentences from students about what they like (e.g. *I like football.*) Remember what they said and model a sentence about one student, e.g. *Mario likes football.* Make the third person *-s* very clear as you model the sentence. Elicit more sentences from students about their partner.

Look at the grammar rules with students. Elicit what other information we can use with the verb *to be* (using their ideas from the lead-in, e.g. *I'm from (a town), I'm in (a class).*

1 Put students into pairs. Ask them what they can see in the photos and pictures. Monitor and help and then elicit sentences. Make sure students are using the third person *-s* form of the present simple. Students now listen to the recording. Elicit the information and elicit that, when we use *like* + verb, we use the *-ing* form (*He likes dancing*). Also elicit that we use *play* + sport (*She plays tennis*) and *play + the +* musical instrument (*She plays the piano*).

Ask students to make sentences about themselves using: *I play (the); I'm good at …* and elicit ideas.

> **Answers**
> **Adrian:** He's from Poland; He's 13 years old; He's really good at football; He likes dancing;
> **Marcia:** She's from France; She plays tennis; She plays the piano.

Track 8

Girl:	Hey! How's school? Do you like it?
Boy:	Yes, it's great and I have some new friends.
Girl:	That's good. Who are they?
Boy:	OK, this is Adrian.
Girl:	Is he from America?
Boy:	No, he isn't. He's from Poland. He's really good at football!
Girl:	How old is he?
Boy:	He's 13 years old. He's cool. He likes dancing, too.
Girl:	OK, and who's this? She looks happy!
Boy:	Yeah, that's Marcia.
Girl:	Oh, cool! Is she from Poland, too?
Boy:	No, she isn't. She's from France and she's 14. She's fantastic.
Girl:	Does she like music?
Boy:	Yes, she does. She loves music! She plays the piano.
Girl:	Does she do any sport?
Boy:	Yes, she does. She plays tennis.
Girl:	Brilliant.

2 Look at the example questions and answers and elicit the negative short form of present simple verbs and the positive short form of the verb to be (*No, I don't, Yes, I am*). Elicit a few examples of questions they could ask, e.g. *Are you good at…? Do you play …?*

3 Elicit what students have to remember about the third person singular form of the present simple (add -s to the end of verbs). Write on the board: *I like football. I don't like football.* Under this write: *He likes football* (using a different colour for the third person -s). *He doesn't like football* (using the same colour for the -es of *doesn't*). Ask: *Do we say 'He doesn't likes'?* (No). Allow students to work in pairs, and monitor and help where necessary. Elicit the answers and elicit or point out that, with the verb to have, we can treat it as a normal present simple verb and say: *Do you have …?* or use the form at the end of the text: *Have you got…?* They are both correct but students have to be careful not to mix them up, e.g. *Do you have got?*

Answers
1 is 2 isn't 3 loves 4 don't like 5 are 6 live 7 go
8 doesn't have / hasn't got 9 are 10 work 11 are

Fast finishers
Tell students who finish early to look through the sentences in Exercise 3 and find new words or phrases which they think would be worth noting down. When everyone has finished the exercise, elicit these words and phrases and encourage everyone to make a note of them.

Students could do Grammar reference: Present simple: *be*, Exercises 1–2, page 106, at this point or for homework.

4 Look at the example and elicit more possible questions, e.g. *Is she tall? Does she like music?* Monitor and help where necessary. When students have finished, nominate different pairs to ask and answer their questions in front of the class.

Extension activity
Students work in small groups. They all think of one person in their family and write four sentences about them, one of which isn't true, e.g. *My dad is 42. He is from Valencia. He likes rock music. He plays the guitar.* The other students guess which sentence isn't true. Elicit some of the untrue sentences students made.

▶ **Grammar reference page 106: Present simple;** *be*
▶ **Workbook pages 4–5**

Vocabulary SB page 11
Family members

Lead-in
Write the numbers 0, 1, 2, 3+ on the board. Say: *Put your hand up if you've got one brother or sister.* Write the number of students next to the number 1. Do the same for 2 and 3+. Then say: *Put your hand up if you haven't got a brother or a sister.* Write the number next to the 0. For those that put their hands up for 3+, ask how many brothers and sisters they have got.

1 Look at the family tree and ask students how many brothers or sisters Carl has (1) and elicit her name (Megan). It might be best to pair weaker students with stronger ones so the stronger students can help them. Monitor and help where necessary. Elicit the answers and what the words mean. Ask students to cover the exercise so that they can only see the family tree diagram. Ask questions to see who can answer them first, e.g. *Who is Janet's husband? (Tom) Who is Megan's mother? (Mary)* Ask the class: What's another word for *mother? (mum/mummy)* What's another word for *father? (dad/daddy).* Elicit that we use *mummy* and *daddy* when we are young.

1

Answers
2 grandad   3 husband   4 wife   5 uncle
6 aunt   7 cousin   8 son   9 daughter   10 sister
11 brother   12 grandson   13 granddaughter

2 Ask students how many aunts, uncles and cousins they have. Elicit numbers from different students and then say: *Only draw two cousins, uncles and aunts on your family tree.* Set a time limit and monitor and help.

Extension idea
The family tree could be extended at home on a large piece of paper with photos of different family members where possible. If so, then students would include both sides of the family. These could then be displayed in the classroom. If this is not possible, ask students to attach them into their notebooks.

▶ **Workbook page 5, page 7**

Reading Part 2 SB page 11

Lead-in
Tell students to think of one family member and to make as many sentences as they can in two minutes. Model some sentences about one of your family members first: *My dad likes… / hates … works in … is … years old, has got a … is good at … .* Students then work in pairs and tell each other what they wrote.

Reading Part 2 (matching)
Tell students that they are going to look at Part 2 of the Reading exam. Look at the exam with the class. As the questions are not in the same order as the text, it is important to read the texts first so that they have an idea of what information each contains so they can answer the questions more quickly.

Exam advice

1 Look at the questions with students. Students decide together if they are similar or different based on their answers to the questions. Elicit ideas.

2 Look at what Ellie says with the class (*my two sisters … and my little brother*). Ask them to read the other extracts and find out why they are wrong (one has no brothers or sisters, one only has a sister).

Answer
Ellie

3 Look at the first question with students. Elicit that most of the words are key words but *and* is very important. Set a time limit for students to do the same for the other questions. Monitor and help where necessary and then elicit the words they think are most important and why.

Answers
2 doesn't like sport   3 wants to go, university   4 oldest   5 pet
6 friend, another country   7 can play, musical instrument

4 Tell students that it is a good idea to read all the texts quickly first and underline key words in the texts. Do this for Ellie's text with the class: *London, two sisters, brother, dog, youngest, at university, Stef, guitar, band.* Allow students to work in pairs or small groups to do the same for the other two texts. Elicit that when they try to answer the questions this will save them from having to look for the key words each time they answer a question. Sometimes key words will appear in more than one text. They then have to read all the sections of the texts containing that key word to find the correct answer, e.g. Question 5: Who has a pet? *Text 1 our dog, 3 don't have any pets, would like a cat.* Students can then find that *1 has a pet but 3 doesn't.* Allow them one minute to underline the key words and then five minutes to do the matching. Elicit the answers.

Fast finishers
Ask the fast finishers to compare the justifications for their answers in pairs.

Answers
1 A   2 C   3 B   4 C   5 A   6 B   7 C

Extension idea
Students look at the text in Exercise 4 on page 10 as a model for a piece of writing about themselves and their family. Tell students to use the verb *to be* and present simple. Re-elicit what sort of information they can write using the verb *to be* and the present simple, e.g. *My brother is 15. My sister likes / plays football.* The writing can be done for homework.

▶ **Workbook page 6**

Grammar SB page 12
Adverbs of frequency

> **Lead-in**
> Write these verbs and phrases on the board: get up at 7 o'clock; do (my) homework; be late for school; go shopping; do the washing-up.
>
> Elicit what these mean. Model some true positive and negative sentences about yourself using the phrases, e.g. *I get up at seven o'clock. I'm not late for school. I go shopping after work. I don't do the washing-up in the morning.* Put students in pairs to make true positive or negative sentences about themselves using these phrases, e.g. *I get up at 7 o'clock. I don't get up at 7 o'clock. I get up at 6.30.*

1 Tell students that, as they can see the first letter of each word, they can complete the diagram without understanding the words.

Elicit the answers and how often they think Ellie does each thing, e.g. *She always gets up at 7.00 am* = every day, seven days a week (or every school day). *She usually does her homework in the evening* = about four school days a week. *She is never late for school* = zero days a week. *She often goes shopping on Saturday* = about three Saturdays a month. *She sometimes does the washing-up* = about two or three times a week.

> **Answers**
> 2 sometimes   3 often   4 usually   5 always

2 Tell students that these are all adverbs of frequency which start with a different letter, so they can just write the first letter of the missing words while they are listening so that they can concentrate on what Stevie says. They then complete the words.

> **Answers**
> 2 usually   3 always   4 sometimes   5 never

> **Track 9**
> **Man:** So, Stevie. Tell me about your week. What time do you get up?
> **Stevie:** I always get up at eight o'clock in the morning. I never get up before that.
> **Man:** How often do you do your homework in the evenings?
> **Stevie:** I usually do it in the morning. Except on Fridays. I do my homework every Friday evening.
> **Man:** Are you ever late for school?

> **Stevie:** I'm always late on Monday mornings. Not very late. Just a bit late.
> **Man:** How often do you go shopping?
> **Stevie:** I go with my mum every Saturday. And I sometimes go shopping on Wednesdays.
> **Man:** How often do you do the washing-up?
> **Stevie:** I never do the washing-up! We've got a dishwasher.

3 Elicit the answers and, if you used the lead-in activity, ask students to talk about themselves in pairs, this time using adverbs of frequency, e.g. *I never get up at 7 a.m.* Elicit sentences and check that they are using the correct word order.

> **Answers**
> 1 after   2 before

4 Look at the example sentence with students and ask why it is wrong. Students can do this alone or in pairs. Monitor and help where necessary.

> **Answers**
> 2 always welcome   3 can usually   4 never forgets
> 5 often goes   6 am usually

Students could do Grammar reference: Adverbs of frequency, Exercises 6–7, page 107, at this point or for homework.

5 Elicit a few more example sentences for different situations, e.g. *I sometimes do the washing-up. I always ride my bike on Saturdays.* Point out that, by giving more details, students can change the adverb of frequency they need to use, e.g. *I sometimes do the washing-up. I always do the washing up on Sundays. It's my job.* Set a time limit of five minutes. If some students finish before this, they can think of more situations to make sentences about.

6 Tell students not to ask questions using the verb *to be*, i.e. not *How often are you happy / hungry?* When students have asked and answered about the other activities in pairs, elicit some questions and answers from different pairs.

Extension idea

Write the sentence beginnings below on the board. Tell students they are going to listen to the recording from Exercise 2 and complete these sentences:

I do my homework …

I go with my mum …

Play recording 09 again and elicit the answers (*every Friday evening, every Saturday*). Elicit that this means the same as always (*I always go shopping with my mum on Saturdays*). Students work in small groups to make sentences about themselves using every + a day of the week.

▶ **Grammar reference page 107: Adverbs of frequency**
▶ **Workbook page 5**

Speaking Part 1 SB page 13

Lead-in

Before students open their books, put them in A/B pairs. A is a new student and B has to look after them. It is now break time. Tell students that they have one minute to get to know each other. The new student should use their imagination and make up answers to any questions they are asked. The other student should answer truthfully. Elicit an example, e.g. *Hi, What's your name?* After one minute, tell students to swap roles and repeat the activity.

Speaking Part 1, Phase 1

Look at the information with students. Point out that the first part of the Speaking is split into two phases; in the first the student gives factual information of a personal kind and then answers questions about daily life, interests, likes, etc. followed by a longer *Tell me something about …* question.

Exam advice

① If you used the lead-in activity, tell students to think about the questions they asked each other. Set a time limit of two or three minutes for students to write the questions and then elicit ideas from different pairs.

② Play the recording before eliciting answers. You could play the recording a second time, this time pausing after each question to elicit the correct answer.

Answer
2 a 3 c 4 b 5 d 6 f

Track 10

Examiner:	What's your name?
Boy:	My name is Gabriel Silva.
Examiner:	Where are you from?
Boy:	I'm from Sao Paulo. In Brazil.
Examiner:	How old are you?
Boy:	I'm 13 years old.
Examiner:	How many people are in your family?
Boy:	There are five people.
Examiner:	Who in your family do you like spending time with?
Boy:	I like spending time with my grandma.
Examiner:	How often do you meet your friends?
Boy:	I meet with them every day.

③ Tell students to pretend they are in the Speaking exam. Only the 'examiner' should look at their book. The other student should look at the examiner as they talk and try to make their answers sound friendly.

Extension idea

Put students into groups of four. They ask and answer the questions again but this time with an audience. This can be more stressful and it is useful to practise speaking in front of others so that students become more used to it. When they have finished, ask the two students listening to give feedback to them.

▶ **Speaking Bank pages 146–147: Speaking Part 1**

Writing Part 6 SB page 13

Lead-in

Before students open their books, write seven gaps on the board: _ _ _ _ _ _ _. Divide the class into two and tell students that the missing word is an adjective. Elicit a letter at a time from students and either write them in the correct places in the word or on the board away from the word. When someone guesses the word (*awesome*) elicit what it means (*brilliant, amazing*). Students then work in pairs or small groups to think of people, places or things which are awesome, e.g. *New York is awesome.*

Background information

Taylor Swift is a singer. She knew she wanted to be a country singer at an early age and visited Nashville when she was 11 with a demo tape of her singing popular songs. The record companies told her everyone was doing the same thing, so she decided she would do something new. At the age of 12 she taught herself to play the guitar and started writing songs. Most of her songs are about experiences from her own life. Her second album, *Fearless,* won four Grammy Awards and she became the youngest ever winner of the album of the year award. In 2018 she had 100 million Instagram followers.

Exam advice: Writing Part 6 (a note or email)
Look at the information with students. Elicit or tell students that the three things they have to write about may be written as questions within a different text, as here, or as bullet points in the instructions.

Exam advice

1 Elicit the questions and ask students how they can answer them. Show students that just the basic answers, e.g. *I've got one brother and one sister, I like doing sports. Yes, I do. I listen to music and play the guitar* add up to 22 words so they don't have to add much more, although if they can make it a little more detailed and interesting, they can get more marks.

> **Answer**
> Have you got any brothers and sisters? What things do you like doing? What kind of music do you like?

2 Elicit the answer and which questions Stef does and doesn't answer (*She answers the question about what she likes doing but not about her family or music*). Elicit what extra information Juan gives (*his name and the name of his favourite singer*).

> **Answer**
> Juan

3 Set a time limit of seven minutes for the writing, as they have already looked at the questions they have to answer and thought about how to answer them. Tell students that, if they have extra time, they can add more details and write some questions back to Alex. When students have finished, put them in pairs. The students read each other's letters to see if they have answered the three questions.

> **Answer**
> Hi Alex,
> My name is Elena. I've got one brother. His name is Javier. I like swimming and playing basketball. I also like reading books. Of course I like music. My favourite singer is Chris Brown.
> Elena

Extension idea
Put students in pairs to brainstorm ideas for questions for Alex. Make sure they are in the present simple. With the class, choose three of the questions and leave these on the board. Rub the other questions off. Tell students that they are now writing a second email from Alex in which they have to answer the three questions on the board. They use their imagination to write a response to these three questions, either in class or at home.

▶ **Speaking bank page 146: Speaking Part 1**
▶ **Writing bank page 139: a short story**
▶ **Complete Key for Schools new edition Test Generator Unit 1**
▶ **Workbook page 6**

Vocabulary

Numbers

a hundred and nineteen	nineteen / ninety
a hundred and ninety	seventeen / seventy
eighteen / eighty	sixteen / sixty
fifteen / fifty	thirteen / thirty
fourteen / forty	

Family members

aunt	grandad	son
brother	grandma	uncle
cousin	grandson	wife
daughter	husband	
granddaughter	sister	

Vocabulary activity 1

Tell students that you are going to write some words on the board but with the vowels missing. (*a, e, i, o, u*). Put students into groups and tell them that, when they know the words, they should put their hand up. The first group to guess wins a point. These should be done by topic, e.g. family members: *sstr – sister, brthr – brother, ncl – uncle, csn – cousin, nt – aunt.*

Vocabulary activity 2

Tell students to choose a family member and make a simple sentence about them, e.g. *My grandma likes making cakes,* but they should write it with the family word missing i.e. *My _____ likes making cakes.* Students think of one similar sentence each for three or four family members. They then swap their gapped sentences with a second student who completes the gaps with the family members they think the sentences refer to. When they have finished, they tell each other what they wrote and see how many they guessed correctly.

2 We're going home

Unit objectives

Topic: home

Listening Part 3: 3-option multiple-choice: listening to identify specific information, feelings and opinions

Reading and Writing Part 1: discrete 3-option multiple-choice: reading for overall understanding of notices, emails and messages

Speaking Part 1, Phase 2: topic-based interview: focus on interactional and social language

Reading and Writing Part 7: short story: writing connected text (a short story or narrative) of 35 words +

Grammar: present continuous; *have got*

Vocabulary: time, rooms, furniture

Pronunciation: word stress: two-syllable words

Starting off SB page 14

Lead-in
Before the students open their books, draw an apartment block on the board with an arrow pointing to the fifth floor. Ask the students how long it took to draw (a few seconds). Tell them to draw the place they live and set a time limit of one minute. Now put the students into small groups to share their pictures and tell each other where their home is.

1 Before the students do Exercise 1, put them in pairs to discuss the photos. Ask them what kind of homes they can see, what they think they are called and where they can see houses like this. Elicit the difference between a flat and a house, (a flat is on one floor of a building, a house is on all the floors of the building; in a house there may be people living next to you but not above or below). Ask students what kind of home they live in and elicit how many people live in houses and how many in flats. Elicit that, in American English, flats are called *apartments*. Elicit the phrase: *I'd like to live in a ... because ...* and an example: *I'd like to live in a big house with a swimming pool because I like swimming.* Put students into small groups to discuss their ideas and help each other with vocabulary. Elicit one sentence from each group.

Answers
A a villa   B a boat house   C a flat/apartment block
D a tree house

2 Give the students one minute to discuss what the words mean and which match to which home. Elicit their ideas and the definitions of each word: ask what each item is for e.g. *Stairs are for walking up and down, a garage is a place to keep your car or bikes, a lift takes you up and down, You can open and close a gate to get into the garden.* NB The first floor in British English is one floor up. The bottom floor is the *ground floor*. In American English, the first floor often refers to the ground floor.

Possible answers
a door: villa, boat house, apartment, tree house
a first floor; villa, apartment, tree house; a garage: villa, apartment
a gate: villa, tree house
a lift: apartment
a roof: villa, tree house
stairs: villa, tree house
a swimming pool: villa
windows: villa, boat house, apartment, tree house

3 If you used the lead-in activity, the students will already have discussed where they live. They can now discuss what their house has got or hasn't got and, if they live in a flat, what floor they live on. Elicit the phrase: *My home has / hasn't got ... .* Elicit that, if the word is singular, they need to say *a/an* (*a garage*). If it is plural, they don't (*stairs, two garages*). Allow students to discuss their ideas in pairs or small groups.

Listening Part 3 SB page 14

Lead-in
Write ten different digital times randomly around the board e.g. *10.45, 1.15, 3.30, 4.40, 5.10, 21.45, 23.20, 2.35, 17.30, 14.15.*

Divide the class into two halves and ask one student from each group to come to the board. Say a time in non-digital form e.g. *quarter to eleven* and the students race to find and touch the correct word. Give a point to the group which finds the correct time first and change the students for the next time. When they have found all ten times, re-elicit what time each says.

1 Set a time limit of about thirty seconds for students to find the information. Elicit the answers and two ways of saying the time (*twelve thirty, half past twelve*).

> **Answers**
> **1** house (warming) party **2** 12.30 **3** the Bakers' (new) house

2 If you did the lead-in, the students could do this activity alone. If not, they can do it in pairs to help each other. Elicit alternative ways to say each time e.g. 2 *four fifteen*.

> **Answers**
> **1** B **2** C **3** E **4** A **5** F **6** D

Listening Part 3

Look at the information with the class. Tell students that, as with the picture multiple-choice, they will have time to read through the questions and think about what they need to listen for before the recording starts. Give them thirty seconds to do this and ask what they are listening for:
1 *how Jarred feels, start time, Gemma's relationship to Rachel, address, Jarred's opinion about music.*

Exam advice

3 Play the recording and allow the students to compare their answers in pairs. If they have any different answers they can try to remember what was said to see who is correct. Play the recording again and elicit the answers and reasons for them.

> **Answers**
> **1** B **2** C **3** C **4** C **5** A

Extension idea

Photocopy the audioscript and put the students into pairs or small groups. Each group or pair looks at one question and finds the information in the Audio script which shows why one answer is correct and why the other two are incorrect. The students then tell the class about their question e.g. *1a Jarred usually worries but not this time b Gemma says: I'm excited. Are you? Jarred says: Yes c It's a surprise party, he isn't surprised.*

Track 11

Narrator: For these questions, choose the correct answer. You will hear Jarred talking to his friend.

Gemma: Hi Jarred!

Jarred:	Hi Gemma.
Gemma:	I'm excited about Jakes' party. Are you?
Jarred:	Yes. I don't usually like parties. I worry that I'm not going to know anyone there. But this is a surprise party and I think it'll be fun.
Gemma:	What time does it start? Is it at 2?
Jarred:	Here, look at the invitation. It's at 3 o'clock. So I'm leaving here at 2:30.
Gemma:	Do you know who's going?
Jarred:	It's family and friends – so Jake's brother, my cousin Martin. Oh, and Rachel, your friend from swimming. She's going too.
Gemma:	Is the party at their new house – number 14 Green Street?
Jarred:	I'm not sure - I thought it was 24.
Gemma:	Oh, no look here. It says 40 on the invitation.
Jarred:	Oh, yes! Haha! So, are you taking any food?
Gemma:	No, I'm taking music.
Jarred:	Oh cool, is it hip hop? Jake really likes hip hop.
Gemma:	No, I haven't got any. I'm bringing mainly pop. I think that's best - I've got lots of rock, but not everyone likes that.
Jarred:	That's true. You need to bring something everyone will enjoy.

4 Elicit good things and bad things about parties from the class and write some ideas on the board e.g. *good: nice food, meet new people; bad: don't know what to say, noisy.* Students then work in small groups and use the ideas to discuss parties in general and Jake's party e.g. *Yes, I like parties because you get nice food and meet new people.* Elicit ideas from each group.

▶ **Workbook page 8**

Grammar SB page 15
Present continuous

Lead-in

With books closed, put the students into pairs or small groups. Ask them to write down as many verbs as they can which describe things they do at parties, e.g. *talk, dance.* It can be things they do at other times as well e.g. *eat, send texts.* Set a time limit of one minute and elicit ideas from each group.

Before the students look at the sentences, ask them to look at the picture and see which verbs that they mentioned in the lead-in are shown in the photo (e.g. *eat*). Students then work in pairs to try to describe what they can see in the picture – objects or activities.

2

1 Students can do the exercise alone. Elicit the answers. Look at the negative sentence 7 (*Martin isn't taking a selfie*) and elicit negative forms for the false sentences as well as true sentences (e.g. 2 *Jenny isn't writing an email. She's reading a book.*)

Answers
3 T 4 T 5 F 6 T 7 F

2 Elicit the answers and ask the students what tense we use to talk about things that usually happen (present simple). NB There are several uses of the present continuous for future arrangements in the listening text. If the students ask, say that this is a different use of the present continuous.

Answers
1 are happening now 2 to be

3 Elicit that we usually use the abbreviated form in speech: *he's, she's, I'm, you're* rather than *he is, she is,* etc.

Answers
2 She isn't writing. She's reading. 3 She isn't watching TV. She's listening to music. 4 They aren't laughing. They're crying.

4 Tell the class to close their books or cover the exercise. Play the recording and pause it after each sound. Students work in pairs and discuss what they think is happening. Students then uncover the exercise, listen again and choose the correct options. Look at how we form short responses in the present continuous and elicit that these are the same as for the verb *to be: Are you English? Are you reading? (Yes, I am. No, I'm not).*

Answers
2 B 3 B 4 B 5 A

Track 12
1 Is he running? *[sound effect of a boy running]*
2 Are they dancing? *[sound effect of people swimming in a pool]*
3 Is she typing? *[sound effect of someone typing]*
4 Is he playing? *[sound effect of a boy or man snoring]*
5 Are they singing? *[sound effect of a choir singing]*

5 Ask the students to work alone. Monitor and help where necessary. Elicit the answers and make sure that the pronouns match the people or things being talked about e.g. *3 your friends = they; your teacher = he / she.*

Suggested answers
2 Are you sitting down? 3 Are your friends sitting near you? 4 Is your teacher helping you? 5 Is it raining?

Students could do Grammar reference: present continuous Exercises 1 and 2, page 108, at this point or for homework.

Fast finishers
Students write more *Are you ...?* questions that they could ask other people in the class. When everyone has finished the exercise, students could ask these questions to the rest of the class and elicit the correct response.

6 Put the students into pairs. Look at the instructions and example with the class and tell the students to look at their photo. Ask how B would respond to the question about Jake; *No, he isn't. He's reading (a comic).* When the students have asked and answered about the people in the pictures, elicit the differences between the two pictures from the class.

Extension idea
Students work in small groups. They each think of an activity that they can show in a mime. They take it in turns to mime and the other students have to say what they are doing, e.g. *You are eating.* Allow them to mime two or three activities each and then choose a few students to do their mime for the class while other students say what is happening.

▶ **Grammar reference page 108: present continuous**
▶ **Workbook page 8**

Vocabulary SB page 16
Rooms

Lead-in
Ask the class what they do at home e.g. *eat breakfast, sleep.* Put the students into small groups and set a time limit of two minutes for them to think of as many things as possible. Elicit ideas and add *have a bath/shower, switch on/off (lights/TV/computers), watch TV* if the students don't think of these.

1 Allow the students to work in pairs to do the labelling. Elicit the answers and ask the students what people do in each room/place e.g. *have a shower in the bathroom, sleep in the bedroom, eat in the dining room, start the car in the garage, cut the grass in the garden, take their shoes off in the hall, cook in the kitchen, watch TV in the living room.*

Answers
2 bathroom 3 garage 4 kitchen 5 hall 6 garden
7 dining room 8 living room

2 Remind the students of the activity in the grammar lesson where they listened to people doing different things and tell them they are going to do the same but this time decide where they are. Play the recording once and then play it a second time, this time pausing after each sound. Elicit the room and a sentence using the present continuous to say what is happening, e.g. *1 Someone is having a shower.*

Answers
2 dining room (or kitchen) 3 garage 4 bedroom 5 hall
6 kitchen 7 living room

Track 13
1 [someone humming in the shower]
2 [the clicking of cutlery, and the sound of eating]
3 [a car starting up in a garage]
4 [an alarm clock going off, being switched off, and the sound of yawning]
5 [door opening, closing, and someone shouting "I'm home!"]
6 [sounds of cooking – frying]
7 [sound of TV channels being changed]

3 If you did the lead-in activity, tell students they can use the verbs they thought of for this exercise, but in the present continuous. Monitor and check the students are using the present continuous correctly.

Extension idea
Put the class into small groups. Each student thinks of an activity that can be mimed but, instead of miming it themselves, they tell the person on their left what they are doing e.g. *You are having a shower.* That person then has to mime the activity. Other students can help them with ideas of how to show the activity if they don't know. The students take it in turns to say an activity for the person on their left to mime.

Reading Part 1 SB page 17

Lead-in
Before the students look at their books, elicit messages that they have written, received or seen and what form they took e.g. *text messages, messages in the school for students, messages to/from their parents, sticky note, letter to parents from the school.* Put the students into small groups to discuss what the last message they wrote, received or saw was about and what form it was in. Set a time limit of two or three minutes and elicit ideas from each group.

1 Elicit the answers and tell the students that, in the exam, the messages will also be designed so it is easy to identify what kind of message they are.

Answers
1 on a phone 2 on a computer 3 on a phone 4 in a restaurant 5 on a computer 6 on a noticeboard

Exam advice: Reading Part 1 (multiple-choice)
Tell the students that they are going to look at Part 1 of the Reading exam. Look at the information in the book and tell the students that in multiple-choice questions, two options are wrong and one is correct. They should think of why the other two options are false to check that their answer is correct.

Exam advice

2 Tell students that there are seven questions to complete in one hour on the Reading and Writing paper. Allow five minutes for the students to find the answers and two minutes for them to check by deciding why the other two choices are wrong. Elicit the answers and reasons for them.

Answers
1 B 2 C 3 B 4 C 5 A 6 A

Grammar SB page 18
have got

Before the students look at the exercise, tell them to look at the pictures and say what is happening in each one: A: *A boy is doing his homework;* B: *A girl is holding a present.* Ask them how they think the two people are feeling and why, (e.g. *He is upset because he is working; She is happy because she is going to a party*).

1 Elicit which sentences match which picture and ask the students when we use *have* and when we use *has got* (*I, you, we, they have; he, she, it has*).

Answers
1 B 2 A

2 Elicit the meaning of *eyes, dark hair, long tail.* For weaker classes, look at the first question with the whole class and elicit the correct form and reason why it is correct (We use *have* after *I*). When the students have chosen the correct verb forms, elicit the answers and then look at the grammar and vocabulary in more detail. Ask the students how to form negatives (add *n't* to *have / has*), questions (reverse the order of the noun/pronoun and *have/has*) and short forms (*Yes, I have / No, I haven't; Yes, he has / No, he hasn't*). Write all the forms on the board for students to note in their books.

Answers
1 have got 2 hasn't got 3 Have / haven't 4 haven't
5 Has / has 6 has

Students could do Grammar reference: *have got*, Exercises 3–4, page 109, at this point or for homework.

3 Elicit what things the students could write about (*brothers and sisters, possessions* e.g. *phone, clothes, pets, hair/eyes*). Point out that they should only form sentences with *have got,* not other verbs. When the students have finished, elicit some interesting information they found out about their partner.

Extension idea
Students work in small groups. They have to find things that are true about all of them e.g. *We've all got a smart phone;* things that are true about some of them, e.g. *Two people have got brothers but one hasn't,* or none of them, e.g. *No students in our group have got green eyes.* Monitor and help where necessary. Note some information that you hear. When the students have finished, write the information on the board e.g. *Mario and Pedro have got ___ but Angelo hasn't.* Then give three choices e.g. *a pet, a sister, blue eyes.* Elicit guesses from the other students then ask the group what the correct answer is. Invite the other groups to write a similar sentence with three choices. Collect these in and read them out to the class, eliciting guesses from the class each time.

▶ **Grammar reference page 109:** *have got*
▶ **Workbook pages 8–9**

Vocabulary SB page 18
Furniture

Lead-in
Draw a square on the board and tell the students this is your bedroom. Add rectangles and squares to the room to denote furniture. Tell the students these are things in your room but don't tell them what they are. Keep the picture on the board until later. The students now do the same, drawing shapes for furniture items but not labelling them. Set a time limit of one minute. Look at your picture with the class and ask them to guess which shape is the bed. When they have guessed correctly put them in pairs. They show each other their diagrams and guess where each other's beds are.

Before the students look at the first exercise, ask them to look at the photo in pairs and say which items they have and haven't got in their homes and where they are if they have got them.

1 Students stay in pairs and to discuss which words they know or think they know. Elicit that a carpet covers the whole floor or a large part of the floor. A rug is a small carpet which only covers a small part of the floor. Elicit why they think carpets are popular in some countries (they make the floor warmer).

Elicit sentences from students about what they have and haven't got in their homes and which things the students can see in the classroom.

Answers
2 bookshelf **3** desk **4** chair **5** lamp **6** carpet **7** bed

/P/ Word stress – (two syllable words)

2 Say the six words and as you say them, tap out the syllables on your hand. Drill the words and tell the students to do the same, tapping the words as they say them. Play the recording and elicit that they all have two syllables.

Answers
bookshelf, carpet, curtain, kitchen, table

Track 14
bedroom
bookshelf
carpet
curtain
kitchen
table

3 Drill the words with the recording and elicit that the words all have the first syllable stressed. In many languages with regular word stress, students may assume that this is always true but say that in English word stress, like spelling and pronunciation of letters, is irregular.

4 Drill the example sentence and ask the students which words are stressed (red, curtains, bedroom). Ask why this is (they contain important information). Elicit another possible sentence students could make e.g. *I've got a big desk in my bedroom*. When the students have talked in pairs, elicit sentences from the class and check the word and sentence stress is correct.

Extension idea
You could extend the students' vocabulary a little here. Introduce *wardrobe, bin, drawers*. If you used the lead-in activity, look again at your diagram on the board. Tell the students to ask questions using *Have you got a ___ in your room?* If you have, label the shape on the diagram that the students ask about, e.g. if the students ask *Have you got a bed in your room?* write *bed* in the appropriate place. Keep going until the students have guessed all the objects. Students now do the same in pairs with their diagrams.

▶ **Workbook page 10**

Speaking Part 1, Phase 2 SB page 19

Lead-in
Before students open their books, elicit topics that they may have to talk about in the speaking exam and write the topics on the board, e.g. home, family, school, friends, hobbies, sports.

Look at the first topic and think of subheadings e.g. *kind of home, rooms, my room, furniture, street, garden*. Put the students into small groups. They think of similar subheadings for the other topics. Set a time limit of three minutes and elicit ideas from each group.

Speaking Part 1, Phase 2
Look at the exam information with the students. Give an example of the sort of questions that could be asked on the topic of homes e.g. *Where do you live? How many rooms are there?* and then, for example, *Tell me about your bedroom?* Elicit how the students could answer the first two questions and three things they may say about their room (e.g. size, things in it, how tidy or messy it is). If you used the lead-in activity, elicit from the students that the subheadings will give them the three ideas they can talk about for different topics.

Exam advice

1 Look at the questions with the students. Tell them not to write anything but to listen and remember. Allow the students to compare answers in pairs and play the recording a second time if necessary. Ask why the girl's answer is better (she uses full sentences and more vocabulary).

Answers
1 about the candidates' home **2** The girl talks about what type of home it is, how big it is, what rooms it has got, and that is has got a garden. (4 things). The boy says what type of home it is and that he likes it. (2 things) **3** The girl gives the best answer.

Track 15

1

Examiner:	Now, please tell me about your home.
Girl:	I live in a house with my family. It's a big house. There's a dining room and a kitchen downstairs. There are three bedrooms upstairs. We've got a garden.

2

Examiner:	Now, please tell me about your home.
Boy:	Er, well … a flat. Er… it's good. I like.

2   If you used the lead-in activity, the students can do this alone as they have discussed their ideas for some of the topics already. If not, allow them to work in pairs to share ideas. Monitor and help with ideas where necessary. Elicit a few ideas from the class.

3   Put the students into pairs. Student A is the examiner and should have their book open. B is the student and should close their books and look at the examiner while answering the questions. Monitor and encourage students to give longer answers where necessary. When students have finished, ask them to swap roles.

Extension idea
Put the students into pairs. Tell them to think of a *'Tell me about …'* question on the topic of daily routine. Not just *Tell me about your daily routine* but something more specific e.g. *Tell me about what you do in the evenings after school.* When they have thought of a topic, they change pairs so they are with someone who doesn't know their topic. The students then take turns to act as the examiner asking: *Please tell me something about …* and the other student has to answer, this time without preparing in advance.

▶ **Speaking Bank page 146–147: Speaking Part 1**

Writing Part 7 SB page 19

Lead-in
Ask the students what the last story they read or film they saw was. Tell the students they have three minutes to show the story in three pictures. When the students have finished, they work in pairs and show each other the pictures. The other student has to guess what the book or film is. To extend the activity, collect in the pictures and number them. Put them around the room and tell the students they have three minutes to walk around the room guessing as many stories as they can. Elicit ideas for each story and the story from the students who drew them.

Writing Part 7 (a story)
Look at the exam information with the students. Elicit that the writing task in Unit 1 was shorter (25+ words). Also elicit that, although there is no right story, there must be a connection to the pictures or they will lose points.

Exam advice

1   Elicit one or two words of objects in the pictures before the students brainstorm together. Elicit ideas and check the meaning of any new vocabulary.

> **Suggested answer**
> **Picture A:** a boy with a rucksack, waking into a building, a door; **Picture B:** the boy in a kitchen, he's looking in the fridge; **Picture C:** the boy's friends, a cake, a 'Happy birthday' sign

2   Give the students two minutes to think alone and note down answers e.g. Picture 1: *Sergio, 13, outside his house.* Tell students not to worry too much about their answers yet as they will have a chance to discuss them later. Allow one or two minutes to discuss their ideas and to see how similar they are. Tell the students to check that their partner has described the events shown in the pictures.

3   Point out that there is no right answer. All three are alright. Students may think 2) is wrong because it uses the present simple to talk about something now but this is just used instead of 'walked' as the students haven't looked at the past simple yet. It may be difficult for the students to articulate why they prefer one sentence to the others. Help them with suggestions.

4 Elicit the words and ideas the students discussed in Exercises 1 and 2 and encourage them to use a few of them in their story. Set a six-minute time limit for the writing. Encourage the students to check their stories for grammatical and spelling mistakes.

Fast finishers
Tell the students that, if they finish early, they should find a picture somewhere in their Student's Book that they can describe using the present continuous. When everyone has finished writing, the students describe their pictures. When they have finished, the other students have to try to find the picture in the book.

Possible answer
Jack is walking home from school. When he gets home, he goes into the kitchen. He's hungry. He opens the fridge. Then his friends come in with a cake. It's Jack's birthday and the friends are giving him a surprise party. Jack is very happy.

Extension idea
Students swap stories in pairs. They check that their partner has talked about each picture in their stories. They find vocabulary or ideas that they like and give feedback to their partner about their writing.

▶ Writing bank page 141: a story
▶ Vocabulary and grammar review Units 1 and 2
▶ Workbook page 10
▶ Complete Key for Schools new edition Test Generator Unit 1
▶ Complete Key for Schools new edition Final test

Vocabulary

Home
boat house	garage	stairs
door	gate	swimming pool
flat	lift	tree house
(first) floor	roof	window

Rooms
bathroom	garden	living room
bedroom	hall	
dining room	kitchen	

Furniture
bed	curtains
bookshelf	desk
carpet	lamp
chair	

Vocabulary activity 1
Tell the students you are going to draw an object from the unit. They can guess whenever they like but, if they get it wrong, they can't guess again. Divide the class into four or five groups. Think of a word (e.g. *carpet.*) Draw one line on the board and ask if anyone wants to guess. If so, elicit the word. If not, draw the next line. Keep going until someone guesses correctly or all the groups guess wrongly and lose.

Vocabulary activity 2
Put the students into pairs. Half of the pairs find six words from one topic and the other half find six words from a different topic. They list these. Pairs then get together making sure the other pair can't see their list. Each pair takes turns to guess as many of the other pair's words as they can in one minute. At the end of the minute, the listening pair tell them how many words they guessed and how many they missed.

Vocabulary and grammar review Unit 1
1
2 live 3 have/have got 4 don't have/haven't got 5 love
6 loves 7 doesn't like 8 is 9 don't like 10 are
11 don't work 12 am

2
2 We **often** go shopping in the evening. 3 My dad **usually** has breakfast at 7.30 am. 4 Dan **never** does the washing-up. 5 Do you **often** do your homework in the morning? 6 I **sometimes** watch TV in the evenings. 7 Maths lessons aren't **usually** fun. 8 Soraya is **always** happy!

3
2 twelve 3 eighty 4 twenty-five 5 eleven 6 one hundred and twenty 7 forty-four 8 fifteen

4
Across 1 husband 3 grandmother 5 uncle 8 sister 9 son
Down 2 brother 3 grandson 4 aunt 6 cousin 7 wife

Vocabulary and grammar review Unit 2
1
2 I haven't got your pen. 3 All my friends have got laptops. 4 My grandfather hasn't got black hair. 5 You have got a nice room. 6 Have you got my book? 7 We haven't got a car. 8 Has your sister got a big desk?

2
2 He's laughing. 3 She's playing football. 4 He's reading. 5 He's swimming. 6 He's writing.

3
2 Three o'clock 3 Twenty to five 4 Half past eleven 5 A quarter past twelve 6 ten past six.

4
2 bathroom 3 kitchen 4 bedroom 5 bed 6 desk 7 chair 8 table

3 Dinner time

Topic: food and drink

Listening Part 2: gap fill: listening and writing down advice (including places, days, prices, numbers, etc.)

Reading and Writing Part 3: 3-option multiple choice: reading for detailed understanding and main ideas

Speaking Part 2, Phase 1: a discussion based on an artwork prompt; focus on organising a larger unit of discourse; comparing, describing, expressing opinions

Reading and Writing Part 5: open cloze reading and identifying appropriate word, with focus on grammar

Grammar: countable and uncountable nouns, *How much / many, a few, a little, a lot of*

Vocabulary: school lunches, food phrasess

Pronunciation: /s/, /z/, /ɪz/

Starting off SB page 22

Lead-in
Put students into small groups. Give them one minute to write down as many food items as they can e.g. *apple*. When they have finished, elicit how many words each group wrote. Elicit the words starting with the group with the fewest. The other groups then add any extra words they wrote.

1 Look at the pictures with students and elicit any food items they mentioned in the lead-in activity. Look at the headings with students and elicit that *dairy* means anything that comes from milk. Set a time limit of one minute to write down other items from the photos. Elicit these and teach other food items not mentioned.

> **Answers**
> fruit and vegetables: apple, banana, lemons, beans, chillies, lettuce, tomatoes, aubergine, asparagus, sweetcorn, red cabbage, broccoli
> meat and fish: steak, mince, fish, burger
> dairy: milk, cheese
> other types of food: bread, oil, beans, rice, sauce, mayonnaise

2 Elicit the names of the items. Elicit that, in British English, we say *chips* but in American English they are called *fries*. Note *potato chips* (US) = *crisps* (UK). Discuss more things which are healthy or unhealthy e.g. *tomatoes are healthy, fried chicken is unhealthy*.

3 Check: *meal* (e.g. breakfast, lunch, dinner). Encourage students to think of all the parts to their favourite meal e.g. not just pizza but what they have on it, a drink and extras as well. Monitor and help with unknown vocabulary where necessary. Students mingle and talk about their meals. When they find someone who has a similar meal, they sit together. Set a time limit and stop the activity even if some students haven't found a partner.

Reading Part 3 SB page 22

Lead-in
Elicit some meals that are popular in a student's country but not well known outside their country. Tell students to work in small groups and choose one of these meals. They work together to decide how to explain it simply to someone from a different country.

Reading Part 3 (multiple-choice)
Look at the advice with the class. Elicit that, in a multiple-choice task, it can help to identify why the two wrong options are wrong as well as identify why the right one is correct. Tell students that the questions are written in the same order as the text.

Exam advice

1 Look at the definition of recipe. Allow students to discuss the questions in pairs or small groups and then elicit ideas from the class.

2 Tell students that, in the exam, there may be words or grammar that they don't know but tell them not to worry. Set a time limit of five minutes. Elicit the answers and the words in the text which show this.

Fast finishers
Students find new or useful vocabulary in the text. When everyone has finished, elicit ideas and write the on the board for everyone to make a written record.

Answers
1 C 2 A 3 C 4 C 5 B

Extension idea
If students did the lead-in activity, put them in pairs with someone from a different group. They take turns to tell each other about the food they thought of.

▶ **Workbook page 12**

Vocabulary SB page 23
School lunches

Background information
In Finland, healthy lunches are very important and vegetables have to cover half the plate. They also give students fresh fruit for dessert. In the UK and USA, school meals were often unhealthy. In the UK in 2004, chef Jamie Oliver started a campaign to improve the quality of the meals and have fewer chips, and less fried food and pizza. Michelle Obama started a similar campaign in the USA in 2010 as part of her 'Let's Move' campaign. However, not all students are happy with their new diet and have posted photos of their lunches online.

Lead-in
Ask students to imagine that they have gone to a different school in a different country and they want to know about lunch at their new school. Give a possible question e.g. *Do you have a lunch break here?* Elicit one or two more questions that students could ask and then put them in groups to think of their own questions. Elicit questions and answers for their country.

 Allow students to work in pairs. Elicit the answers and ask students which lunch they prefer and why. Elicit ideas of other items they could include in lunch box e.g. *carrot, yoghurt.*

Answers
2 water 3 cheese 4 biscuits 5 apple 6 banana 7 cake
8 orange juice 9 ice cream 10 lemonade 11 salad
12 chicken 13 rice

2 To help students decide the answers, they can tick the food and drink items in the pictures that each person mentions. They can then write the correct letter next to each name. When they have listened to the recording, elicit the answers.

Answers
Becky B Murray A Tina C

Track 16
Man: Becky, what do you usually have for lunch at school?
Becky: My mum makes my lunch every day. She always gives me sandwiches and fruit – usually a banana, and I have orange juice to drink. Sometimes, she gives me cake.
Man: Murray, what about you? Does your mum or dad make your lunch?
Murray: Yes, my mum does. I have sandwiches too, and cheese. I love cheese! She also gives me an apple, some biscuits, and a bottle of water.
Man: And Tina. What do you usually have for lunch?
Tina: I buy a hot meal in the school café. It's different every day. I usually have meat and vegetables. Today, we're having chicken and rice and a salad. I always drink lemonade with my meal and have an ice cream afterwards.

 Set a time limit of one minute for students to discuss their lunches. Elicit ideas and ask: *Do you make your own lunch or does your mum or dad make it for you?*

Extension idea
Set a time limit of one minute and tell students to think of an empty lunch box and write five things they would have in it. They shouldn't tell their partner what they are writing. When they have finished, put them in pairs. They take turns to tell their partner what is in the lunch box while the other person has to draw the items. When they have both done this, they compare their pictures with their partner's list.

▶ **Workbook page 13**

3

/P/ /s/, /z/, /ɪz/

4 When students have listened and identified the differences, ask which two words have the same sound (*his, mum's* – /z/). Drill the four words with the class to make sure they say them correctly. Start by drilling the whole class then smaller groups, pairs and individually.

Answers
Murray likes his mum's chicken sandwiches.

Track 17
Murray likes his mum's chicken sandwiches.

5 Before students listen, put them in pairs to say the words together and try to guess the correct s sounds. Elicit how they think the words should be pronounced and then play the recording to drill the words before they complete the table.

Answers
/s/: chips, wants; /z/: onions, apples; /ɪz/: dishes, fridges

Track 18
apples, chips, dishes, onions, wants, fridges

Grammar SB page 24
Countable and uncountable nouns

Lead-in
Elicit food items from students. Write these on the board in two columns. One column has only countable nouns in it and the other only uncountable nouns. Don't tell students this. When you have about ten items in total, put students into small groups to try to work out what the two groups are. Elicit ideas but don't tell students if they are right or wrong yet. Leave the lists on the board. They decide the difference between the two groups in Exercise 2 and add the items to their vocabulary lists in Exercise 3.

1 Tell students to cover the sentences so they can just see the two baskets. Students work in pairs and take turns to say a food item they can see. The other student points to it. They then uncover the sentences and do the matching.

Answers
Mia – A Noah – B
Mia's – uncountable, Noah's – countable

2 Elicit the answers and tell students that later in the unit, they will look at ways of making uncountable items countable. Also elicit that some words, such as *chocolate*, can be countable or uncountable e.g. we can have a box of small, individual chocolates which are countable.

Answers
• uncountable nouns do not take *a/an* or a number.
• countable nouns have a singular and a plural form.
• uncountable nouns do not have a plural form.
• countable nouns can take *a/an* or a number.

3 If you used the lead-in activity and the words are still on the board, students can use them to help them and to add extra words to the table in the book after they have completed the activity.

Answers
Countable: biscuits, chips, grapes
Uncountable: milk, rice, tea

4 Students could work in pairs and read the conversation aloud first. Elicit the answer. Tell the class when we use questions to offer something or ask for something, we use *some* not *any*. Elicit the examples from the dialogue.

Answers
1 We usually use *some* in positive sentences, offers and requests.
2 We usually use *any* in negative sentences and in questions.

5 Do the first one with the class. Ask: *Why does Dad say 'an apple'?* (it is a countable noun beginning with a vowel). If students ask why there is no article before *apples* in the next line, point out that, when we talk about something in general, we don't use an article before the plural noun e.g. *Dogs are friendly*. Students can complete the exercise alone or in pairs.

Answers
1 an 2 some 3 any 4 any 5 some 6 a

Fast finishers
If any students finish early, ask them to find three words in the conversations which have silent letters in them. When everyone has finished, elicit what these are (*biscuits, fridge* and *cupboard*).

28

Track 19

Mia:	Dad, I'm hungry.
Dad:	Would you like an apple?
Mia:	No, thanks. I don't like apples. Can I have some cheese?
Dad:	No, we haven't got any, I'm afraid.
Mia:	Have we got any biscuits?
Dad:	Oh yes. There are some in the cupboard.
Mia:	Great! I'll have a biscuit, then!
Dad:	Me too!

6 Set a time limit and then elicit the answers and why the sentences are wrong.

Students could do the Grammar reference: Countable and uncountable nouns, Exercises 1–3, page 110–111 at this point or for homework.

Answers
1 Can I have <u>an</u> orange?
2 On Sundays, we have <u>a</u> great time together.
3 I start ~~a~~ work at eight o'clock.
4 I bought ~~a~~ black trousers and a pink T-shirt.
5 Don't forget to buy (<u>some</u>) milk.
6 Do you know <u>any</u> shops near here?

7 Ask students to follow the instruction and use the example conversation to help them. Model the activity with a strong student. While students are talking, go around the class and monitor students' intonation, modelling questions and answers.

Extension idea
Tell students they are going to play a memory game. Say: *I need an apple.* Elicit that *apple* begins with an *a* and ask for a food beginning with *b* (e.g. *bread*). Now say: *I need an apple and...* elicit *some bread.* Ask students if they can think of something beginning with the letter c and ask that student to continue e.g. *I need an apple, some bread* and *a cake.* Elicit that we only use and before the last item. Keep going for as long as possible.

▶ Grammar reference pages 110–111: Countable and uncountable nouns
▶ Workbook page 14

Listening Part 2 SB page 25

Lead-in
With books closed, write the words *competition* and *prize* on the board and elicit meanings or examples. Put students in small groups to think about competitions they know and the prizes for the winners, e.g. *Good exams – Students get a certificate from the head teacher and sometimes get a book.* Set a time limit of two minutes.

1 Look at the picture with students and ask if they think the cake looks nice or not. Students could stay in the same groups as for the lead-in or work in pairs to discuss their ideas. Elicit ideas and ask them what kind of cake they like best e.g. *chocolate cake.*

Listening Part 2 (gap fill)
Discuss the exam advice with students. Tell students to write numbers in numerical form, not words and say: *You can only write one word in each answer, so don't write articles (a/the).* Also, tell students that spelling is important and there may be one name which is spelled out for them. They won't get a mark if they spell this wrong.

Exam advice

2 Set a time limit of about 30 seconds for students to do this alone and elicit the answers. Elicit which answer would be spelled out for them (4 a person's name).

Answers
b 3 c 4 d 2 e 1 f 5

3 Tell students to quickly look through the text and ask what kind of competition it is (cake making). Play the recording twice. When students have written the answers, elicit these and how the name was spelled (with the speaker saying: *double 'l'*).

Answers
1 9.45 (am) 2 425 3 eggs 4 Pallister 5 (a) camera

3

Track 20

Narrator: You will hear a teacher talking to her class about a cake competition. Write one word or a number or a date or a time.

Woman: At cooking club next week, we're having a cake competition. You can make the cake at home over the weekend and bring it to school.

Here's the information. It's on Monday the third of May. School starts at 9 o'clock as usual, and all cakes need to be on their plates and ready at 9.45 – that's when the head teacher will look at them and decide which one is best.

The competition will be in the room next to the school kitchen, that's room 425. All cakes must include flour, eggs, butter and sugar. You can include other things too, like fruit or chocolate, if you want.

If you have any questions, ask Mrs. Pallister – that's P-A-double-L-I-S-T-E-R. When you arrive, she will give you a number and ask for your name. Put the number next to your cake.

Last year's prize was a scooter, but this year we're giving the winner a camera – so we're hoping for some really good cakes!

Extension idea
Put the class into small groups. Each student thinks of a competition e.g. *a painting competition*. Students take turns to try to guess each other's competitions by asking Yes/No questions. Give some examples before they start e.g. *Is it a sports competition? Is it a competition you can do at school?*

▶ **Workbook page 13**

Grammar SB page 25
How much / many; a few, a little, a lot of

Lead-in
Remind students about the competition they heard about in the listening activity. Tell them that they want to win the competition. In small groups they should decide what to put in their cakes.

1 As an alternative, tell students to close their books and listen to the recording to see what kind of a cake Mia wants to make (*lemon*). They then open their books and read through the dialogue in pairs, discussing which words to use in the gaps before listening again to check.

Answers
2 a few 3 a little 4 much 5 a lot 6 a few 7 many

Track 21

Mia: I want to make a cake for the cake competition.
Dad: What do you need?
Mia: Let's see … eggs.
Dad: How many do you need?
Mia: Just a few! Three, I think. I also need a little milk for my recipe.
Dad: How much do you need?
Mia: I don't need a lot of milk. Just half a cup. And it's a lemon cake, so I think I'll need a few lemons.
Dad: Really? How many?
Mia: Let me see – oh, actually I only need one.

2 Tell students that all the answers can be found in the conversation they have just completed. Ask them to find the quantifiers first and then discuss their use in pairs. Elicit the answers and ask students for the quantifiers and nouns from the conversation e.g. *How much – milk, How many – eggs, lemons, a few – eggs, lemons, a little – milk, a lot – milk.*

Answers
With countable nouns: a few, a lot of, How many
With uncountable nouns: a little, a lot of, How much

3 Look at question 1 with the whole class. Elicit which words are correct and why (*much* because chocolate is uncountable), a *lot* because it is a positive response. Elicit that, if it was a negative response, they could answer *Not much* or *Not a lot*. Students then work alone or in pairs to complete the exercise.

Fast finishers
Students write sentences about what they've got in their school bags or in their room at home e.g. *I've got a lot of books in my bag. I've got a few old CDs at home.* When everyone has finished the activity, elicit these sentences.

Students could do Grammar reference: *How much / many; a few, a little, a lot of* Exercise 4, page 111, at this point or for homework.

Answers
1 much; a lot of 2 much; a little 3 many; A few 4 many; a lot of 5 many; a few

4 Look at the instructions and elicit that, if the answer is zero, the usual way to say this is *I haven't got any* but that we can also give a one word answer: *none*. Elicit or point out that, in English, we don't use double negatives, so we don't say: *I haven't got none*. If you think students need more help, tell them to decide whether each item is countable or uncountable before they start. Elicit questions and answers from different students.

▶ **Grammar reference page 111:** *How much / many; a few, a little, a lot of*

▶ **Workbook page 14**

Vocabulary SB page 26

Food phrases

> **Lead-in**
> Tell students to think about breakfast. Write the following question words on the board: *Who, What time, Where, How often, Do.* Elicit questions they could ask other students about breakfast using these words, e.g. *Who makes breakfast in your house?* Students work in pairs and ask and answer the questions.

1 Look at the menu and check that students understand all the food items by asking questions like: *What is your favourite cereal?* Students think alone for one minute and then discuss their ideas.

2 Play the recording once for students to write the letters next to the food. You could play the recording a second time and pause it after each person to elicit what food and drink they talked about.

> **Answers**
> cereal T, M, cheese B, cake -, toast T, sausage -, cake, fruit M, eggs B, tea, juice, coffee T, mineral water M, milk B

> **Track 22**
> **Man:** Becky – what do you usually have for breakfast?
> **Becky:** I have a glass of milk and some eggs.
> **Man:** How many eggs do you have?
> **Becky:** Two usually. And sometimes a piece of cheese.
> **Man:** Tina – what do you usually have for breakfast?
> **Tina:** I usually have a slice of toast and a bowl of cereal.
> **Man:** And to drink?
> **Tina:** Coffee.
> **Man:** How many cups?
> **Tina:** Just one.
> **Man:** Murray – how much coffee do you drink at breakfast?

> **Murray:** None. I don't drink coffee. I have a healthy breakfast.
> **Man:** What do you usually eat?
> **Murray:** A plate of fruit, and a bottle of mineral water. Sometimes mum buys a box of cereal and I have a bowl of that, too.

3 Tell students that they are now going to look at ways of making uncountable nouns countable. Put students into pairs to see if they can name the items in the photos. Elicit the answers and check what each word means e.g. *a slice* is a flat piece of food cut from a larger piece, such as *a slice of bread*).

> **Answers**
> A bottle of water, a piece of cake, a cup of tea, a glass of milk, a bowl of fruit, a box of cereal, a can of cola, a plate of meat, a slice of bread

4 Tell students to write the quantifiers in their notebooks: *a glass of, a piece of.* When the minute starts they just need to write food and drink items after each one. Elicit ideas e.g. *a slice of meat* and check the meaning if necessary.

> **Possible answers**
> A glass of: water, juice, cola, lemonade.
> A piece of: chocolate.
> A cup of: coffee.
> A bottle of: milk, cola, lemonade.
> A bowl of: cereal, soup, ice cream.
> A box of: biscuits.
> A can of: lemonade (In British English food comes in a tin e.g. a tin of tomatoes. In American English can is used with food and drinks).
> A plate of: biscuits, food, chips.
> A slice of: cheese, cake, meat.

5 Encourage students to use as many of the phrases in this section and earlier sections as possible e.g. *I have a slice of bread with a little butter and a lot of jam.* Before they start, allow them to think of their ideas alone and monitor and help with vocabulary if necessary.

> **Extension idea**
> Students work in small groups. They think of a food item and describe it e.g. *It is a countable word. We use it in cakes. We can eat it for breakfast. We can eat one cold on a picnic. We often buy 6, 10 or 12 of them in a box.* (eggs).

▶ **Workbook page 13**

Reading Part 5 SB page 26

Lead-in
Write the word *party* in the middle of the board. Leading from it, have lines making a mind map. Each one leads to another word: *invite (who), where, when, what for, food and drink, music.* Elicit a type of party e.g. a birthday party for friends. Put students into small groups and set a time limit of three or four minutes to think of what they need for a good party under each heading. Elicit ideas from each group.

Reading Part 5 (open cloze)
Look at the advice with students. Elicit that the words will be mainly grammatical items and there will usually only be one possible answer. If more than one answer is possible, it doesn't matter which one students use. Encourage them to read the text when they have written the words to make sure that it sounds correct.

Exam advice

1 Set a time limit of about 30 seconds. If you did the lead-in activity, elicit that it is an invitation and also ask what other advice for the headings on the mind map it answers (who – Sue, Tom and Sophie; where – Teri's house; when – Friday; what for – birthday; food and drink – dinner, cake, lemonade; music – not mentioned).

Answer
an email invitation

2 Go through the different types of words and elicit more examples of each. Make sure students are clear that they need to find the kind of word needed, not the actual word. Look at the example with students and elicit that the correct answer in this exercise is 'preposition', not 'on'. Before eliciting the answers, tell them to just tell you the type of word.

Answers
1 verb **2** quantifier **3** verb **4** a question word
5 a preposition which is part of a quantifier **6** preposition

3 Set a realistic time limit of 3–5 minutes for the class. Elicit the answers and how students know e.g. 1 can't be *want* because we say: *Do you want*; 2 can't be *little* as *friends* is countable. It can't be *lots* because that would be followed by *of*; 3 needs the correct form of

the verb *to be* to complete the present continuous, etc. Tell students that *lots (of)* is an informal way of saying *a lot of.*

Answers
1 like **2** few **3** are **4** What **5** of **6** on

Extension idea
Put students into pairs. Tell half the class to look at a reading text in Unit 1 and the other half to look at a reading text in Unit 2. They find a sentence which includes a word which could be removed but which could still be guessed by someone else. Re-elicit the sort of words students can remove. They write the sentence with the word gapped. When they are ready, they swap sentences with a second pair and try to complete each other's sentences.

▶ Workbook page 14

Speaking Part 2 SB page 27

Lead-in
With books closed, ask students to think about a great restaurant they know. It can be in their town or somewhere they know from a holiday. Ask them to work alone for one minute listing the things they like about it e.g. *food, people, place.* They then work in pairs and tell each other about their restaurant.

Speaking Part 2 (a discussion)
Look at the exam advice with students. Elicit how they will talk to each other, e.g. by asking and answering questions and responding to each other's ideas.

Exam advice

1 Discuss the pictures with students and elicit what they can see and what kind of food the people are eating. Set a time limit of two minutes for them to match the pictures and answer the question in the Student's Book. Have a class vote on which place students like most and least to eat in.

Answers
(top left): restaurant; (top right): fast food place; (middle left): beach; (middle right): home; (bottom): school

2 Play the recording and elicit the places they talk about (restaurant, home). Ask which one the conversation was mainly about and why (the restaurant – the boy only talks about eating at home to compare it to eating at restaurants). Play the recording again and elicit the good and bad things they mention about eating in restaurants.

> **Answers**
> the picture of the restaurant

Track 23

Boy:	Do you like eating in a restaurant?
Girl:	Yes, I do.
Boy:	Why?
Girl:	Because restaurants have usually got different kinds of food. What do you think?
Boy:	I don't like restaurants.
Girl:	Why not?
Boy:	They're usually busy or expensive. I prefer to eat at home. I like my mum's cooking!

3 This could be done alone or in pairs.

4 When they have competed the rules, elicit what they are. Say some sentences and elicit questions from the class.

> **Answers**
> **1** Why **2** Why not

5 Look at the example with the class and elicit why it is *Why not?* (It's a negative sentence). Students work alone. Elicit the correct answers and then put students into small groups. They work together to think of reasons for these opinions e.g. *I don't like fast food. Why not? Because it's unhealthy and not tasty.*

> **Answers**
> **2** Why? **3** Why not? **4** Why? **5** Why not?

> **Extension idea**
> Ask students to write down three things they like and three things they don't like. These can be on any topic. They have similar conversations to those in Exercise 5 using *Why/Why not … because.*

6 You could do this activity in groups of three. Make sure that students are not working with the same person they worked with in Exercise 3. Students take turns to be the examiner who asks the questions and the other two students work together to answer them. The examiners can then give feedback on how long the two students talked for and whether they asked and answered each other effectively. They then swap roles and repeat the activity.

7 Remind students to think of reasons for their opinions. Allow them one minute to think alone and then put them in pairs or small groups to discuss their opinions and reasons. Elicit ideas from each group.

▶ **Speaking bank page 147: Part 2**
▶ **Complete Key for Schools new edition Test Generator Unit 3**

Vocabulary

Food

bread (u)	fish (u)	recipe (c)
burger (c)	fruit (u)	tea (u)
chef (c)	grape (c)	vegetable (c)
chip (c)	meat (u)	
dairy (u)	milk (u)	

School lunches

apple (c)	cheese (u)	orange juice (u)
banana (c)	chicken (c/u)	rice (u)
biscuit (c)	lemonade (u)	salad (c/u)
cake (c/u)	ice cream (c/u)	water (u)

Food phrases

(a) bottle (of)	(a) can (of)	(a) piece (of)
(a) bowl (of)	(a) cup (of)	(a) plate (of)
(a) box (of)	(a) glass (of)	(a) slice (of)

Vocabulary activity 1

Divide the class into two groups. One student from each group comes to the front of the class and sits facing the other students. Write a word behind them on the board. Tell the class that the two students at the front can't look at the word and the other students can't say it, spell it or translate it. They have to define, describe, give examples or mime the word. The two students at the front listen to their group's ideas and try to guess the word. The first student to guess wins a point and two new students come to the front for the next word.

Vocabulary activity 2

Put students into pairs. Each student chooses three words from the word list. One of these they have to define, one they have to draw and one they have to mime. The two students take it in turns to present their words for the other to guess.

4 I'm shopping!

Topic: clothes and shopping

Listening Part 5: matching: listening to identify specific information (objects, places, feelings, opinions, etc.)

Reading and Writing Part 4: 3-option multiple-choice cloze: reading and identifying the appropriate word

Speaking Part 1, Phase 2: topic based interview: focus on interactional and social language

Reading and Writing: Part 7: writing a story: writing connected text (a short story or narrative) of 35 words +

Grammar: present continuous and present simple; *too* and *enough*

Vocabulary: clothes and accessories, adjectives, shops

Pronunciation: /ɪ/ and /iː/

Starting off SB page 28
Clothes and accessories

Lead-in
Before the students open their books, write the word *clothes* vertically on the board. Then write the word *jacket*, horizontally so that the letter *c* intersects with the *c* in *clothes*. Tell the students to work in pairs and try to complete the word grid so that each letter in the word *clothes* is part of an item of clothing. When the students have finished, elicit a word for each letter and what each item is.

1 Students stay in their pairs and talk together about what they can see in the photos.

Suggested answers
In a shop; In a shopping mall; At a fashion show; In a changing room.

2 Set a time limit of two minutes and allow the students to work in pairs. Elicit the answers and, for each word, ask if anyone is wearing or has the items with them, e.g. *Is anyone wearing a belt? Has anyone got a hat in their bag?*

Answers
2 I 3 L 4 A 5 D 6 F 7 E 8 G 9 H 10 K 11 J 12 B

3 Look at the first question with the class. Elicit answers which the students could give, e.g. *I go shopping every Saturday. I love shopping for clothes. I like looking at different styles. I don't always buy things but I find things I want to buy in the future.* Tell the students to try to talk about each question for 30 seconds and to ask more questions if their partner can't think of anything else to say. Elicit ideas when they have discussed all four questions.

Extension idea
Put the students into different pairs. Tell them to stand up and look at each other for ten seconds. They then sit down and sit back to back. Tell the students to take turns to describe what their partner is wearing without looking at each other again. They should try to remember as much detail as possible, e.g. *You are wearing a black top, blue jeans and black boots.* Ask pairs how well they managed to remember each other's clothes and what their partner got right or wrong.

Listening Part 5 SB page 28

Lead-in
Write the words: *fashion show* on the board. Ask the students if they follow fashion and elicit the names of any famous models or designers, e.g. Yves Saint Laurent (designer); Kate Moss (model). Put the students into small groups and ask them to discuss what things are fashionable at the moment. Set a time limit of one minute and then elicit ideas from the class.

1 For stronger classes, you could make this a race and ask students to close their Student's Books as soon as they find and remember the answers. Remember who the first student to do this was and elicit the answers from them.

Answers
1 Park Hill School 2 Local clothes shops 3 Students

2 Play the recording once and elicit the answers and then play it again for the students to hear the conversation again, already knowing the answers.

Answer
E A hat

Listening Part 5 (matching)

Look at the information with the class. Elicit that, in addition to the two unused words, one has also been used in the example. They can cross out 'E hat' to avoid using it again by mistake.
Ask: *How many items match each person?* (one) *How many times can each item be used?* (once).

Exam advice

Track 24

Sara: Hi Pip – nice hat! Are you having fun?

Pip: Oh, hi Sara. Yes, I'm really enjoying this fashion show. That's a lovely dress!

Sara: Thanks. It's fun being a model.

Pip: It is, isn't it?

3 Discuss the instructions and tell students that, in the example, the two people are referring to each other's clothes but that, later on, they discuss other people's clothes. Play the recording and allow students to compare answers in pairs. Don't elicit any answers yet. Play the recording again and elicit the answers. It would be a good idea to photocopy the Audio script and ask students to underline the distractors, e.g. *Have you seen Ben? No – is he wearing a jacket with jeans? No. He's in a really nice blue sweater.*

Answers
1 H 2 A 3 F 4 B 5 G

Track 25

Narrator: For these questions, choose the correct answer. You will hear Pip and Sara talking. What is each person wearing?

Sara: Hi Pip – nice hat! Are you having fun?

Pip: Oh, hi Sara. Yes, I'm really enjoying this fashion show. That's a lovely dress!

Sara: Thanks. It's fun being a model.

Pip: It is, isn't it?

Sara: Have you seen Ben?

Pip: No – is he wearing a jacket with jeans?

Sara: No. He's in a really nice blue sweater.

Pip: Oh yes, I see him. Is that Amy with him, in the yellow dress?

Sara: I don't think so. Amy's wearing trousers with an interesting belt tonight.

Pip: Look! Is that George? It is! He looks great in smart trousers and a jacket, doesn't he!

Sara: It's a bit different from his usual jeans and boots, isn't it!

Pip: It's a shame he hasn't got a tie.

Sara: True. Alice looks amazing, doesn't she? She looks like Taylor Swift!

Pip: Her boots are too high! I hope she doesn't fall.

Sara: She'll be fine. But look at Katy - she doesn't look comfortable. Why doesn't she take off that heavy coat?

Pip: That's not Katy. That's her sister. Katy's over there.

Sara: Oh yes, of course. She's wearing a T-shrt and jeans! And looks very comfortable!

Extension idea

Students act out their own fashion show. Talk about fashion shows with the students and how they are organised – models walk on a catwalk and someone describes their clothes. Put the students into small groups. In each group, one person will be the presenter who describes clothes and where they are from and the others will be models. They discuss what the presenter will say. Set a five minute time limit and then invite the groups to act out their fashion shows in front of the class.

▶ **Workbook page 16**

Grammar SB page 29
Present continuous and present simple

Lead-in

Divide the class into two halves. Put the students in each half into pairs. One half of the class look back to Unit 1 at the present simple and one half look at Unit 2 and the present continuous. Tell them to make notes about: form, i.e. how we form the structure, questions, negatives and short answers; use: what we use it for. Set a time limit of about three minutes. The students then join together in groups of four with one pair who looked at the present simple and one pair who looked at the present continuous and tell each other about each tense.

1 Look at the instructions with the students. Set a time limit of one minute and elicit the answers. Elicit that the verb *to be* on its own is a form of the present simple.

Answers
is enjoying the school fashion show. Cool. Are you a model? Or are you watching? I'm a model! What are you wearing, George? I'm wearing a suit. Look. Ha ha! You look funny. Now I know why you usually wear jeans and a T-shirt. I think you look great, George.

2 Look at rules 1 and 3 with the class first. This is what they looked at in Units 1 and 2 and the lead-in activity. Elicit more examples of each, e.g. *1 I go to school every day. 3 I'm learning English now.* Now look at rule 2. Elicit examples of a state, e.g. *I'm 15. I like tennis.* When the students have matched the rules to the examples elicit or point out that, even though *I think* and *you look* refer to *now*, we don't say: *I'm thinking* or *you're looking.* We always talk about states using the present simple not the present continuous.

> **Answers**
> **1** b **2** c **3** a

3 Before the students look at the exercise, tell them that some verbs have both a state form and an action form. Write the verb *have* on the board. Under this, write *have a pet, have a shower.* Ask the students which is a state (*have a pet*) and which is an action (*have a shower*). Allow the students to work in pairs and elicit the answers with reasons for them (1 it's happening now 2 usually 3 *know* is a state verb 4 this is an action not a state 5 *understand* is a state verb, 6 this is an action not a state).

> **Answers**
> **1** is playing **2** don't usually wear **3** Do you know
> **4** 're having **5** don't understand **6** is having

4 If you think that the students need more help, elicit which questions will be in the present simple and which in the present continuous before they start. Look at the example with the students and elicit that the adverb *usually* means it is an example of rule 1 in Exercise 2 and needs the present simple. You may also want to point out that although *think* is usually a state verb, *think about* is an action verb and can be used in the present continuous. Encourage students to write the questions in full before they start asking and answering them. Monitor and correct where necessary.

Students could do Grammar reference: present continuous and present simple Exercises 1 and 2, page 112, at this point or for homework.

> **Fast finishers**
> Tell students who finish early to think of three more questions using the present continuous, present simple for a habit or routine and present simple with a state verb. They can ask these to the class when everyone has finished the activity.

> **Answers**
> **2** Does your dad often wear jeans? **3** Are you enjoying this exercise? **4** What time do you usually go to bed? **5** What are you thinking about at the moment? **6** What is the teacher doing now?

5 Look at the example question and response. Elicit something else the person answering the question could say, e.g. *I usually listen to pop music. I find music on YouTube and Spotify. I always listen to music when I'm in my bedroom.* Set a time limit of three minutes and then invite students to ask and answer the questions in front of the class.

> **Extension idea**
> Students work in small groups. They take it in turns to start a question using the words: *do, does, is* or *are.* The person on their left has to add one word, e.g. *you, your, Maria, the.* The students keep going, adding one word at a time until they have completed a question or they think the question is now grammatically incorrect, e.g. *Are – you – knowing … wrong. 'Know' is a state verb.* Monitor and make sure students are making grammatically correct questions. Elicit some of the questions asked at the end of the activity.

▶ **Grammar reference page 112: present continuous and present simple**
▶ **Workbook page 16**

Vocabulary SB page 30
Adjectives

> **Lead-in**
> Write: *man / woman* and *black / white* on the board. Elicit or tell the students that these are opposites. Tell students you are going to dictate some words and they should write the opposites.
> Say: up (down), hot (cold), good (bad), young (old), happy (sad), wrong (right). Students compare their answers in pairs. Elicit the answers and the meanings of the words.

1 If you used the lead-in activity, they will have seen *old–young* already but not *old–new*. Elicit the answers and the meanings of each adjective. Elicit that we use *young* for living things and *new* for non-living objects, e.g. a car. Elicit an alternative opposite for *short* (*tall*) and elicit the difference between *long* and *tall* (*tall* is a vertical measurement; *long* is a horizontal measurement – demonstrate this by looking at a desk or the board).

> **Answers**
> expensive > cheap; light > dark; new > old short > long; small > large

2 Tell students to work alone and then compare their answers in pairs.

> **Answers**
> **2** old **3** small **4** dirty **5** dark **6** expensive

> **Fast finishers/Extension idea**
> Say: *Look at the words in the box that you didn't use in Exercise 2.* Choose one word and think of a similar sentence to show what your word means. When everyone has finished Exercise 2, elicit students' ideas. As an extension idea, students work in pairs to think of a new situation, e.g. someone trying to get a pair of skis into a small car and saying: *These skis are very long. I can't get them into the car.*

3 Allow the students to do this in pairs or small groups. When each pair or group read out their statements, the other students race to decide the incorrect one. Make sure they put their hands up and don't shout out and only allow each group one guess. The first group to give the correct answer wins a point.

▶ **Workbook page 18**

Reading and Writing Part 4 SB page 31

> **Lead-in**
> Before the students look at their books, discuss why people leave their country and move to other countries, e.g. *job, be with family* and to think of any famous people who have left their country to live somewhere else. Give one or two examples, e.g. *Cristiano Ronaldo – Portugal to England/Spain.* In stronger classes, students could try to think of other examples in small groups. Set a time limit of two or three minutes and elicit ideas from each group.

> **Background notes**
> Alex Wek was MTV's Model of the Year in 1997 and became the first African model to appear on the cover of Elle magazine. She had to leave South Sudan in north-east Africa because of war, so now she tries to help other refugees. She helps Doctors Without Borders, UNICEF and World Vision. She also talks to children in American schools about having belief in themselves because she looked different to other models and had to believe in herself.

1 Put the students in pairs and tell them to try to talk about the two photos for one minute. They can talk about what they can see, what they think her job is and why, what she is doing in the photo where she is helping people, what she is wearing in both photos, where they think she is from, etc.

> **Answer**
> A model; She's meeting people

2 Look at the questions with the students and ask if they talked about any of these things in Exercise 1. If so, elicit ideas. If not, elicit guesses before the students look at the text. Set a one-minute time limit for them to find the information. If possible, show the students where South Sudan is on a map or IWB.

> **Answers**
> **1** South Sudan **2** London **3** She is a model and works to help people in South Sudan.

> **Reading Part 4 (multiple-choice gap fill)**
> Look at the information with the students. Tell them that up to two options may be grammar items. Elicit that when they have chosen their answers, they should read through the text to make sure it makes sense. Tell students they may see some words they don't know but higher level words aren't tested. In this text, there are examples of the past tense, e.g. *she had, she left* but, as the students haven't looked at this tense yet on this course, the answers don't check their knowledge of past simple.
>
> **Exam advice**

3 Tell the students to cover the choices. Allow them to discuss their ideas in pairs. When they have finished, ask the students how many words they are sure they know, even without looking at the choices. Elicit ideas here to see how well the students have guessed or you could go straight to the actual reading task.

4 As the students have already spent some time on this task, set a shorter time limit than usual of about three minutes. Tell them to first check the choices to see if their ideas from Exercise 3 are mentioned but even if they are, they should look at the other choices to make sure they are wrong.

> **Answers**
> 1 A 2 A 3 B 4 A 5 C 6 B

> **Extension idea**
> Put the students into pairs. Tell them to imagine that they are interviewing Alek Wek for a school magazine. The questions shouldn't be about her past life but her likes, favourite clothes, current work, etc. so that the questions are in the present simple or present continuous, e.g. *What's your favourite clothes shop?* Set a time limit of three minutes for the students to write the questions then another three minutes to imagine the answers and practise acting out the interview. Invite students to act out their interviews in front of the class.

▶ **Workbook page 17**

Grammar SB page 32
too and enough

1 Tell the students to look at the picture and describe the hat (it's small). When they have listened, ask them what the difference between *small* and *too small* is (one is a problem, the other isn't – it's just a fact).

> **Answers**
> 1 small 2 big

> **Track 26**
> **Girl:** Oh dear. I think this hat is too small.
> **Shop assistant:** You're right. It isn't big enough for you.

2 Elicit the rules. If students did the lead-in activity, elicit two of the opposites they wrote down, e.g. *dark/light* and a way of using them with too and enough, e.g. *I can't see anything. It's too dark. It isn't light enough.* Students work in pairs and do the same with the other opposites they wrote. Elicit examples from different pairs.

> **Answers**
> 1 too 2 enough

3 Before the students start, elicit how they could rewrite the example using *enough* (*It isn't hot/warm enough to go out today*).

> **Fast finishers**
> Tell students to rewrite some of the other sentences in the same way as in the example above, i.e. use *too* instead of *enough* or *enough* instead of *too*. Elicit the alternative versions when you elicit the answers.

Students could do the Grammar reference: *too* and *enough* Exercises 3 and 4, page 112, at this point or for homework.

> **Answers**
> 2 old enough 3 too heavy 4 fast enough 5 too expensive
> 6 clean enough

4 Look at the example sentence with the students. Encourage students to think of different adjectives for each item. Elicit ideas from different pairs, e.g. *A horse is too expensive/isn't small enough.*

> **Extension idea**
> Look at sentences 1 and 2 in Exercise 3 and tell the students that we often follow *too* and *enough* with *to* + verb saying what we can't do because of the problem. Elicit more examples, e.g. *I'm not rich enough to buy a car. I'm not strong enough to lift this suitcase.* The students work in pairs and look at the adjectives they used in the lead-in and make sentences using *to* + verb, e.g. *It's too dark to ... take photos.* Set a time limit of two or three minutes and elicit ideas from different pairs.

▶ **Grammar reference page 112: *too* and *enough***
▶ **Workbook page 17**

Vocabulary SB page 32
Shops

> **Lead-in**
> With books closed, put students in small groups and ask them to tell each other their favourite shop in their town. They have to say what it sells, where it is and why they like it. Set a time limit of two minutes and elicit ideas from the class.

1 Look at the photos with the class and elicit what they can see. When they have done the matching activity, ask for examples of these shops in their town.

> **Answers**
> A department store B supermarket C bookshop D chemist

2 Put the students into small groups and set a time limit for them to write down as many items as possible for each shop. When they have finished, ask how many items they wrote for each kind of shop.

Answers
bookshop: magazines, CDs, posters
chemist: shampoo, plasters
department store: clothes, jewellery
supermarket: fruit, milk, bread

3 Encourage the students to think of other questions to ask each other, e.g. *Do you go alone or with parents or friends? Do you ever go there just to look, not to buy?* Elicit interesting information that students found out.

/P/ /ɪ/ and /iː/

4 Drill the two sounds before students listen to the sentence and elicit a few words in which the sounds appear, e.g. *sit / seat, ship / sheep, fit / feet*. When they have listened, drill the four words in which the sounds appear: *we, cheese, it, chemist*.

Track 27 Answers
We like the cheese shop. It's next to the chemist.

5 Put the students into pairs to say the words and try to decide which words have the same sound. Play the recording for the students to check and then play again to drill the words with the same sound. Elicit which syllable of the longer words the sound appears in: *T-shirt, department, swimsuit, aspirin*

Answers
1 free expensive clean **2** jeans jacket T-shirt
3 department store swimsuit cheap **4** aspirin beans big

Track 28
1 free, expensive, clean
2 jeans, jacket, T-shirt
3 department store, swimsuit, cheap
4 aspirin, beans, big

Extension idea
Read out a list of words and ask the students to write down what they hear. When they have finished, allow them to compare in pairs. Write pairs of words on the board and ask them which you said.
Dictate: *sit, feet, bit, will, heat, bin, feel, eat*
Write: *sit / seat, fit / feet, bit / beat, will / wheel, hit / heat, bin / been, fill / feel, it / eat*

▶ **Workbook page 18**

Speaking Part 1, Phase 2 SB page 33

Lead-in
Put the students in pairs and tell them to think of questions they could ask somebody on the topic of clothes, e.g. *Where do you usually buy your shoes?* Set a time limit of two minutes and then elicit ideas from each group.

Speaking Part 1, Phase 2
Look at the information with the students. Elicit/explain that the first part of the Speaking exam is split into two parts: general questions and then questions on a topic, for example school, family, free time. Elicit why it is important to listen to the instructions (if they don't listen, they won't know what to say and that giving full answers shows you can use grammatical structures in English).

Exam advice

1 Tell the students not to write anything in the gaps yet. Elicit ideas but don't comment on their answers unless their ideas are grammatically wrong, e.g. if they think gap 2 is *evening* or *school* elicit that we say *in the evening* or *at school*). When they have listened to the recording, elicit the correct answers.

Answers
1 clothes **2** weekend **3** colour **4** school **5** Who **6** party

Track 29
Examiner: Now, let's talk about clothes. What clothes do you wear at the weekend? What colour clothes do you like to wear? What clothes do you wear to school? Who helps you buy your clothes? Now, please tell me something about the clothes you like to wear to a party?

2 Tell the students to cover the dialogue while they listen a first time. Before they listen, ask them to decide who should get the best marks for speaking. Elicit their ideas, then play the recording again while the students read as well. Elicit the answers with examples of the structures Marco uses, e.g. present simple with *usually, like -ing*.

Answers
1 both **2** Marco **3** Marco

4

Track 30

Examiner:	Now, let's talk about clothes. Marco, what clothes do you wear at the weekend?
Marco:	I usually wear a T-shirt and trousers. I wear trainers.
Examiner:	What colour clothes do you like to wear?
Marco:	I like black.
Examiner:	Maria, what clothes do you wear when you go to school?
Maria:	Jeans. In winter – boots.
Examiner:	Who helps you buy your clothes?
Maria:	My mum. And my friends. They help.
Examiner:	Now, Marco, please tell me something about the clothes you like to wear.
Marco:	I like wearing T-shirts. I like T-shirts with pictures on. I like black or white T-shirts. I don't like yellow, or red T-shirts!

3 Tell the students to try to continue the conversation for two minutes each. Only the student playing the part of the examiner should look at the book. The other student should try to look at the examiner while speaking.

Extension idea
If the students did the lead-in activity at the start of the lesson, put them in different pairs from the lead-in. They do the same as in Exercise 3 but this time the questions won't be known in advance, so the students will really have to listen carefully to the examiner and think quickly of how to answer the questions.

▶ **Speaking Bank page 146: Speaking Part 1**

Writing Part 7 SB page 33

Lead-in
Students work in small groups. Give each student a letter, A, B, C, D (if the group has four people). Tell student As to think of two characters in a story, e.g. 15-year-old boy and his father. Tell student Bs to think of a place where the story takes place, e.g. *the seaside, school*. Student Cs think of two things which appear in the story, e.g. *a house, a dog*. If there is a fourth student in the group, they can think of two verbs which the story must include, e.g. *steal, run*. The students then share their ideas and have three minutes to discuss what their story could be about.

Writing Part 7 (story)
Before students look at the advice, tell the students you are going to dictate a sentence. They should write it down on a piece of paper without discussing it with other students. Say: *My sister Maria goes to watch Barcelona play football every Saturday.* Look at the exam advice with students and then tell them to swap sentences with a partner. Tell them to put their hands up if the other student wrote *My* with a capital letter. Do the same with *Maria, Barcelona* and *Saturday*. Elicit words we always use with capital letters (days of the week and months of the year). Now ask them to put their hands up if the students used a full stop.

Exam advice

1 Allow the students to work in pairs. Give them one minute to think of vocabulary items for the things they can see and then another minute to think of sentences they could use. *A boy is taking off his clothes.* Elicit ideas from different pairs.

> **Answers**
> **1** A boy by a lake **2** A boy swimming in the lake and a dog running off with his shoe
> **3** The boy is in the kitchen with his mum. He looks cross because his shoe is missing

2 Tell the students that the sentence needs capitals, full stops and a different form of punctuation. While the students are correcting the sentence, write it as it is in the book on the board. Elicit what has to be changed and change the sentence on the board for everyone to see.

> **Answers**
> Noah is in the park. He's feeling hot and wants to go in the pool.

3 Before they start writing, elicit that the story should be at least 35 words long. The sentences in Exercise 2 use 15 words, so they still need at least 20 to describe pictures 2 and 3. Set a time limit of five minutes for students to complete their story. Tell students who finish early to try to add information to their story.

> **Answers**
> **2** While he is swimming, a dog runs away with his shoe.
> **3** He walks home with one shoe. His mother is angry with him.

Extension idea
Put the students into small groups. Tell them to think of another story on the topic of clothes, which could be shown in three pictures. They don't have to draw the pictures but describe what is in each, e.g. *1 A teenage boy and his mother are in a clothes shop. He is looking at a leather jacket.* Elicit ideas from each group and ask them to write their stories in class or for homework. When they have finished writing, students swap stories with a partner and check each other's punctuation.

▶ **Writing bank page 141: A story**
▶ **Vocabulary and grammar review Units 3 and 4**
▶ **Workbook page 18**
▶ **Complete Key for Schools new edition Test Generator Unit 4**
▶ **Complete Key for Schools new edition Term test Units 1–4**

Vocabulary

Clothes and accessories

belt	jacket	trainers
boots	jeans	trousers
dress	shirt	sweater
hat	shoes	sunglasses

Adjectives

dirty – clean	new – old
expensive – cheap	short – long
light – dark	small – large

Shops

| bookshop | department store |
| chemist | supermarket |

Vocabulary activity 1
Tell the students to think of a clothes item and how it can relate to their lives, e.g. *Boots: I've got some brown ones. I wear them when I go on long walks.* They are very comfortable. They then tell their partner about the item without mentioning what it is. Their partner has to guess what they are talking about.

Vocabulary activity 2
Put students into groups. Tell students that you are going to dictate three words and one of them is the odd one out. Students work in groups and put their hands up if they know the answer. The first group who guesses correctly wins a point, e.g. *light large dark (large – the other two are*

opposites), jeans, trousers, sweater (sweater – the other two we wear on our legs), chemist, supermarket, trainers (trainers – the other two are shops) small, cheap, shirt (shirt – the other two are adjectives).

Vocabulary and grammar review Unit 3

1 **2** an **3** a **4** some **5** any **6** milk
2 **2** How much milk is (there) in the fridge? **3** How many bottles of water do you drink every day? **4** How many students are (there) in class 3B? **5** How much chocolate does she eat? **6** How much money have you got?
3 **2** B **3** C **4** A **5** C
4 **2** Can I have a pencil and **some / a piece of** paper? **3** I want to buy some new **T-shirts / a** new T-shirt. **4** My house has seven **rooms**. **5** Do we have **any** bread? **6** We haven't got any **homework** tonight!
5 **2** some tomatoes **3** some cheese **4** a cake **5** an apple **6** some grapes
6 **2** ice cream **3** fish **4** biscuit **5** pizza **6** meat
7 **2** bowl **3** cups **4** plate **5** bottles **6** bowl **7** pieces

Vocabulary and grammar review Unit 4

1 **2** am **3** live **4** love **5** 'm listening **6** listen **7** Do you like **8** 'm sending
2 **2** is dancing **3** don't understand **4** isn't wearing **5** Do you like **6** is Leila reading
3 **2** I'm too short. **3** These exercises aren't hard enough. **4** It's too dangerous. **5** The end of this film isn't happy enough. **6** This car isn't fast enough.
4 **2** expensive **3** light **4** dirty **5** new **6** long
5 **2** shirt **3** bookshop **4** trousers **5** trainers **6** dress **7** supermarket **8** socks **9** sweater **10** chemist **11** tights **12** jacket

5 It's my favourite sport!

Topic: sports

Listening Part 4: 3-option multiple-choice: listening to identify the main idea/message/gist/topic/point

Reading and Writing Part 3: 3-option multiple-choice: reading for detailed understanding and main ideas

Speaking Part 2, Phase 1: a discussion based on an artwork prompt. Focus is on organising a larger unit of discourse; comparing, describing, expressing opinions

Reading and Writing Part 6: an email: writing a communicative note or email of 25 words +

Grammar: comparatives and superlatives; prepositions of time (*at, in, on*)

Vocabulary: *do, play, go* with sports; nationalities

Pronunciation: schwa /ə/

Starting off SB page 36

Lead-in
Before students open their books, ask them what sport they do at school. Put them into pairs to discuss which of the activities they like and which they don't like and why. Elicit ideas and have a class survey of the most and least popular activities.

1 Elicit the answers and drill the words, making sure students put the stress on the first syllable of each one. If the activities in the pictures weren't mentioned in the lead-in, ask if students do these activities and, again, ask which they like and don't like and why.

Answers
A football B badminton C basketball D judo E table tennis

2 Set a time limit of two minutes. Make sure students only write the names of sports they know in English. Elicit the sports.

3 Play the recording once and elicit the favourite sports. Play the recording a second time for students to listen for reasons why they like the sports and how often they play. Elicit adjectives that the two people use: *fast, exciting, the best* and time expressions: *every week, every day after school.*

Answers
Xuan: badminton, Paolo: football

Track 31

Boy:	Hi. What's your name?
Xuan:	Hello! I'm Xuan.
Boy:	And what's your favourite sport?
Xuan:	I love badminton – it's really fast and exciting. I play it in the sports centre every week.
Boy:	And what's your name?
Paolo:	I'm Paolo.
Boy:	What is your favourite sport?
Paolo:	Football! It's the best.
Boy:	How often do you play it?
Paolo:	Every day after school.

4 Tell students to take turns to ask the questions. When they have finished, tell students that, in the speaking exam, there may be a general question such as: *Tell me about a sport you like to play.* Their answer to this question could include what the sport is, why they like it and where and how often they play it.

Extension idea
Put students into pairs. Ask them to think of a different general question about sports e.g. *Tell me about a sport you like to watch on television. Tell me about a sport you don't like.* Change the pairs. They take it in turns to act as the interviewer.

Reading Part 3 SB page 37

Lead-in
Talk to the class about sports that they can do in after-school clubs, either run by the school or in their town. Have a class survey of who practises a sport or activity after school.

Reading Part 3 (multiple-choice)
Look at the exam advice and tell students to look at the photo and the heading as well as any words in bold. Elicit that the text is an interview about a gymnast's life.

Exam advice

1 Discuss the two questions with the class. Point out that they can train alone e.g. by jogging regularly. Elicit that the teacher who helps you get better at a sport is called a *trainer*.

2 Encourage students to make a note of the words: *gymnast / gymnastics*. Elicit answers to the questions from students.

3 Remind students about the exam advice. Set a time limit of five minutes.

Answers
1 C 2 B 3 C 4 A 5 B

Fast finishers
Students should find the parts in the text which show why the other two choices are wrong. When you elicit the answers, these students can say why the incorrect choices are wrong.

Extension idea
Put students into pairs. Tell them to choose a sport they like/do. When they have thought of one, they take it in turns to interview each other, using the four questions in the reading.

▶ **Workbook page 20**

Grammar SB page 37
Comparatives and superlatives

Lead-in
With books closed, elicit a sport e.g. *football* and write the word in the middle of the board. Elicit adjectives which students can use to describe it. Make a mind map by writing the adjectives around the word *football* on the board and leave this on the board until the Extension activity after Exercise 3. Students now work in pairs or small groups to do the same for a different sport. Tell them all to write the adjectives they think of.

1 Allow students to work in pairs to discuss their ideas. Elicit ideas but don't say what the correct answers are until they have listened. When they have listened to the recording, ask who they agree with; the person who prefers football or basketball.

Answers
2 best 3 faster 4 interesting 5 harder 6 popular 7 cooler

Track 32

Boy:	Why do you like football so much? Basketball is better.
Girl:	No, it isn't. Football is the best game in the world.
Boy:	But basketball is faster and more exciting.
Girl:	You're joking! Football is a much more interesting game than basketball.
Boy:	Ha ha! Why do so many football games finish 0–0?
Girl:	Because scoring a goal is harder than scoring a basket.
Boy:	In basketball, they often score more than 60 points in one game!
Girl:	Yes, I know. But football is the most popular game in the world.
Boy:	I don't understand why! Basketball is cooler.

2 Look at the rules with students. Look at Exercise 1 and elicit which two things are being compared in 1, 3, 4, 5 and 7 (1, 3, 4, 7 football and basketball 5 scoring a goal and scoring a basket). Then ask which groups the superlatives refer to in 2 and 6 (all the games in the world). You could also refer to the spelling rules in the Grammar reference section page 113.

Answers
1 b 2 a

3 Look at the example with students and elicit what the mistake is (using *more* with a superlative form instead of *most*) and why it is a superlative (the speaker isn't comparing rugby to one other sport but to all sports). Allow students to work in pairs to correct the sentences and say what the problems are.

Answers
2 faster 3 best 4 the slowest 5 the most popular sport
6 easier

Fast finishers
Tell students to look at question 4 and make similar sentences about people in their class but positive ones, e.g. *Juan is the tallest person in the class. Isabel is the best basketball player in the class.*

Students could do Grammar reference: Comparatives and superlatives, Exercises 1–2, page 113, at this point or for homework.

Extension idea
Tell students to look at the sport they thought of at the beginning of the lesson and the adjectives they wrote. Give them three minutes to write comparative and superlative sentences for their sports. Elicit ideas from different groups or pairs, e.g. *I think that swimming is healthier than jogging.* Depending on the adjectives elicited, this could be an opportunity to check the spelling rules.

/P/ schwa /ə/

4 Before students listen to the sentences, model the schwa sound on its own. Play the recording once and then say each word which contains the schwa sound to model the sound again. Allow students to practise saying the sentences before they listen again. Play the recording, and drill each sentence.

Track 33
Scoring a goal is harder than scoring a basket.

5 Tell students to work in pairs and to say the sentences, trying to listen to where there is a schwa sound. Elicit their ideas then model and drill the sentences in sections, making sure students say the schwa sound correctly: *I'm a / faster / runner / than your / brother. / Mike is a / better / basketball player / than me./*

Track 34 Answers
1 I'm a faster runner than your brother.
2 Mike is a better basketball player than me.

6 Look at the box with students and elicit some comparative adjectives that they could use for each topic. Set a time limit of two minutes for students to work together to add more adjectives. Look at the example dialogue with students and give them two or three minutes to have similar conversations.

▶ **Grammar reference SB page 113: Comparatives and superlatives**

▶ **Workbook pages 20–21**

Vocabulary SB page 38

do, play and *go* with sports

Lead-in
Write *judo / karate* and *baseball / cricket* on the board. Put students into small groups and ask: What do you know about these sports? What are the main similarities and differences between each pair. Set a time limit of two minutes and elicit any ideas they have.

Before students look at the first exercise, ask them to stay in their groups and describe what they can see in each photo, how they think the people are feeling and which sports students would prefer to do. Elicit ideas from groups.

1 When students have done the matching, ask them to compare the three sports using comparative and superlative adjectives from the last lesson e.g. *Cricket is more boring than judo. Rock climbing is the most dangerous of the three sports.*

Answers
1 C 2 B 3 A

2 When students have looked at the rules, elicit or tell them that we also *play* sports which have something like a ball e.g. badminton has a shuttlecock, ice hockey has a puck. There are one or two activities ending in *-ing* which we use with *do* (boxing, wrestling).

Answers
1 play 2 go 3 do

3 Allow students to do this in pairs. Elicit the answers and reasons why e.g. baseball is a ball sport, judo is a non-team sport and *running* ends in *-ing*.

> **Answers**
> play: baseball, volleyball; do: judo, yoga; go: running, surfing

4 Look at the example dialogue with the class. Ask why the first question uses *play* and the second question uses *do* (football is a ball game, yoga is a non-team activity). Ask what grammar form the speaker uses in their third answer (a comparative adjective). Elicit or point out that we could also use a superlative form here: *Running is the cheapest sport*. Set a time limit of five minutes for students to think of ideas and practise their conversations. Monitor and help where necessary.

> **Extension idea**
> Put students into small groups. Ask one group to choose a sport or activity and mime it. They can use one or more person in the mime. Tell the other students to put up their hands when they have guessed the activity. They then have to form a present continuous sentence with the correct verb e.g. *You are playing football*. If they do this correctly, they win a point. If not, a different group can guess.

▶ **Workbook page 22**

Listening Part 4 SB page 39

> **Lead-in**
> Put students into small groups. Write on the board: *Buying clothes for sports*. Ask the class what is important and why and where they go to buy them e.g. *comfortable, look good, cheap*.

> **Listening Part 4 (multiple-choice)**
> Look at the exam advice with students. Elicit that there are three choices to choose from.

Exam advice

1 Look at the instructions. Elicit ideas from students and then ask students to choose one word which they think is the most important. Elicit ideas and reasons e.g. *Why*: the answers all start *because*, so the reason is the important information to listen for.

> **Answers**
> You will hear a <u>girl</u> talking to her friend about a pair of <u>shoes</u>. <u>Why</u> does she <u>buy</u> them?

2 Tell students to ignore the options in in Exercise 1 for now and to concentrate on the questions in Exercise 2. Elicit the answers.

> **Answers**
> **1** the girl's friend **2** no **3** training

> **Track 35**
> **Narrator:** You will hear a girl talking to her friend about a pair of shoes. Why does she buy them?
> **Girl:** Hey, Pedro. Look – what do you think of these shoes?
> **Boy:** They look comfortable. But that colour is horrible.
> **Girl:** Oh, it's not too bad. Anyway, they're for training – not for school, or going to parties.
> **Boy:** Well, if you want them for training, they're fine. The colour isn't important.
> **Girl:** You're right. I'm buying them!

3 Tell students to look at the choices in pairs and try to decide which is the correct answer. Don't elicit ideas yet. Play the recording again and elicit the correct answer and why the other choices are wrong (A – the price isn't mentioned B – She says: *it's not too bad* but not that she likes it. C – *they're for training*).

> **Answer**
> C

4 Set a 45-second time limit for students to look at the key words. Encourage them not to choose more than one or two for each question. Don't elicit ideas before playing the recording.

> **Answers**
> **2** A **3** B **4** C **5** C

> **Extension idea**
> Make a photocopy of the Audio script and ask students to look at the reasons why the two wrong options were incorrect. Elicit that the information in the options is often mentioned but in a way that shows it is the wrong choice e.g. *3 A You just had breakfast*.

Track 36

Narrator: For these questions, choose the correct answer.

2

Narrator: You will hear a football manager talking to his team at half-time. What does he want them to do?

Man: OK, you are playing really well – and that's good. I just want you to think a bit more about what you're doing. It's great to see you trying to get the ball. When you get it, try to keep it for a while. Don't give it to somebody else immediately, and don't just run towards the goal. Play a slower game.

3

Narrator: You will hear a woman talking to her son. Why doesn't she want him to go out?

Woman: Are you going out on your bike now, John?

Boy: Yes – I'm training for the race on Saturday. It's not raining.

Woman: I know, but it's very early. You just had breakfast, and it's still dark!

Boy: That's OK – the roads are quiet.

Woman: I don't like you going out when people can't see you properly.

Boy: I've got lights, Mum.

Woman: I don't think that's enough.

4

Narrator: You will hear a woman talking about surfing. What advice does she give to someone who wants to start the sport?

Woman: Well, the first thing I'd say is get the best board you can. The cheap ones are no good. Then be ready to make a lot of mistakes – it takes time and practice to be a good surfer. You can do it without a teacher, though – there are plenty of good lessons available on the internet.

5

Narrator: You will hear a girl talking about running. While she's training, what does she think about?

Girl: When I'm training, I feel like I'm in my own little world. I don't worry about winning the next big race, or trying to run faster than before. That's only for the competitions. I just enjoy the beautiful countryside and the clean air. I might think about what to have for dinner, or what's on TV that night – anything, really.

▶ **Workbook page 21**

Grammar SB page 40

Prepositions of time: *at, in, on*

Lead-in

Ask students to think of one Olympic athlete who they know something about. Put students into small groups to discuss the athletes and what they know. If possible, allow students to research their athlete online so they have some information to share with their group. Elicit one sportsperson that each group discussed and why they like them.

Background information

Yusra left Syria in 2015. She travelled through Lebanon to Turkey and then by dinghy to Greece. When the boat stopped working, Yusra, her sister and two other refugees swam and pushed the boat and saved the lives of the 20 people on board. Yusra has talked at the UN, met Barack Obama and the Pope and is now a global ambassador for the UNHCR, the United Nations refugee agency.

1 Tell students to look at the picture and, without looking at the text, guess where she is from and the connection between her and the word *refugee*. Set a time limit for students to find out the information and the answer to the question in the book, (she is from Syria and she is a refugee living in Germany now; she didn't represent a country at the Olympics, she represented people who are refugees).

Answers
Every morning at 6 am, every afternoon and at the weekend

2 Elicit the rules. Elicit or point out that when we have a day of the week and a time of day, we use *on* e.g. *on Saturday morning*; we say *at night*; we don't use prepositions of time with *yesterday, tomorrow* or expressions with *next / last*; in American English, we use *on the weekend*.

Students could do Grammar reference: Prepositions of time: *at, in, on* 3–4, page 114, at this point or for homework.

Answers
1 at **2** in **3** on

3 If you think students need more help, look at the example and elicit alternative questions and answers from the class, e.g. *When are the school holidays? They are in July and August. When do you have English classes? On Tuesdays and Thursdays.* Set a time limit of two minutes for students.

Fast finishers

Students think of one or two more questions that they could ask. When everyone has finished the exercise, allow these students to ask the class their questions.

Extension idea

Tell students to write down some of their answers from Exercise 3 on a piece of paper e.g. *on 13 June, at 6.30, in July.* Collect the answers and redistribute them randomly. Students think of questions which match each answer e.g. *When is your birthday? What time do you wake up? When do you go on holiday?* When they have finished, students mingle and ask each other the questions to try to find out whose answers they have got.

▶ **Grammar reference page 114: Prepositions of time:** *at, in, on*
▶ **Workbook page 21**

Vocabulary SB page 40
Nationalities

Lead-in

Split the class into two groups: A and B. Divide these groups into pairs. Set a time limit of one minute. A pairs write as many countries as they can in English. B pairs write as many nationalities/languages as they can. Now put A and B pairs together in groups of four. They share their information and try to match countries, nationalities and languages.

1 Tell students that one of the missing words is in the text in the previous section. Allow students to work in pairs and elicit the answers.

> **Answers**
> 1 German 2 Syrian

2 Look at the table with students and elicit that sometimes they can just add a suffix e.g. *America – American,* but sometimes they will have to make other spelling changes to the country words, not just add the correct suffix e.g. *England – English.* Allow students to work in pairs and check the spellings of each word when you elicit the answers. Elicit that in English both countries and nationalities are written with a capital letter.

> **Answers**
> 1 Indian 2 Italy 3 Mexican 4 China 5 Japanese
> 6 Portuguese 7 British 8 Irish 9 Spain 10 Swedish
> 11 France 12 Greek

3 Look at the example questions and answers with students. Give a time limit of two minutes for students to ask and answer the questions. Elicit the questions and answers from the class.

Extension idea

Ask each student to write down the name of a famous person from a different country. Put students into groups of four and tell them not to show each other their famous person's name. They take turns to guess each other's person using the same question form as in Exercise 3.

▶ **Workbook page 22**

Writing Part 6 SB page 41

Lead-in

Write *surfing* on the board. Elicit what clothes or equipment you need to go surfing e.g. *surfboard.* Ask if anyone in the class goes surfing and, if so, elicit questions from other students about where they go, what it's like, how easy or difficult it is etc. Now put students into small groups and tell them to do the same with *horse riding.* Set a time limit of two or three minutes and elicit ideas from different groups of what to bring (e.g. clothes – *hat, boots.*).

1 Encourage students to use adjectives to describe the different sports and comparatives and superlatives to compare them e.g. *I'd like to try fishing. It's more relaxing than the others and exciting when you catch a fish.*

> **Writing Part 6 (writing short messages)**
> Discuss the information with students and elicit examples of 'little words' that could be tested e.g. prepositions *(on, in, at)*, articles *(a, the)*, auxiliary verbs *(do, be, have)*.
>
> **Exam advice**

2 Tell students to cover Exercise 3 so that they don't get any ideas from that. Elicit the first thing they would do in their email e.g. *say hello.* Allow two minutes for students to think of what is needed. Elicit ideas.

> **Suggested answer**
> Say hello, ask her about going surfing (Would you like / Do you want), tell her what to bring (e.g. swimming costume, towel, warm clothes) say when you want to meet (e.g. in the morning, at 9 o'clock)

3 Tell students there is no correct answer as long as it is grammatically correct. You can set rules for the gaps e.g. one word only or a maximum of three words or leave it up to students. Remind students that the task in the exam isn't to complete a note like this but to write the whole thing.

Possible answers
tomorrow / on Saturday / at the weekend; bring; nine o'clock

4 If you think students need more help, allow them to discuss their ideas as you did in Exercise 2 before they start writing. When they are ready, set a time limit of five minutes for students to write their email. Remind students to read their emails and check for mistakes. When students have finished, put them in pairs and ask them to read each other's notes to see if they can spot any mistakes.

Fast finishers
Tell students to think of a new set of instructions for a different activity using three bullet points as in Exercises 2 and 4.

Possible answers
Hi Sam,
Would you like to come horse riding with me on Sunday? I want to go riding in the fields behind our house. You can ride Misty, my mum's horse. Don't forget your hat and boots!
See you then,
Niki

Extension idea
If any students finished early and wrote a new set of instructions, collect these and choose one to dictate to the class for them to write an email for homework.

▶ **Writing Bank page 139: Writing Part 6**
▶ **Workbook page 22**

Speaking Part 2, Phase 1 SB page 41

Lead-in
Put students in small groups. Give them one minute to find a sport or activity that none of them have tried before. When they are ready, they imagine that someone asks them to do this activity and they discuss what their reactions would be e.g. *No way! It's dangerous; Yes, that sounds really exciting.* Elicit the activities students discussed and their reactions.

Speaking Part 2, Phase 1 (a discussion based on an artwork prompt)
Look at the advice with students. Tell students that the examiner won't interrupt unless you can't think of anything to say. It is important that this doesn't happen because the examiner wants you to discuss something together. Elicit that it is useful to ask each other questions because it gives students more to talk about and shows the examiner that they can form questions correctly.

Exam advice

1 Tell students that, in the exam, they will have just a few seconds to look at the pictures and think about the English words for what they can see. Say: *If you don't know what the word is you can describe or explain it,* for example, *'I'm not sure what this sport is called. It's popular in America. They hit a ball with a bat and run.'* (baseball). Tell students to imagine that they don't know the names of the sports in the pictures. Elicit how students could describe them.

Answers
A tennis B basketball C table tennis D skiing E football

2 Look at the phrases with students. Point out that *I've never tried it* is a new structure. Tell them you won't look at how other verbs are formed in this tense now. They should just use this phrase for something they don't do now and never did in the past. Also elicit how they could finish the sentence: *It's exciting, but … (e.g. it's dangerous/expensive.).*
Play the recording twice if necessary. Elicit the answers.

Answers
tennis: girl – It's fun
football: boy – I like it.; girl – I don't like it.
table tennis: girl – I really like it.; boy – It's boring.
skiing: girl – I've never tried it; boy – It's exciting, but …
baseball: boy – I don't understand it; girl – I hate it.

Track 37
Examiner: Do you like these different sports? Say why or why not.
Girl: What are these sports?
Boy: This is tennis, and this is football.
Girl: Right, and this is table tennis, I think, oh and skiing!
Boy: And baseball! So do you like playing tennis?
Girl: Yes, I do.
Boy: So do I. Why do you like it?
Girl: It's fun!

Boy:	OK. What about football? I like it because I play with my friends. We play on Wednesdays in the park. And you?
Girl:	No, I don't like it.
Boy:	Why not?
Girl:	I don't like team sports. And do you play table tennis?
Boy:	No, it's boring.
Girl:	Oh? I really like it.
Boy:	Why?
Girl:	I play with my mum! She's really good.
Boy:	Now what about skiing. Can you ski?
Girl:	No. No , I've never tried it. It looks cold!
Boy:	Oh. I can ski! We go to the mountains and we ski. It's exciting, but it is very cold!
Girl:	Do you like baseball?
Boy:	Not really. I don't understand it. We don't play it in my country. What about you?
Girl:	No, I hate it.

3 Look at the example questions with the class. Elicit or tell students that they could first ask: *Do you ever play / go …?* and then only ask the next two questions if the answer is *Yes*. Tell students to ask each other about the seven activities and then discuss the last question (using comparatives) together, giving reasons for their answers.

Extension idea
Put students into groups of three so that they can take turns in playing the part of the examiner. Each examiner decides what to ask about the seven sports; one of the questions they discussed in Exercise 3 or a new one if they can think of one. Students do the same as in Exercise 3 but this time with an examiner listening. After each student has played the role of the examiner, they give the two students feedback.

▶ **Speaking bank pages 146–147: Part 1**
▶ **Complete Key for Schools new edition Test Generator Unit 5**

Vocabulary

Sports
badminton   judo
basketball   table tennis
football

do / play / go with sports

do		play		go	
	karate		baseball		running
	judo		hockey		surfing
	gymnastics		cricket		climbing
	yoga		volleyball		skating

Countries – nationalities
Australia – Australian   Italy – Italian
Britain – British   Japan – Japanese
China – Chinese   Mexico – Mexican
France – French   Portugal – Portuguese
Greece – Greek   Spain – Spanish
India – Indian   Sweden – Swedish
Ireland – Irish

Vocabulary activity 1
Put students into small groups. Tell them that you are going to think of a word and give them five clues. They can only have one guess. If they guess the word correctly after the first clue, they get 5 points but, if they are wrong, they are out. After two clues they get 4 points, 3 clues – 3 points, 4 clues – 2 points and 5 clues – 1 point. After each clue, the groups decide whether to guess and risk being wrong or wait for another clue and hope that no other group guesses correctly.
e.g. sports:
Clue 1: We play it with a ball. (Ask if anyone wants to guess.)
Clue 2: It is a team game. (Ask if anyone wants to guess.)
Clue 3: Players hit the ball. (Ask if anyone wants to guess.)
Clue 4: It is an American game. (Ask if anyone wants to guess.)
Clue 5: Players wear a special cap. The cap has the same name as the sport (This is the last chance for groups to guess.) The answer is baseball.
Ask each group to find another word from the wordlist and write five clues of their own. The groups then take it in turns to give their clues to the class as you did in the example.

Vocabulary activity 2
Put students into small groups and give each group a number. Tell students that they have to define a word from the list e.g. *Football – it's a sport with two teams who try to score goals by kicking a ball*. They then choose three key words from their definition and write these on a blank piece of paper (e.g. sport, goals, kicking) and add their group number. Collect the key words and place them around the room. Students walk round the classroom and try to guess each word from the key words written. When they have finished, elicit guesses and ask the groups who wrote the key words if the guesses are correct.

6 Have you got any homework?

Unit objectives

Topic: school

Listening Part 3: 3-option multiple-choice: listening to identify specific information, feelings and opinions

Reading and Writing Part 2: matching: reading for specific information and detailed comprehension

Speaking Part 2, Phase 2: a discussion based on an artwork prompt; the focus is on organising a larger unit of discourse; comparing, describing, expressing opinions

Reading and Writing Part 5: open cloze; reading and identifying appropriate word, with focus on grammar

Grammar: *have to*, object pronouns

Vocabulary: school subjects, classroom objects, education verbs

Pronunciation: /v/ and /f/

School subjects SB page 42

Lead-in
Put students into small groups. Tell them to think about their favourite school day of the week and reasons why it is their favourite. Students then take turns to say which day they like best and why.

1 Often school subjects are similar in English and other languages, so students might be able to match the subjects to the pictures alone. Elicit the answers and model and drill the words.

> **Answers**
> **B** geography   **C** chemistry   **D** history
> **E** biology   **F** art   **G** maths
> **H** English   **I** music

2 Put students into small groups. One person in each group writes the answers on a piece of paper. Tell them they will get two points for a correct answer and one point if the answer is correct but spelled incorrectly. When they have finished, students swap answer sheets with a different group and turn to Student's Book page 149 to check their answers and add up the marks.

> **Answers**
> **1** Mount Everest **2** elephant **3** worse **4** 9 **5** both the same
> **6** salt **7** (November 11th) 1918 **8** Paris **9** guitar

3 Students work alone. Elicit the answers and check the pronunciation of the subjects.

> **Answers**
> **1** geography **2** biology **3** English **4** maths **5** physics
> **6** chemistry **7** history **8** art **9** music

4 Put students into pairs and set a time limit of one minute. When they have finished, elicit ideas and have a class vote on the best/worst subjects.

Extension idea
Students work alone. Tell them that they are going to create a timetable for one of their days at school. They should draw a grid showing the number of lessons and the time each one begins and ends. They then join together in pairs. They take turns to ask and answer about each other's timetable. Elicit some possible questions they could ask, e.g. *What do you have at 9 o'clock? What's your second lesson?* They note their partner's answers and guess the day they are talking about. If there are any other subjects needed, try to give the class the English equivalent or ask them to look them up.

Listening Part 3 SB page 43

Lead-in
Ask students to think about different schools either in their town or that they have seen in films from different countries. Put them into small groups and set a time limit of two minutes to think of differences between the schools.

1 Look at the first question with students and elicit other answers they could give, e.g. *I wear different clothes every day. In the summer, I wear shorts.* Tell students to try to give long answers with reasons for their answers to questions 2 and 3.

Listening Part 3 (multiple-choice)
Elicit that all three options will probably be mentioned and students have to understand why one is correct and the other two aren't. Also elicit that they will hear the recording twice and should listen carefully both times.

Exam advice

2 Set a time limit of one minute for students to read the questions and the options and do the matching. Elicit the words that helped them do the matching (1 sport – sport; 2 clothing – wear; 3 action – speak, laugh, explain; 4 time – start at; 5 topic – English homework).

> **Answers**
> 2 1 3 3 4 2 5 4

3 Tell students to listen alone but allow them to compare their answers after they have listened once. If they have different answers, they should try to justify their answer to their partner from what they heard and listen carefully on the second listening. Don't elicit any answers yet.

4 When students have listened again, elicit the answers and anything they can remember from the dialogue which helped them to identify the correct answer.

> **Answers**
> 1 C 2 C 3 C 4 C 5 A

Track 38

Narrator: For these questions, choose the correct answer. You will hear Louis and Rachel talking about their new schools.

Rachel: Hey Louis, how's your new school

Louis: Hi, Rachel – I love it. What's your new school like?

Rachel: It's great. But I don't like the uniform!

Louis: I don't have that problem, because there isn't one! I usually go in trousers and a T-shirt. The school rules are that I can't wear jeans or trainers, that's all.

Rachel: What time does your school start?

Louis: I catch the eight-thirty bus, which gets me to school at about quarter to nine. Lessons don't start until nine o'clock, so that gives me plenty of time to talk to my friends. What are the teachers like at your school?

Rachel: Great – especially my maths teacher. She's from the US and she uses different words for some things. But she speaks slowly. She isn't funny, but she's kind. I think the best thing about her is that she tells us how to do things really clearly, you know, so we understand!

Louis: What about English?

Rachel: It's fine. We have homework for tomorrow. We have to write about a famous person. I talked about it with my family. My dad said I should write about a famous actor, but I think I want to write about a football player. What sports do you play at school?

Louis: It's different each term. At the moment, it's basketball. Next term I think it's hockey or football. And of course, I have badminton on Fridays at my mum's club.

Extension idea
Photocopy the audioscript and ask students to work in pairs to find why the incorrect options were incorrect, (1 There's no uniform; You can't wear jeans or trainers; 2 I catch the 8.30 bus. It gets me to school at about quarter to nine; 3 She isn't funny. She speaks slowly (quietly isn't mentioned); 4 her family talked about a famous actor; 5 Next term it's hockey. I have badminton at my mum's club)

▶ **Workbook page 24**

Grammar SB page 43

have to

> **Lead-in**
> Put students into small groups. Elicit one or two things that teachers tell them to do, e.g. *Be quiet*. Set a time limit of two minutes for students to add more ideas. Tell them not to use negative verb forms. Elicit ideas from each group.

1 To help weaker students, tell them there is one positive, two negatives and one question, so they know what to look out for.

> **Answers**
> *have to*: get up early; *don't have to*: get a bus, wear a tie. Question: Does everyone have to wear it?

2 Allow students to work in pairs so they can help each other. Tell students that *have to/has to* has the same form as the verb *to have*. If students ask if we can use *have got to* instead, it is possible but informal and almost always uses an abbreviated form (*I've got to …* rather than *I have got to*).

> **Answers**
> 1 F 2 T 3 T 4 T

3 Elicit the answers and ask students to make sentences about Rachel and Simon to make sure they use the third person forms correctly, e.g. *Rachel doesn't have to get a bus to school.*

> **Answers**
> 1 necessary 2 not necessary

/P/ /v/ and /f/

 Play the recording once for students to listen. Ask if they notice any difference in the way the verb is pronounced. Then play it again, pausing after each sentence for them to repeat.

Track 39

1 I have three sisters.
2 I have to go to school.
3 We don't have to wear a uniform.

> **Answers**
> /hæv/
> Sentences **2 3** /hæf/
> /hæv/ sounds longer

5 Look at the rules with the class and model and drill the two ways of saying the verb *have* again using the two examples sentences in the rules box. Monitor and check students' pronunciation while they are practising the conversation.

Track 40

Boy: Have you got any homework?
Girl: Yes, I have. But I don't have to do it now.
Boy: When do you have to hand it in?
Girl: On Thursday.
Boy: Then you have to do it now, because you have a piano lesson on Wednesday evening.

6 Look at the first sentence with the class and elicit an answer from one or two students. Check that they use the correct form by asking follow-up questions. If a student says *have to*, ask them what their uniform is. If they say *don't have to*, ask what they wear to school. Also make sure students use the correct pronunciation. Allow students to work in pairs to complete the exercise. Elicit the answers and check pronunciation.

Students could do Grammar reference: *have to*, Exercises 1–2, page 115 at this point or for homework.

7 This could be done in pairs with students working on the questions together. They then take turns to ask and answer them.

> **Answers**
> **2** Do you have to wash the dishes? **3** Do you have to clean your room? **4** Do you have to go shopping? **5** Does your mum or dad have to wake you up in the morning?

> **Fast finishers**
> If students finish early, ask them to write one or two more questions using *Do you have to …* . They can then ask other students their questions when everyone has finished the exercise.

▶ **Grammar reference page 115: *have to***

▶ **Workbook page 25**

Vocabulary SB page 44

Classroom objects

> **Lead-in**
> Ask students to look in their school bags and find three things they know the words for in English and one thing they don't know the word for in English. In pairs, they tell each other what they have got and see if their partner can name the other item.

1 Allow students to do this in pairs. Elicit the answers and model and drill the words. Ask students: *Which part of the longer words is stressed?* Model these words again if necessary and elicit that all the longer words have the stress on the first syllable.

> **Answers**
> **1** board **2** textbook **3** pencil case **4** desk **5** ruler **6** pen **7** dictionary **8** pencil **9** timetable **10** notebook **11** rubber

2 Re-elicit the form *have to*. Look at the example question with students. Elicit the pronunciation of *have* in the question and answer, then ask them to answer it so that it is true for them, e.g. *No, I can remember it. Yes, I do.* Elicit questions and answers from different pairs.

> **Extension idea**
> Tell students to work in small groups and, together, put ten items on the desk between them including, if possible, a ruler, rubber, pen, pencil, textbook and notebook. They can add other personal items such as money, phone. They then take it in turns to tell the others to close their eyes and then hide one of the objects. They can move the other objects around as well if they wish. When the other students open their eyes they race to say what the missing item is.

▶ **Workbook page 24**

Reading Part 2 SB page 45

Lead-in

Write on the board: _ _ _ _ _ _ _ _ _ _ _ (*drama school*). Divide the class into two groups. Elicit one letter at a time from each group. Every time their letter appears in the words, they get a point (e.g. a = 2 points). The groups keep guessing letters until the words are complete. They cannot guess full words. The team with the most points wins. If students guess a letter that doesn't appear in the words, write these on the board away from the gapped words so that they can see what letters have been used. When the word has been completed elicit what students think a drama school is.

Reading Part 2 (matching)

Discuss the advice with students. Tell students to look at the title and photos and try to think what the text might be about. Elicit that the questions in this part of the test are not written in the order that the texts are written i.e. the first answer may refer to text 3, the second answer to text 1.

Exam advice

Background information

Perhaps the most famous fictional boarding school is Hogwarts in the Harry Potter books. In the stories, Harry sleeps in a room with four other boys and all students eat together in the Great Hall. The most famous real boarding school in the UK is probably Eton College. Its past students include Prince William and Harry, and Eddie Redmayne.

One of the most famous schools for drama and performing arts in the UK is the BRIT School for Performing Arts and Technology in London. It is the only free drama school for 14–19 year olds and its famous students include singer Adele.

1 Tell students that it is very important to read the texts quickly and elicit why (because they will have an idea of where the relevant information is, which will make it quicker to find). Set a time limit of one or two minutes for students to read through the text. Elicit which text matches each photo and, if you did the lead-in activity, which photo shows a drama school.

> **Answers**
> Sara: C Marian: B; Freddy: A

Extension activity

Students work in pairs with their books closed. They talk together about what they remember about each text they have just read. Set a time limit of one minute then ask the first question from Exercise 2 and elicit which text students think it refers to and any details they can remember.

2 Set a time limit of five minutes for the reading. Elicit the answers and ask students if reading the texts quickly first helped them to find the information more quickly.

> **Answers**
> 1 C 2 B 3 C 4 A 5 C 6 B 7 A

3 Elicit what the three types of school are (one you live in, one to learn drama, one studying at home). Elicit one advantage or disadvantage for each from the class. Set a two-minute time limit for students to discuss more advantages and disadvantages.

Extension idea

Ask students to work in pairs to prepare a short dialogue between two students. One has left their school and is now either at a boarding school, drama school or is studying at home. They can be happy or unhappy about this. The other student thinks of questions to ask them. Allow five minutes for students to write and practise their dialogues.

▶ **Workbook page 25**

Grammar SB page 46

Object pronouns

Lead-in

Tell students you are going to tell them some sentences about yourself and they should guess what you are talking about. Students work in small groups and have ten seconds to write an idea for each sentence. Say: 1 I love it; 2 I can't stand him; 3 I like her; 4 I hate them.

Elicit ideas for each sentence from different groups. If any answers don't make grammatical sense, write these words on the board next to the number they refer to, e.g. *1 dogs 2 Emma Stone 4 English*. At the end of the activity, ask the class: *What is wrong with these answers?* Elicit that the nouns students used don't match the pronouns.

1 Tell students to work in pairs and describe one photo each, saying what is happening. Set a time limit of 30 seconds for each student and then elicit ideas.

Look at the sentences with students. Elicit that in the second sentence there are two verbs (*make, laugh*). We are interested in the first verb here as that's what the teacher does (*She makes (does something to make) students laugh*). Elicit more examples of things that people make us do (e.g. *My parents make me tidy my room*). In the other two sentences, it appears twice. In the first sentence it is an object, so it comes after the verb. In the second, it is the subject, so comes before the verb.

> **Answers**
> **1** her = teacher; them = children; it = homework; him = the boy **2** after

2 Elicit the four object pronouns in Exercise 1 (*her, them, it, him*) ask students to write these in the correct place in the table. Students then work alone to try to complete the table with *you / us*.

> **Answers**
> it = it; you = you; we = us; he = him; she = her; they = them

3 Look at the example with students. Elicit what it refers to (*geography*) and why it is the correct word to use (*geography* is a singular noun). Allow students to work in pairs to complete the sentences. Elicit the answers.

> **Fast finishers**
> Tell fast finishers to look at question 4 and make similar sentences about other things or people, e.g. *My brother complains a lot. No one listens to him! Our English teacher is great. Everyone likes him.* When everyone has finished the exercise, ask fast finishers to read out one or two of their sentences.

> **Answers**
> **2** us **3** them **4** her **5** it **6** him **7** you **8** me

Students could do the Grammar reference: object pronouns, Exercises 3–4, page 115, at this point or for homework.

4 Before students do the activity, elicit that, when we refer to things in general, e.g. hamburgers, we use a plural form (if the word is countable) and use the object pronoun *them*. If the food is uncountable, we use *it* (e.g. *What do you think of pizza? I love it*). We also refer to music bands as plural (*What do you think of Imagine Dragons? I love them*). Allow students time to think alone about examples and then two minutes to ask and answer in pairs.

> **Extension idea**
> Tell students they are going to do a quick survey. Tell them you are going to read out some topics and they should choose their favourite example of each.
>
> Choose some or all of the following to read out: animals, day of the week, shop, actor/actress, singer, sports star, town, book, film, shop.
>
> Students then work in small groups and tell each other their choices. The others agree or disagree as appropriate.

▶ **Grammar reference page 115: Object pronouns**
▶ **Workbook page 26**

Vocabulary SB page 46

Education verbs

> **Lead-in**
> Write the word *learn* on the board. Tell students that, in our lives, we learn to do many things. Elicit the first thing a child has to do (e.g. *learn how to walk*). Put students into small groups and allow two minutes to think of other things people have to learn to do in their lives. Elicit ideas from each group.

1 When students have found Rachel's best subjects ask them to underline the verbs in the text. Elicit: *teaches, leave, want, go, study, learning, play, taking, get.*

> **Answers**
> maths and science

2 Allow students to work in pairs if necessary. Elicit the answers and the meanings of the different words: teach – help someone else learn, learn – a skill, study – reading or doing exercises to get better in a subject, pass a test – get the marks you need, fail a test – not get the marks you need, take an exam – answer the exam questions.

Answers
1 teaches 2 learn 3 study 4 pass 5 taking 6 fails

3 Students can work together or alone to complete the sentences. Elicit the answers.

Fast finishers
Ask students to write more sentences which include some of the phrases from the exercise, e.g. *learn how to …, pass your …, study … at university, … teaches … take an exam.* When everyone has finished, ask students to read out their sentences.

Answers
1 learn 2 pass 3 study 4 teaches 5 fail

4 Set a time limit of four minutes for pairs to ask and answer the five questions. Encourage them to give more details, e.g. *I'd like to learn the guitar because I want to be in a band when I'm older.* When they have finished, elicit answers from different students.

Extension idea
Put the class into small groups. Ask students what other skills schools should teach students, e.g. *We should learn to cook at school. Healthy food is very important in life.* Set a time limit of three minutes.

▶ **Workbook page 24**

Reading Part 5 SB page 47

Lead-in
Write the word *forget* on the board. You could tell them about something you sometimes forget as an example. Elicit the meaning and ask students to work in small groups to talk about things they sometimes forget to bring to school, e.g. *I sometimes forget my PE kit.*

Reading Part 5 (open cloze)
Discuss the advice with students and elicit what kind of little words from this unit may be tested (e.g. object pronouns) and other kinds of small words, e.g. articles (*a, the*), prepositions (*in, on, at*), linking words (*and, but*), auxiliary verbs (*do, be, have*).

Exam advice

1 Look at the words in the box with students and elicit what they are (*she* – subject pronoun, *him* – object pronoun, *you, it* – subject or object pronoun, *my, their* – possessive adjectives). When students have finished, elicit the answers and why each word is used.

Answers
1 my 2 him 3 she 4 their 5 it 6 you

2 Elicit that *forgot* is past form of forget. Tell students not to worry about the gaps yet. Set a time limit of about 30 seconds and elicit the answers.

Answers
Matt wants his dad to bring his trainers and a snack to school; His father says she will bring them, and asks if he wants his pencils.

3 Set a time limit of five minutes for students to do the gap fill. Students choose one of the three texts and think of one word which could be gapped in each sentence and what kind of word each is. When everyone has finished the exercise, elicit ideas of which words could be gapped.

Answers
1 them 2 with 3 any 4 the / your 5 Do 6 They

4 Set a length for the text (e.g. 25–35 words). Elicit that, in the text in Exercise 2, a past form is used (*I forgot*). Tell students they can use this but that they shouldn't try to use any other past forms unless they are sure of them. If you think students need more help, elicit other useful phrases from Matt's note, e.g. *Can you (bring) … .* Set a time limit, then students swap messages with a partner to check their work.

Extension idea
When students have checked each other's messages, they choose one and rewrite it with three gaps. Remind students of the sort of words that can be gapped. When they have finished, they swap texts with a different pair and try to complete the missing words.

▶ **Workbook page 26**

Speaking Part 2, Phase 2 SB page 47

Lead-in

Write the question prompt on the board: *Do you prefer … or …?* Elicit what this means (*Which one do you like best?*) and that, if the words used are verbs, they need the *-ing* form, e.g. *Do you prefer running or swimming?*

Put students into pairs to think of three or four questions to ask using this structure and encourage them to think of related pairs of words (burgers or pizza, football or basketball) rather than random ones (burgers or football). When they have finished, they work together to answer the questions, giving reasons.

Speaking Part 2 (a discussion based on an artwork prompt)

Look at the advice with students. Elicit that, first of all they will discuss the picture together and then the examiner will ask questions on the same topic. Look at the third piece of advice and explain to students that they should try to give more details like these before they are asked by the examiner.

Exam advice

1 Look at the question with students. Elicit what 'arts' subjects are (all the school subjects which aren't maths or science-based, e.g. English, history, art). Elicit other subjects that would go under each heading, e.g. *sciences: maths; arts: history.*

Answers
sciences: physics, biology, chemistry;
arts: music, English, drama

2 Play the recording and elicit the answer and why Claudia gives the better answer: she uses longer sentences with reasons linked with linking words; Jorge gives short answers with no linking words.

Answers
Claudia

Track 41

Examiner: Claudia, do you prefer studying science or arts subjects?
Claudia: I prefer the sciences.
Examiner: Why?
Claudia: Because I like to learn about the world. I like arts too, but I don't like studying them.
Examiner: And what about you, Jorge. Do you prefer studying science or arts subjects?
Jorge: Arts.
Examiner: Why?
Jorge: I don't like science. It's difficult. I like music.
Examiner: Claudia, what's your favourite school subject?
Claudia: Hmm … I think it's biology.
Examiner: Why biology?
Claudia: Because it's interesting. And I'd like to be a doctor when I am older.
Examiner: What about you, Jorge? What's your favourite school subject?
Jorge: English.
Examiner: Why do you like English best?
Jorge: I like my English teacher. She's nice.

3 Ask students to read the sentences before they listen again and try to remember or work out the missing words. Elicit ideas and then play the recording for students to check.

Answers
1 because **2** but **3** because, and

4 Tell students that they can link everything in one sentence or in two sentences, starting the second sentence with a linking word as in sentence 3, Exercise 3.

Fast finishers

Tell students to continue Jorge's answers with a reason why he likes music and his geography teacher. Elicit ideas when everyone has finished.

Suggested answers
1 I don't like science because it's difficult, but I like music.
2 I like my English teacher because she's nice.

5 Encourage students to use the ABBA system for taking turns so that student A answers question 1 first, followed by student B. Student B then answers the second question followed by A. This makes it fairer and enables both students to listen to some ideas from their partner before speaking.

Extension idea
Students work in pairs to ask and answer similar questions to those in Exercise 2 but on different topics, e.g. food, music, sports. When students have finished, elicit questions and answers from different pairs.

▶ Speaking bank pages 147–148: Part 2, Phase
▶ Vocabulary and grammar review Units 5 and 6
▶ Complete Key for Schools new edition Test Generator Unit 6

Vocabulary

School subjects

art	English	maths
biology	geography	music
chemistry	history	physics

Classroom objects

board	pen	ruler
desk	pencil	textbook
dictionary	pencil case	timetable
notebook	rubber	

Education verbs

fail	study
learn	take
pass	teach

Vocabulary activity 1
Tell students to choose a word from the wordlist. They then think of three related words or phrases, e.g. *fail an exam – low marks, difficult, take again*. They then tell their partner the three related words and see if the partner can guess the original word. They then work together and write one or two sentences using them.

Vocabulary activity 2
For this activity, provide squared paper for students to draw a crossword on. Alternatively, get them to draw a grid in their notebook. Put students into pairs. Discuss crosswords and how we make them (connecting words going up or across). Show students an example if you think it will help. Elicit that letters can't appear next to each other unless they form a word. Students work together to make a small, five word crossword, e.g.

```
      r u b b e r
      u   o
pencil   a
      e   r
      r   d e s k
```

Do the example as a class if you think it will help. Then ask students to draw a blank grid and write clues for the words. When they have finished, pairs swap puzzles with another pair who try to complete the puzzle.

Vocabulary and grammar review Unit 5

> **1**
> **2** the best **3** the most interesting **4** happier **5** more expensive **6** the most beautiful **7** harder **8** the worst
> **2**
> **2** in **3** on **4** at **5** on **6** in **7** in **8** At **9** in **10** On
> **3**
> **2** cricket **3** yoga **4** judo **5** cycling **6** gymnastics **7** football **8** tennis **9** swimming
> **4**
> You play: cricket, football, tennis
> You do: yoga, judo, gymnastics
> You go: surfing, cycling, swimming
> **5**
> **2** Mexican **3** Japanese **4** Swedish **5** French **6** Italian **7** Greek **8** Australian

Vocabulary and grammar review Unit 6

> **1**
> **2** don't have to **3** have to **4** doesn't have to **5** has to **6** Do you have to **7** Does your mother have to
> **2**
> **2** him **3** her **4** them **5** you **6** me
> **3**
> **2** C **3** B **4** A **5** C **6** B
> **4**
> **Across: 3** uniform **5** notebook **6** board **7** break
> **Down: 1** dictionary **2** rubber **4** ruler

7 Let's go to the museum

Starting off SB page 50

Lead-in
Before students open their books, elicit a famous city, e.g. London or students' capital city, and ask students what they would write about in a fact box about the city. Elicit ideas and write these on the board, e.g. population, famous buildings. Elicit or give some ideas. Students then work in pairs or small groups and make a fact file about the city. It should have five headings.

1 Elicit how we compare two different things (using comparatives) and elicit a few examples, e.g. *better, worse, more interesting*. Put students in pairs and set a time limit of one or two minutes for students to discuss the questions. Elicit ideas.

> **Suggested answers**
> City: more work, More things to do, exciting, better shops
> Village: Quieter, more friendly, safer, cleaner,

2 Play the recording once and allow students to compare what they heard in pairs. Allow them to listen again to check or complete their answers.

> **Answers**
> 1 Ellie lives in a little village. Rory lives in a city.
> 2 She likes it because it's safe and quiet. He likes it because it's exciting.

Track 42

Girl: We moved to this little village last year and I like it. I can cycle to my friends' house through the beautiful countryside, and my parents don't worry about me because there isn't much traffic – so it's very safe. All the families here know each other. There's only one café, but the coffee is good. It's also very quiet – some people say it's boring, but I don't agree. I like it.

Boy: Dad bought a flat in the city two years ago, and I love it here. It's a really exciting place to be because there's always something to do. OK, it's a bit noisy, some areas are a bit ugly, and it can be a bit dangerous – especially at night. But I wouldn't want to be anywhere else. I love living in a big city.

3 Give students examples of some adjectives that aren't in the exercise, e.g. *old, happy* and elicit the opposites (*young, sad*). Elicit the answers to the activity and ask students to match the adjectives to the places the boy and girl talked about i.e. the village and the city.

> **Answers**
> safe – dangerous; quiet – noisy;
> boring – exciting; little – big

4 It would be good to have students who live in different places together in pairs so that they can tell each other about their town. If they live in the same town, they see if they agree about what their town is like. Encourage students to give reasons for their opinions where possible.

Extension idea
Put students into small groups. Ask them to take turns to tell their group which town or city they would like to live in and why. Set a time limit of two minutes.

Reading Part 1 SB page 50

Lead-in
Put students into three groups. Give each group two writing tasks of 20 words: 1 Write a short advert you might see in a shop window. 2 Write a text message about a meeting to a friend. 3 Write an email to a friend asking for something. 4 Write a text to a friend who has been ill. 5 Write a notice you may see in a hospital. 6 Write a notice you may see on a school notice board. Set a time limit of three minutes.
When they have finished, groups swap messages to decide what the other group's messages are about and what type of text they are.

Reading Part 1 (multiple-choice)

Look at the advice with the class and elicit why it is useful. The first point helps students to understand the text and helps them decide the correct answer. The second point is useful because students can't lose marks for a wrong answer.

Exam advice

1 Look at the question with students and elicit one or two examples, e.g. *a cinema, a café*. Put students into pairs or small groups and set a time limit of one minute for them to brainstorm ideas.

2 Ask the class what kind of message this is (an advert). Elicit the answers and ask what other special offers there could be, e.g. buy one coffee, get one free.

Answers
1 special offer 2 half-price

3 Tell students to work in pairs and think of reasons why the incorrect options are wrong. Elicit the answers and the reasons why. (A The offer only lasts from 9 am – 10 am. We can see the café is open longer because lunch is from 12–12.30. B There is no special offer for food advertised. C True. The time is 9 am–10 am).

Answer
C

4 Set a time limit of eight minutes. Elicit the answers and the words in the options and texts which helped them (*1 couldn't catch – missed 2 give me in class – take to school 3 Our history homework is – tell about the homework 4 two visitors – OK for two people to visit 5 give me their names by Friday – Tell Mr Smith soon*).

Answers
1 A 2 C 3 B 4 C 5 A

Extension idea

Put the messages and options the fast finishers wrote during the reading activity around the room. If there were no or very few fast finishers and students didn't do the lead-in activity, put students into small groups to write a short message similar to those in the reading task and to write three options for it. Then put the messages and options around the room. Students walk round looking at the different messages and trying to choose the correct option for each.

▶ **Workbook page 28**

Grammar SB page 51

Past simple

Lead-in

Write two answers on the board:

Q: ?   Q: ?

A: I am at school now.   A: I live in Toledo.

Elicit the questions (*Where are you now? Where do you live?*), write them on the board and elicit the structures in each (*verb to be, present simple*). Put students into pairs to think of two answers of their own using the two structures. Set a time limit of one minute. Students then swap answers with a different pair and write the questions.

1 Before students look at the text, ask them to describe the girl and what she is doing and use their imaginations to say where she lives and where she is from.

Set a time limit of two minutes for students to read the text and find the answers. Elicit adjectives she uses to describe Sydney (*beautiful, exciting*) and ask what the opposites are (*ugly, boring*).

Answers
She lives in Australia. Yes, she loves living there.

2 Tell students to look at the events and work in pairs to order them. They can then quickly find the events in the text and check that their order is correct.

Answers
2 d 3 b 4 g 5 f 6 a 7 c

3 Elicit or check that regular past simple verbs are formed by adding -*ed* to the end of the verb. Irregular ones have different forms. *Was* and *were* are the past forms of the verb *to be*. Students work in pairs to find the verbs. Elicit each one and their base forms.

7

> **Answers**
> I liked living in our little village in Spain, so when my parents got new jobs in Australia, I felt sad. All my friends were in the village, and I didn't want to leave them. I didn't know anybody in Sydney!
>
> Last year we left our old home and got on a plane to a new life in a new country.
>
> How did I feel about that? I hated it at first. My new school was much bigger than my old one, and I felt very small and alone. I didn't speak much English, so it was difficult to make new friends. I wanted to go back to our village.
>
> But slowly I began to feel happier. My parents gave me a camera for my birthday. Then I joined the school photography club and I met some interesting people. Last month, there was a competition called 'Pictures of the City' and I decided to enter it. I won a prize, and they showed my photograph in the city library.
>
> I love living here now. It's a beautiful place, and much more exciting than my old village.

4 When students have found the examples, elicit how they are formed (did / didn't + base form of the verb).

> **Answers**
> past simple question: How did I feel about that?
> past simple negative: didn't want, didn't know

5 Allow students to work in pairs to complete the rules, then go through them with the class, eliciting examples from the text, e.g. *1 Last year we left.*

> **Answers**
> 1 finished 2 adding –ed or –d 3 did 4 didn't 5 was and were

Extension idea
If you used the lead-in activity, look at the two questions and answers and change them to:

Q Where _____ you yesterday? Q: Where _____ you live last year?

A: I _____ at school yesterday. A: I _____ in Toledo last year.

Students now change their original questions and answers into the past tense, changing or adding time expressions where necessary. Elicit questions and answers from pairs.

6 Look at the first sentence with students and elicit what the student has done (used the present form of the verb instead of the past). Allow students to work in pairs and elicit the answers and what mistakes students made.

> **Answers**
> 2 stayied stayed 3 played play 4 costed cost
> 5 maked made 6 have watched watched

7 Allow students to work in pairs. Monitor and help where necessary. Elicit the answers and model and drill the pronunciation of some of the difficult irregular past forms, e.g. *saw, knew, bought*.

Fast finishers
Tell fast finishers to think of more questions that Tom could ask Sandra, e.g. *What prize did you win? What did your school friends say?* When everyone has finished the exercise, elicit some of these questions and ask other students to answer them.

> **Answers**
> 2 took 3 went 4 was 5 were 6 decided 7 did you take
> 8 weren't 9 Were you 10 knew 11 didn't think 12 Did you have 13 bought

8 Elicit when we use the verb to be and when we use *did* (We use *did* before a verb, we use *was/were* before other words, e.g. nouns, adjectives and prepositions, e.g. *Were you happy? Was he a tall man?* Elicit the answers and, for stronger classes, what kind of word follows each question (1 verb; 2 preposition; 3 verb; 4 verb; 5 noun + adjective; 6 verb; 7 noun + adjective; 8 preposition).

> **Answers**
> 1 did 2 Were 3 did 4 Did 5 Was 6 did 7 was 8 were

Students could do Grammar Reference: Past simple, Exercises 1–2, page 117, at this point or for homework.

/P/ past simple -*ed* endings

9 Model and drill the three sounds and then play the recording. Tell students that all verbs ending in -*ded* or -*ted* have the sound /ɪd/. Students sometimes try to pronounce verbs which should end with the /t/ sound with an /ɪd/ sound, e.g. *like-ed*. Correct any pronunciation mistakes that you hear or encourage self-correction. To do this, you could say: Not *'like-ed'* to elicit the correct pronunciation or say *like-ed?* with a questioning intonation. Alternatively, say the base form *like* and see if the student can say the past form correctly.

Track 43
showed
finished
started

10 Put students into pairs. Students say the sentences together and decide the sound of each verb. Play the recording and drill the three verbs.

> **Answers**
> /d/ lived /t/ liked /ɪd/ wanted

Track 44
She lived in a village. She liked it. She wanted to stay there.

11 Again, see if students can guess the correct pronunciation before they listen. When the table is complete, model and drill all the verbs in each column.

> **Answers**
> /d/ joined, arrived /t/ worked, asked /ɪd/ visited, waited

Track 45
asked arrived joined waited worked visited

12 You could write the words on the board in four columns and tell students to do the same in their notebooks. They can then add ideas to each column apart from the second. Elicit a question one word at a time and, as you do so, link the words used with a line. Set a time limit and monitor and help where necessary.

13 Encourage students to give extended answers. Monitor and help where necessary. Invite pairs to ask and answer their questions in front of the class.

Extension idea
Divide the class into three groups. Groups 1 should write down all the regular verbs from the lesson which end with a /d/ sound. Groups 2 the verbs ending in a /t/ sound and Groups 3 the verbs which end with an /ɪd/ sound. They write a sentence or sentences using some or all of their verbs. Set a time limit and elicit ideas from groups.

Students could do Grammar reference: Past simple, Exercises 1–2, page 117 at this point or for homework.

▶ **Grammar reference page 116: Past simple**
▶ **Workbook pages 29–30**

Vocabulary SB page 53

Buildings

Lead-in
Draw a very simple picture of the Eiffel Tower on the board and elicit what it is. Put students into small groups to think of another famous building they could draw. Invite groups to draw their buildings on the board and ask the other students to guess what it is.

1 Students stay in the same groups. Ask them to cover the box and try to name the buildings in the photos in English before looking at the words and doing the matching. Model and drill the words and elicit that they all have the first syllable stressed except for *hotel* and *museum*.

> **Answers**
> 1 hospital 2 church 3 cinema 4 factory 5 train station
> 6 hotel 7 mosque 8 museum 9 post office 10 stadium

2 Look at the first place (hospital) with students and elicit if there is one in their town and, if so, where it is, how big it is, etc. Students then discuss the other places in pairs.

Extension idea
Write on the board: *A: What's wrong? B: I don't know. Owww! A: Quick, get a doctor.*
Ask students where they think that the people are (in a hospital). Put students into pairs and give them two minutes to write a similar short dialogue that takes place in one of the buildings in Exercise 1.

▶ **Workbook page 29**

Listening Part 4 SB page 53

Lead-in
Write the name of a place on the board, e.g. *New York*. Now ask students to think of an adjective to describe New York. Elicit ideas and write three on the board, e.g. *exciting, crowded, expensive*.

Now write a sentence about New York which matches one of the adjectives but doesn't mention it, e.g. *I loved New York. There were lots of things to see but they all cost so much money!* Elicit that this matches *expensive*.

Students now work in small groups and do the same. Set a time limit of two minutes and elicit options and sentences from groups and ask other students to say which adjective the sentences matched.

Listening Part 4 (multiple-choice)

Discuss the advice with students. Elicit why the key words are important: they help students to decide what information to listen for and why students should check their answers; because it is always possible that they made a mistake or misheard something.

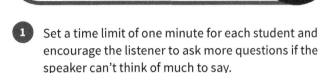

Exam advice

1 Set a time limit of one minute for each student and encourage the listener to ask more questions if the speaker can't think of much to say.

2 Allow students one minute to read the questions and underline the key words. Look at the first question with students and elicit that they should underline the three adjectives; *expensive*, *small*, *boring*. Don't elicit any answers after the first listening.

Track 46

Narrator: For these questions, choose the correct answer.

1

Narrator: You will hear two friends talking about a place they visited. What did they think of it?

Boy: That museum trip was great, wasn't it?

Girl: Yes. It's a pity we only had a little time to spend there.

Boy: Oh, I thought two hours was enough. I'm glad mum paid for the tickets though!

Girl: Yes, twenty pounds is a lot, isn't it?

Boy: I didn't like the long train journey, though.

Girl: Me neither. That wasn't much fun.

2

Narrator: You will hear a teacher talking to her class about a trip Where did they go?

Teacher: For your homework, I'd like you to write about today's trip. Think about the people who lived in that building, what sort of food they cooked, what they did in their spare time, and their work. We didn't have time to visit the factory, but we do know what they made there. How were their lives different from ours today?

3

Narrator: You will hear two friends talking about their town. Why do they both like it?

Girl: Our town's great. Especially our museums. Lots of people come to visit them.

Boy: I guess they're interesting - but I don't go to them very often.

Girl: Nor me. I prefer going to the football.

Boy: We haven't got a a great team, though. What I like is that we're so near the beach.

Girl: Yeah, it's great for surfing, isn't it?

Boy: The best!

4

Narrator: You will hear a father asking his daughter about what she did last night. What did she do?

Girl: I had a lovely time last night.

Dad: You went to the cinema, didn't you?

Girl: No, I was at Olivia's house. The film was on Thursday.

Dad: Oh, right.

Girl: Last night we played games on the internet. I won all of them!

Dad: Well done. Did you have dinner?

Girl: Yes, Olivia's dad cooked it. He's a really good chef.

5

Narrator: You will hear a boy leaving a message for his friend. Where does he want to meet?

Dave: Hi Dan, it's Dave. The match starts at three, and I've got your ticket. We should meet either at the stadium or somewhere in town. Actually, I need to do some shopping and post a letter before the game, so let's not meet in town. I'm too busy. Meet me at the main entrance at two forty-five. Don't be late!

3 When students have listened a second time, ask if anyone changed any answers when they listened again. Elicit the answers.

Answers
1 A **2** C **3** C **4** B **5** A

Extension idea

Put students into pairs and photocopy the Audio script enough times for each pair to have one dialogue or monologue. Tell the pairs to look at what was said and find the information that showed which option was correct and why the other two options were wrong.

▶ **Workbook page 29**

Grammar SB page 54

Imperatives

Lead-in

With books closed, tell students to imagine they are a teacher coming into a new class. In pairs, they think of things they may say to the class. Set a time limit of one minute and elicit ideas. Write any ideas which are imperatives (e.g. open your books) on the board. Elicit or tell students that this kind of structure is called an imperative and that they are now going to look at this structure in more detail. 1 Elicit the answers and elicit that we also don't use pronouns, e.g. We don't say *You meet* or *You don't be*.

1 Students work in pairs and underline the verbs in the sentence. Elicit the answers.

Answers
<u>Meet</u> me at the main entrance. <u>Don't be</u> late!

2 Look at the imperative forms and elicit who might say them and why, e.g. a *A teacher to a noisy class*. Play the recording once all the way through then play it again pausing after each sound to elicit the command.

Answers
a 4 b 6 c 1 d 5 e 7 f 3 g 2

Track 47
1 [sound of a phone ringing]
2 [sound of a child jumping up and down on a bed]
3 [sound of a boy laughing]
4 [sound of a noisy classroom]
5 [sound of a cat miaowing]
6 [sound of a girl crying]
7 [sound of a person snoring]

Students could do Grammar reference: Imperatives, Exercises 3–4, page 118, at this point or for homework.

3 Encourage stronger students to use more verbs. Set a time limit for students to think of some ideas and then tell them to use the ideas in a role play with one of them the visitor asking questions and the other the local giving advice.

Extension idea
Tell students to work in pairs. They make a similar dialogue this time with a new student at their school. The new student keeps doing wrong things, e.g. starting to use their phone or not listening. The other student has to give commands, e.g. *Don't use your phone in class. Listen to the teacher.* Set a time limit for students to plan their dialogue.

▶ **Grammar reference page 117: Imperatives**
▶ **Workbook page 30**

Vocabulary SB page 54
Directions

Lead-in
Draw a square on the board and tell students that this represents the school. Draw the road the school is on. Tell students you want something, e.g. a sandwich/a bank and invite students to come to the board to extend the map showing where you can find different things. Make sure the roads are clear and draw arrows to show the routes.

1 When students have matched the words, elicit what each one means and where there are examples of each near the students' school. They could draw these on the map from the lead-in activity.

Answers
2 E 3 C 4 B 5 D

2 Look at the first set of directions with the whole class. Read the directions and use gestures to show 'turn left' and 'straight over'. Elicit the place and then students do the other two alone or in pairs. Elicit the places and tell students to make a note of the imperatives used in the three sets of directions: *turn left, go straight over, come out of, go over, turn right, take the first turning* and the phrases used to show where something is: *it's on … Street, it's on the left/right*. Elicit what all these mean.

Answers
1 theatre 2 police station 3 supermarket

Extension activity
Look at the map on the board and elicit how students could give directions to the places marked on it. Start with: *Come out of the school and turn left/right/cross over the road.* Elicit one direction at a time from the start so they get as much practice as possible. This will prepare them for the next exercise.

3 Look at the example with students. Elicit the directions to the cinema. Monitor and help students where necessary.

▶ **Workbook page 29**

Speaking Part 2, Phase 1 SB page 55

Lead-in
Put students into pairs or small groups. Ask students to think about one place they like going to, e.g. *the cinema* and one place they don't like going, e.g. *the supermarket*. Students share their ideas and tell each other why they like or don't like going to these places. Ask the pairs or groups about places they all like or dislike.

Speaking Part 2, Phase 1 (a discussion based on an artwork prompt)
Look at the advice with students. Elicit why giving reasons is important: it gives them a chance to use more language, including adjectives to describe places and verbs to talk about activities.

Exam advice

1 Elicit the answers and then ask students which speaker likes each place and which speaker dislikes each place, (the boy likes shopping centres but doesn't like sports stadiums; the girl doesn't like shopping centres).

Answers
shopping centre, sports stadium

Track 48

Boy:	Do you like going to the shopping centre?
Girl:	No, I don't.
Boy:	Why not?
Girl:	I don't like shopping centres because I don't like shopping. What about you?
Boy:	I love going to them!
Girl:	Why?
Boy:	The reason I love them is that I often meet my friends there.
Girl:	Do you like going to the sports stadium?
Boy:	No, I don't.
Girl:	Why not?
Boy:	I don't go to the stadium because I'm not really interested in sport.

2 Tell students to read the sentences before they listen again and try to work out what the missing words might be. When they have listened, elicit the answers and when we use each expression. You could write the following on the board for them to make a note of. Elicit that they would use the same words in the gaps in both sentences. Provide an example to illustrate. Leave the prompts on the board for Exercise 3: *I like X because ... . The reason I like X is that ... .*

Answers
1 because 2 The reason 3 because

3 Look at the example sentences and show how they follow the form in the prompts on the board. Monitor and help where necessary.

Answers
2 I hate the beach because I don't like sand. 3 The reason I don't like museums is because they're boring.

4 Encourage students to vary the way they answer the questions; sometimes using *because* and sometime using *the reason why*. Elicit ideas from students.

Extension idea
Put pairs together. Each pair takes turns in playing examiners. They ask the other two students to look at the five pictures in Exercise 1 and discuss which they like going to and which they don't like going to. You may want to play the recording again to remind students about how the two students asked and answered questions. Elicit some useful questions that they used, e.g. *Why not? What about you? Why?* When the first pair has finished, they swap roles.

▶ Speaking Bank page 147: Speaking Part 2, Phase 1

Writing Part 6 SB page 55

Lead-in
Create a mind map on the board: write *interesting places* in a circle at the centre of the board. Elicit a place in the students' town/city which could be described as interesting, e.g. *museum*. Write this around the circle. Put students into small groups and ask them to think of other interesting places in their town. Set a time limit of one minute and then elicit ideas and write them around the circle as well. Students now discuss which they like and which they don't like in their groups, giving reasons using *because / The reason why*.

1 Set a time limit of one minute and then elicit which questions are answered and what the answers are.

Answers
1, 3, 4

2 Tell students to do this exercise alone. When they have finished, ask how many mistakes they found. Tell them that there are three but don't say what they are yet.

> **Answers**
> Hi Sandra
> Yesterday I <u>go</u> to the car museum in town. My friend Julie <u>were</u> with me. I didn't <u>liked</u> it because I think cars are boring!
> Jenny

3 Allow weaker students to work in pairs to discuss what they think the mistakes are and how to correct them. Other students can work alone. Elicit the mistakes, what kind of mistakes they are (all grammatical) and what the correct forms are.

> **Answers**
> Hi Sandra
> Yesterday I **went** to the car museum in town. My friend Julie **was** with me. I didn't **like** it because I think cars are boring!

> **Writing Part 6 (short messages)**
> Discuss the advice with students and elicit what kind of mistakes they might make, e.g. wrong tenses, spelling mistakes, missing off words like *the*.
>
> **Exam advice**

4 Look at the instructions with students. If you did the lead-in, students can use some of the ideas on the board in their messages. Set a time limit of five minutes for students to write their messages and another minute to check and correct them if necessary.

> **Extension idea**
> For homework, tell students that someone has written a message on the internet. They are coming to the student's town and want to know about places to visit. This time students should write a message about a place they regularly go to. They should include: why they like going there, what they do there, the last time they went there.

▶ **Writing bank page 139: Reading and Writing Part 6**
▶ **Workbook page 30**
▶ **Complete Key for Schools new edition Test Generator Unit 7**

Vocabulary

Describing places

beautiful	exciting	safe
big	little	ugly
boring	noisy	
dangerous	quiet	

Buildings

church	hotel	stadium
cinema	mosque	train station
factory	museum	
hospital	post office	

Directions

bridge	come out of
cross (v)	go (straight) over
crossing (n)	it's on the left/right
roundabout	take the first turning on the
square	left/right
traffic lights	turn left/right

▶ **Workbook page 30**

Vocabulary activity 1

Students need some blank paper to write on. Tell students you are going to read a sentence which has an adjective missing. You are going to think about one adjective from the word list to complete the sentence. The other students should write the adjective they think you are thinking of in letters big enough to see from the front of the class. Say: *I went to a beach in Greece. It was* (BLANK). Give everyone time to write one adjective then say your word (beautiful) and ask everyone to hold up their word. Anyone with the wrong word is out. Choose one of these students and ask them to sit at the front. Repeat the process but with this student choosing an adjective. Keep going until there is a winner or as long as time permits, with a different student choosing the adjective each time. Ideas for sentences: *Our school is …; This town is …; Big cities are … .*

Vocabulary activity 2

Put students into small groups. Tell students you are going to draw one of the nouns in the wordlist. Choose one, e.g. a bridge. Draw one line and ask students if they can guess what it is. Elicit a guess. If the student guesses *bridge*, tell them they are correct. If not then draw a second line and elicit a second guess from someone else. Keep going until someone guesses correctly. Students then continue in small groups.

8 Did you get my message?

Unit objectives

Topic: school

Listening Part 5: matching: listening to identify specific information (objects, places, feelings, opinions, etc.)

Reading and Writing Part 2: matching: reading for specific information and detailed comprehension

Speaking Part 1, Phase 2: topic-based interview: focus on interactional and social language

Reading and Writing Part 5: open cloze: reading and identifying appropriate word, with focus on grammar

Grammar: past continuous; *can/can't, could/couldn't*

Vocabulary: technology verbs; music

Pronunciation: *can/can't*

Starting off SB page 56

Lead-in

If students can use phones at school, ask: *How many of you use your phones just before or after lessons? How many of you use your phones just before you get to or after you leave school?* Put students into small groups and ask them what they did on their phone before the lesson / school started today. Allow one minute for students to share ideas, then elicit information from each group.

Look at the pictures with the class. Elicit what they show. Ask: *How do we connect to the internet or other devices?* (using wifi). Ask what the following mean: *chat, smartphone, computer game*.

1 Either students take turns to ask their partner the questions and note their answers or students ask alternate questions and mark both their own and their partner's answers. Set a time limit of about four minutes for the activity but allow longer if necessary.

2 When students have finished and checked their answers on page 149 elicit how many points different people got (ask if anyone scored 16) and if they agree with the comments.

Extension idea

Students work in pairs. They think of another question they could ask about computers, phones or the internet. They then join together with a second pair and ask and answer each other's questions. They try to answer them as if they were in the speaking exam i.e. giving extra details, e.g. *1 I spend about 20 hours a week on the internet. I use it to check social media and I write a blog. I don't often watch videos.* Elicit the most interesting things students found out.

Listening Part 5 SB page 57

Lead-in

Ask students to close their books and think about different gadgets or items connected with computers and technology. Draw two examples on the board, e.g. a laptop and a memory card and write *laptop, memory card*. Put students into small groups. Tell groups to think of something they know the word for in English but that other students might not. Invite each group to draw their object. They get a point if no one else knows the name of their object.

Listening Part 5 (matching)

Elicit ways that something can be mentioned but is not the correct answer.

Exam advice

1 Tell students to discuss their ideas in pairs and choose words or phrases which helped them to decide. Elicit answers and key words which helped them decide (*discount prices* – this means that they can buy something there).

> **Suggested answer**
> It's a place where you can buy computers, phones, cameras, games, etc.

2 If you did the lead-in activity some or all of these things may have been drawn by students, so this will help to reinforce what they learned earlier. Elicit the answers and ask which of the objects students have at home.

Answers
A camera B mouse C memory card D smartphone
E laptop F keyboard (The mouse isn't shown in the advert).

3 Look at the instructions with students and make sure students understand they don't have to identify the correct answer at this point. This is practising the second piece of advice in the exam advice box. Tell students the same item may match more than one person.

Answers
1 E, G 2 H, B 3 F, A 4 F, A 5 G, D

Track 49

Narrator: For these questions, choose the correct answer. You will hear Marta talking to her dad about what she and her friends bought at the computer fair. Write two things that are mentioned for each person.

Dad: How was your trip to the computer fair, Marta? Did you get the game you wanted?

Marta: Yes, I did.

Dad: What about Ollie, did he get a new laptop?

Marta: No, he's still saving money for that, but he did buy a mouse. Everybody bought something, actually.

Dad: What did they get?

Marta: Well, Susie's parents gave her a smartphone for her birthday, and she's worried about breaking it.

Dad: She's always dropping things!

Marta: I know, so she bought a phone case for it.

Dad: Good idea! What did Anna buy?

Marta: She bought a memory card for the old camera her dad gave her.

Dad: She likes taking photos doesn't she?

Marta: Yes, she does, and you know how Pedro always copies Anna?

Dad: Did Pedro buy a memory card too?

Marta: No! He bought a camera. It was really expensive!

Dad: Miguel was looking for a present for his sister's birthday, wasn't he?

Marta: Yes, he was thinking about getting her a mouse like the one I bought, but he changed his mind. I think she'll like the nice keyboard he bought for her.

Dad: I'm sure she will.

4 This time the correct answers can only match one person and only five of the eight items are needed. When students have listened, elicit the correct answers and ask what the speakers said about the other options (1 saving up for it 2 parents gave her one for her birthday 3 dad gave her 4 in the question 5 thinking about getting one).

Answers
1 G 2 B 3 F 4 A 5 D

Extension idea
Put students into small groups. Tell them to imagine there is a computer fair and they have decided to go. They should tell each other what they would like to buy at the fair and why, e.g. *I'd like a memory card to keep a copy of my photos on.* Set a time limit of one or two minutes and elicit ideas from groups.

▶ **Workbook page 33**

Vocabulary SB page 57

Technology verbs

Lead-in
Write *social media* on the board. Ask the class what question they could ask someone about social media, e.g. *What social media websites do you use?* Put students into small groups and set a time limit of one minute for them to think of more questions they could ask. Elicit ideas and write the verbs they use on the board.

1 Elicit the meanings of the verbs in the questions before students start. Set a time limit of 1–2 minutes for students to read the questions and discuss them, then elicit their ideas. If you didn't elicit the meanings before they started, elicit them now. You could point out we can either use the verb *to send + emails/texts/messages* or use *email/text/message* as a verb as in the fourth sentence.

2 Students could do this alone or in pairs. Check that students have used the correct form.

Answers
2 downloads 3 text 4 uploaded 5 checked

3 Set a time limit of two minutes for students to discuss the questions. When students have finished, elicit true sentences for them.

Extension idea
Put them into small groups to think of new questions to ask about technology. Monitor and help where necessary. They then work in pairs with someone from a different group to ask and answer their questions.

▶ **Workbook page 32**

8

Grammar SB page 58

Past continuous

> **Lead-in**
> Put students into small groups. Tell them they are each going to mime something to the class. They should come to the front in their groups and each mime at the same time, e.g. one may be cooking, one may be playing the violin and one may be having a shower. The other students have to watch and try to remember but they can't write anything. When everyone has mimed, the other students work in their groups to try to remember what each person was doing. At this stage, they may use the present continuous to describe the mimes.

1 Look at the definition and the example sentence. Elicit which verb we use before the word *viral* (*go*). Elicit one or two examples of videos that went viral, then set a time limit of 1–2 minutes for students to discuss other ideas. Elicit ideas and whether students like the videos or not.

2 Tell students to look at the photo and describe what they can see. Set a time limit of two minutes for students to read the text and find the answer. Ask students what the surprising news was and what the viral video was of (surprising news – a video he uploaded got 100,000 views: the video was of his baby sister dancing at a party).

> **Answer**
> He was in bed

3 Elicit the answers and also elicit that the actions in the first sentence were longer activities whereas the actions in the second sentence were all short.

> **Answers**
> 1 Music was playing and Meg was walking around.
> 2 Meg stopped, dropped her biscuit, and danced.

4 Elicit the answer and again elicit that a longer activity (Meg walking) was interrupted by a single, short action (the song coming on the radio). *Came on* has the same meaning as *started*.

> **Answers**
> before

5 Ask students: *Which was the longer activity?* (I was sleeping). *Which happened first?* (I was sleeping). Students then complete the answers.

> **Answers**
> I was sleeping when my phone rang. (sleeping started first)

6 Look at all three rules with the class. Point out that the first use of the past continuous is similar to the present continuous, e.g. *I am working now; I was working at 10 o'clock yesterday*. The second use is useful for the start of stories to set the scene, e.g. *The sun was shining and the children were lying on the beach*. The third use is also useful in stories to say that something, often dramatic, happened while something else was happening, e.g. *They were playing tennis when a dog took their ball*.

> **Answers**
> 1 past simple 2 past continuous 3 in the middle of

7 Look at the example sentence and ask students which rule in Exercise 6 this corresponds to (2 – two actions happening at the same time). Before students start, tell them that not every sentence needs the past continuous. One sentence is similar to the second sentence in Exercise 3 with two actions happening one after the other. Elicit the rules that the sentences correspond to (Rule 1: 3, 4 (wasn't happening), 6, 7; Rule 2: 1; Rule 3: 5).

> **Answers**
> 2 texted, woke up 3 was sleeping 4 wasn't raining, went
> 5 came, was watching 6 was reading 7 were you doing

Students could do Grammar reference: Past continuous Exercises 1–2, page 119 at this point or for homework.

> **Extension idea**
> If you did the lead-in activity, elicit what different students were doing in their mimes and check the use of the past continuous. Use a variety of *was/were*: *What was Sergio doing? What were Maria, Elmira and Isabel doing?*

8 Students would then need to change partners for Exercise 9 where they have to guess what their partner was doing. Monitor and help where necessary. Elicit the answers.

Fast finishers

Ask students to write similar questions but about other students in the class, e.g. *What was Pedro doing at 7 pm yesterday?* When students have finished Exercise 9, allow the fast finishers to ask their questions to the class. Students guess and then the actual students give the true answer, e.g. *Pedro was doing his homework. No, I was watching a film.*

Answers
1 What were you doing at 9 o'clock last night?
2 What were you doing at 1 o'clock yesterday afternoon?
3 What were your parents doing at 8 o'clock last night?
4 What were you doing ten minutes ago?
5 Were you sleeping at 11 o'clock last night?
6 Were you doing your homework at 7 o'clock last night?

9 Look at the example question and elicit that it has the same form as questions 5 and 6 in Exercise 8. Elicit more possible questions that students could ask for questions 1 and 2, e.g. *Were you watching TV at 9 o'clock? Were you eating lunch at 1pm?* For weaker classes, you could elicit possible questions for questions 3 and 4 as well, e.g. *Were your parents eating dinner at 8 o'clock yesterday? Were you writing ten minutes ago?* Monitor and help where necessary.

Extension idea

Tell students to think of other longer activities in the past. Give them a few ideas and elicit more, e.g. *I was walking to school when ... .* Now elicit some ideas of something that happened in the middle of the activity, e.g. *I was walking to school when I saw an accident.* Students work in small groups to think of two or three different ideas. Monitor and help where necessary.

▶ **Grammar reference page 119: Past continuous**

▶ **Workbook page 33**

Reading Part 2 SB page 59

Lead-in

Tell students you want to relax tonight by watching some videos on the internet. Put students into small groups and set a time limit of two minutes for them to agree on one video you should watch and how they can describe it. Elicit ideas from each group.

Reading Part 2 (matching)

Discuss the advice with students and elicit why it is a good idea, e.g. it helps them to check their answers at the end. Elicit that they should also read the texts quickly before they start as this will help them to decide where the information is and be able to find it more quickly. This will mean they don't have to keep reading each text for every question and give them more time.

Exam advice

1 Keep students in the same groups as for the lead-in. Set a two-minute time limit and elicit ideas from the class. Ask if any of the videos they recommended in the lead-in are by the video makers they discussed here.

2 Set a time limit of one minute for students to read the texts quickly. Tell them that, even if they find the information in the first line, they should still quickly read the text.

Answers
Davina: animals Sonja: daily life Joana: games

3 Students underline key words in each question, e.g. *1 Who, funny; 2 a year ago.* This will make it easier for them to find the information they need. Give students two minutes to read the text and find the answers. Elicit how the information in the key words was written in the text (*a year ago – twelve months ago, good wishes – lots of nice messages*).

Answers
2 and 5: twelve months ago; I get lots of nice messages

4 Tell students to cross out the two questions they've already matched and to read the other five sets of key words again. Set a time limit of four minutes and again elicit the answers and the words which helped them, (*funny – makes people laugh; can do –I'm really good; likes, questions – they just need to ask me/ makes me feel good to help them, more than one a week – every three days, earn money – pay me*). When you have elicited the answers, ask how this method is useful – it means students don't have to keep re-reading the same texts to see where the answers are.

Answers
1 B 2 A 3 C 4 C 5 A 6 B 7 C

Extension idea
Put students into small groups. Set a time limit of three minutes for them to think of an interesting idea for an online video that they think might become popular, then some details of exactly what they would show. Allow each group to present their idea to the class and have a class vote on which one, apart from their own, students liked best.

▶ **Workbook page 34**

Vocabulary SB page 59

Music

Lead-in
Put students into small groups. Set a time limit of one minute and ask them to list groups and singers who they like. Elicit a few ideas from different groups and elicit recommendations of less well-known singers or musicians that other students should listen to.

1 Teach the word *genre* (a particular type of art, writing, music, etc.) and elicit genres of music or literature, e.g. horror, musicals, fantasy. Look at the playlist in Exercise 1 with students and elicit examples of each type of music and what it sounds like.

Answers
1 C 2 E 3 F 4 A 5 G 6 D 7 B

Track 50
A [pop music]
B [electronica/dance music]
C [classical music]
D [rock music]
E [jazz music]
F [opera music]
G [R&B music]

2 Elicit other types of genres from the class and what they sound like. If you did the lead-in activity, students may be able to say what kind of genre of music the musicians they recommended sing, e.g. blues, rap. Write these on the board then put students into pairs to think of singers or bands for each type of music. Elicit ideas.

3 This would work best by putting students in new groups so that they are with students whose music tastes they don't know as well. Set a time limit of three minutes for students to discuss the questions.

4 Tell the groups that they are going to present their findings to the class and that each student should report the answers to one of the questions to the class. If the groups have fewer than four students, one student can report the results of two of the questions.

Extension idea
Students work in small groups. They imagine they are a band. First they decide the genre of music they will play then try to think of a good name for their band. Set a time limit of one or two minutes and then elicit band names. Have a class vote on the best name.

▶ **Workbook page 32**

Grammar SB page 60

can/can't, could/couldn't

Lead-in
Give examples of things you can and can't do, e.g. *I can speak ... I can cook ... I can't write computer code*. Tell students to write something unusual they can do and something they can't do. Students then mingle and tell each other what they can't do. If they find someone who can do the same thing, they make a note of their name. When students have talked to several people, they sit down again. Elicit things that students can't do and who could help them with these things.

1 Tell students to cover the photos and sentences in Exercise 2. Look at the question with the class and elicit a reason why it has and hasn't made lives easier, e.g. *It is easy to find directions using your phone. It is more difficult to relax.* Put students into pairs or small groups to think of more ideas. Set a time limit of one minute and elicit ideas from different groups.

2 Look at the photos with students and elicit descriptions of what they can see. Ask how many of the photos show things they talked about in Exercise 1, then ask them to do the matching.

Answers
1 E 2 B 3 C 4 G 5 F 6 A 7 D 8 H

3 Elicit the rules and the sentences in Exercise 2 that are examples of rule 1 (2, 5, 7, 8) and rule 2 (1, 3, 4, 6). Look at rule 3 with students and elicit the verbs which come after *can/can't/could/couldn't* in Exercise 2 (*find, carry, put, get*).

Answers
1 present 2 past

4 Look at the first sentence with the class and elicit that this is an example of a problem with rule 3 (we use the infinitive without *to* after *can/could*). Students work alone or in pairs to find and correct the other mistakes. Elicit the answers and, in each case, elicit that the verbs following *can/could* are not the infinitive without *to*.

Answers
1 couldn't find 2 can play 3 couldn't listen 4 can't get
5 could use 6 can't help

Students could do the Grammar reference: *can/can't/ could/couldn't*, Exercises 3–4, page 120 at this point or for homework.

▶ Workbook page 33

/P/ can/can't

5 Play the recording and drill each sentence. Then play it again and drill just the word *can* or *can't* each time.

Track 51
Boy: My phone can do lots of things.
Girl: Can it take photos?
Boy: Yes, it can, but it can't do my homework.

6 Model and drill the three sounds represented by the phonetic script. Students do the matching then practise the dialogue from Exercise 5 again in pairs. Listen and check they are saying the words *can* and *can't* correctly.

Answers
2 c 3 a

7 Look at the ideas in the box with the class. Tell students to work alone and underline the things they could do when they were four. Now look at the example dialogue with students. Ask two students to model it for the class and check their pronunciation of *can* in the question and short response. Students do the same in pairs for all the activities in the box. Elicit some ideas of things students could and couldn't do when they were four.

Extension idea
Give students one or two statements, e.g. *I could do it when I was young but I can't do it now. I couldn't do it last year but I can do it now.* Students have to think of something that would make these sentences true, e.g. *I could walk on my hands when I was young but I can't do it now. I couldn't understand the past simple last year but I can understand it now.* Put students into small groups to share ideas for each statement and see whether the other students' sentences are also true for them.

▶ **Grammar reference page 120:** *can/can't, could/couldn't*
▶ **Workbook page 33**

Reading Part 5 SB page 61

Lead-in
Write the following on the board: *Can ride bike?; Could ride bike when you four?; How friends have you got social media?* Ask students what words are missing and what the full questions are. Students work in pairs to write the full questions. Elicit these (*Can you ride a bike? Could you ride a bike when you were four? How many friends have you got on social media?*). Now ask students to discuss what kind of words the missing words are and elicit these (*you* – pronoun, *a* – article, *were* – verb, *many* – quantifier, *on* – preposition).

1 Look at the words in the box with students and elicit one more verb that could be tested (*do/did* in present/ past simple sentences). Look at the example sentence with students and ask why *the* is the correct word (Dad has his own bank which he goes to, so he uses *the* as we know which bank he went to.) Allow weaker students to work together. Elicit the answers.

Answers
2 were 3 off 4 many 5 me 6 a 7 Can/Could

2 Set a time limit of one minute and tell students not to write anything at this point. Look at the example and elicit what kind of word this is (verb) and re-elicit that all they are doing in this exercise is thinking of the type of word missing.

Answers
1 article 2 modal 3 verb 4 preposition 5 pronoun
6 quantifier

Reading Part 5 (open cloze)

Ask why it is useful to know what kind of word is missing (knowing the type of word missing limits the choice of words and makes it easier to think of the correct word for the gap.) Discuss the advice with students and ask them when the tense of the sentence is important (if the missing word is a verb).

Exam advice

3 Set a time limit of about five minutes. Students may not need that long. Elicit the words and how students know that they are the correct ones, e.g. the example is a past continuous verb, so we need the past form of *to be* and we use *was* with *I*: (2 there is only one internet; 3 we need a modal to ask permission; 3 present simple; 4 we use *on* with radio and television; 5 object pronoun from *they*; 6 we use *much* when talking about price).

Fast finishers

Ask fast finishers to think of one or two alternative gaps in the same text that could be tested. When everyone has finished, fast finishers can say which they chose, and what kind of words they are, e.g. in (*my room*) = preposition.

Answers
1 the 2 Can/Could 3 Do 4 on 5 them 6 much

Extension idea

Put students into small groups. They look at earlier pages in the Student's Book and choose one sentence each to write on a piece of paper with one word gapped, similar to those tested in Exercise 3. They can't gap words that are impossible to guess or negative contractions such as *don't*. They then swap sentences with a different group and try to complete the sentences. The groups then tell each other their answers and see if they are correct.

▶ Workbook page 34

Speaking Part 1, Phase 2 page 61

Lead-in

Write the question prompt: Tell me about the last ... . Elicit how the question could be completed and what it means, e.g. *Tell me about the last English lesson you had. Tell me about the last thing you ate.* It means the most recent one before now.

Put students into pairs and ask them to think of three more questions they could ask using this prompt. They should both write the questions down. They then change pairs and ask and answer each other's questions.

1 Tell students to look at the gapped questions and think of the kind of words missing (1 nouns; 2 verb; 3 adjective/noun to form compound noun (noun made up of two nouns); 4 noun; 5 Question word; 6 verb; 7 verb *to be*. When students have listened, elicit the missing words.

Answers
2 use 3 puzzle 4 music 5 How 6 listened to 7 was

Track 52

Examiner:	Raquel, tell me about your computer or smartphone.
Raquel:	I don't have a smartphone, but I have a computer.
Examiner:	What do you use it for?
Raquel:	I use it for homework every day. Sometimes I play games on it.
Examiner:	Marco, do you have a computer or a smartphone?
Marco:	Yes, I've got a smartphone.
Examiner:	What do you use your smartphone for?
Marco:	I use it for listening to music and messaging my friends.
Examiner:	Now, Raquel, tell me something about the games you play on your computer.
Raquel:	I like to play car racing games.
Examiner:	Do you like puzzle games?
Raquel:	No, not really.
Examiner:	Now let's talk about music. Marco, do you like music?
Marco:	Yes, I like it very much.
Examiner:	What kind of music do you like?
Marco:	I like rock and pop.
Examiner:	What kind of music do you like, Raquel?
Raquel:	I like pop, too. I also like classical.
Examiner:	How do you listen to music?
Raquel:	I listen to it on my phone.
Examiner:	Now, Marco, tell me something about the last piece of music you listened to.
Marco:	Oh, that was a pop song by Taylor Swift. She's my favourite singer.
Examiner:	What was the song about?
Marco:	I think it was about love.

2 Elicit the answer and ask why they are in the past simple, (the question is about the last piece of music you listened to, i.e. at some time in the past).

> **Answers**
> 6 and 7

Speaking Part 1, Phase 2 (topic-based interview)
Look at the exam advice with students and ask why it is useful, e.g. if the examiner asks about routines, you should talk about routines not one specific time. If they ask about a past time, you should use past tenses. If the examiner stops you it means you have probably answered the question in enough detail.

Exam advice

3 You could play the recording again until the girl says: *Sometimes I play games on it.* Elicit a possible follow-up question that the examiner could ask, e.g. *What's your favourite game?* Monitor and help students where necessary. When both students have answered the questions, invite pairs to ask and answer one of the questions for the class.

Extension idea
Tell students to look at questions 4, 5 and 6 from Exercise 1 and to change these to questions about films or video clips, e.g. *How do you watch films? Tell me something about the last film you watched. What was the film about?* Students work in pairs and ask and answer the questions, adding follow-up questions where possible. Ask students what they found out about their partner.

▶ **Speaking bank page 146: Part 1, Phase 2**
▶ **Vocabulary and grammar review Units 7 and 8**
▶ **Complete Key for Schools new edition Test Generator Unit 8**

Vocabulary

Technology
followers	smartphone
internet	social media
online	wifi
post	

Technology verbs
check	text
download	upload
email	

Music
classical	pop
electronic/dance	R&B
jazz	rock
opera	

Vocabulary activity 1
Put students into small groups and give each student a word from the word list. They shouldn't tell anyone what their word is. Tell students that they are going to have a conversation about technology. During the conversation they should use their word. Set a time limit of two minutes and when the time is up, students have to guess what each other's words are.

Vocabulary activity 2
Put students into small groups and tell them to choose one of the music genres in the wordlist or a different type of music that they named during the lesson. When they are ready, each group should mime a concert showing the band playing their instruments or singing. They do this silently and the other students have to guess what kind of music it is.

Vocabulary and grammar review Unit 7

> **1** 2 met 3 gave 4 didn't feel, didn't go 5 didn't like 6 drank 7 didn't win 8 began
> **2** 2 Did they enjoy the party? 3 Where did she go? 4 Did it rain yesterday? 5 Why did you laugh? 6 Who did you speak to? 7 How did they get there? 8 Were you late?
> **3** 2 Don't write 3 Don't walk 4 Listen 5 Don't call 6 Eat 7 Don't go
> **4** 2 bridge 3 mosque 4 factory 5 church 6 hotel 7 roundabout 8 hospital 9 square 10 stadium
> **5** 2 factory 3 bridge 4 stadium 5 cinema 6 hotel
> **6** 2 straight 3 turn 4 Take 5 over 6 on 7 traffic 8 second

Vocabulary and grammar review Unit 8

> **1** 2 d 3 b 4 a 5 e 6 c
> **2** 2 were you doing 3 wasn't raining 4 Were your parents sleeping 5 were having 6 weren't watching
> **3** 2 couldn't do 3 can you use 4 can show 5 can tell 6 could do 7 could see 8 can switch 9 can't see 10 can
> **4** 1 check 2 download 3 email 4 send 5 upload
> **5** 2 pop 3 rap 4 opera 5 rock 6 jazz

9 I love that film!

Unit objectives

Topic: entertainment

Listening Part 2: gap fill: listening and writing down information (including places, days, prices, numbers, etc.)

Reading and Writing Part 4: 3-option multiple-choice cloze: reading and identifying the appropriate word

Speaking Part 2, Phase 2: a discussion based on an artwork prompt; the focus is on organising a larger unit of discourse; comparing, describing, expressing opinions

Reading and Writing Part 7: a story: writing connected text (a short story or narrative) of 35 words +

Grammar: verbs with *-ing* or *to* infinitive; the future with the present simple; present continuous and *will*

Vocabulary: suggesting, accepting and refusing; adjectives

Pronunciation: *-ing* forms

Starting off SB page 64

Lead-in
Before the students open their books, write the word *Entertainment* on the board and ask or tell the students what things can be described as entertainment, e.g. *films, theatre, exhibitions, concerts, dance*.

Put the students into small groups and tell them to imagine that a friend is coming to stay with them. Set a time limit of one minute for students to discuss what entertainment they would take their friend to in their town and why. Elicit ideas from each group.

1 Keep the students in the same groups as for the lead-in. Ask them to discuss the questions and see if the web page has given them more ideas than they had in the lead-in. Elicit ideas from different groups.

2 Look at the words in the box with the class and elicit what kind of words they are and what they mean (an *actor* is a person who acts in films or plays; a *band* is a group of musicians, *dancers* are people who dance; *photographers* are people who take photos; *play* can be something you watch at a theatre or a verb). Students then do the gap fill alone. Elicit the answers and the words in the text which helped them (1 camera, exhibition; 2 songs, album; 3 film, Tom Hanks; 4 dance group 5 theatre, *Just you, me and Bobby*). Elicit examples of exhibitions, songs, albums, movies and plays that students know.

Answers
1 photographers 2 bands 3 actor 4 dancers 5 play

Extension idea
Put the students into small groups. Each group chooses one of the things from Exercise 1 that they can do where they live and decide how they can get other students to go to it. Set a time limit of 2–3 minutes for the groups to think of what they can say and then invite each group to tell the class about their activity.

Reading Part 4 SB page 65

Lead-in
Put the students into small groups. Ask them to tell each other about their favourite books or stories when they were young. Elicit ideas from different students.

1 Look at the instructions with the students. Tell them that this is an example of a new tense that they will look at later in the book. For now, tell them that, to answer the question, they can say: *I have seen it … times*. Students can stay in the same groups as they were in for the lead-in. Elicit ideas from different groups.

Extension idea
Ask the students: *Are there any stories or books that you like or liked when you were younger that are also films?* Elicit some examples and ask students if they liked the film version or not and why.

Background information

The *Winnie the Pooh* stories are the 3rd best selling story franchise in the world after *Disney Princess* and *Star Wars* and are worth about $5 billion a year. 18th January is Winnie the Pooh day and a good day to play Pooh Sticks, a popular game from the book where you throw sticks from a bridge into a stream and see whose comes out the other side first. *Kung Fu Panda* started as a film by Dreamworks. There have been three films, a TV series and a video game. 391 artists worked on the first film and most of them had to learn kung fu and other martial arts to understand the moves that they had to draw.

In the stories, Paddington came to England from Peru and was discovered at Paddington Railway station. There is now a statue of him there and a Paddington Bear gift shop. When French and English engineers connected the two ends of the Channel Tunnel, they passed each other presents. The English gave the French a Paddington soft toy.

2 Elicit any names of the bears that students know in English (they may have different names in the students' own language). Students can then discuss what they know in small groups or pairs. Ask the students if they have read any books about these characters or seen any films.

Reading Part 4 (multiple-choice cloze)

Look at the advice with the class and elicit why it is useful. The first point helps them to understand the text and help them decide the correct answer for the context. The second gives them more detailed information about the word needed. The last point helps because, sometimes, seeing different options can make us less sure of what is correct. If we have already chosen a word and see it as one of the options, we can be confident that it is correct.

Exam advice

3 Tell the students to follow the advice, starting by reading the text quickly and then looking at the text around the gaps in more detail. Ask them to cover the options so that they guess the words themselves. After five minutes, tell them they can now uncover the options and complete the reading task. Elicit the answers and ask the students how many of the words they guessed before looking at the options were the correct ones.

Fast finishers

Tell students to think of another word in the text which could be gapped and three options they could write for it. Elicit some of their ideas when everyone has finished the exercise.

Answers
1 B 2 C 3 A 4 B 5 A 6 B

4 Put the students into small groups to discuss their ideas, whether they have seen films of these stories or read books about them and why they like them. Elicit ideas from different groups.

Extension idea

Students work alone and write down five different animals that appear in famous stories, e.g. *lion, tiger, dog, snake, frog*. They should try to think of animals from five different stories. They then join together in pairs and take turns to tell each other their animals. The other student has to guess the story, e.g. *A: Lion B: Lion King? B: No. A: Madagascar? A: Yes!*

▶ **Workbook page 36**

Grammar SB page 66

Verbs with *-ing* or *to* infinitive

Lead-in

Write the following on the board: *I enjoy ...; I want ...; I'd like ...; The best thing about ... is... .*

Tell the students to write full sentences in their notebooks using these prompts. When they have finished, they compare ideas in pairs.

1 Look at the photo with the students and ask: *Do you like clowns? Can you juggle?* Mime juggling and, if students say *Yes*, ask what they can juggle and how many they can juggle at one time.

Students then work in pairs to answer the questions. Elicit ideas from different students.

Answers
A clown. She is juggling.

2 Tell the students to first read through the interview and work in pairs to try to match the words in the box to the correct gaps, then play the recording. When they have listened, elicit the answers and how many they got right before listening.

> **Answers**
> **2** to laugh **3** to do **4** to learn **5** being **6** making **7** doing **8** to work **9** talking

> **Answers**
> **2** working **3** to help **4** cleaning **5** sleeping **6** to do **7** coming **8** reading **9** to buy **10** waiting

/P/ -ing forms

5 Elicit the verbs: *working, cleaning, sleeping, coming, reading, waiting*. Play the recording then model the verbs with the /ŋ/ sound.

> **Track 54**
> working, cleaning, sleeping, coming, reading, waiting

> **Track 53**
>
> **Man:** Why did you decide to become a clown?
>
> **Girl:** Well, I love to laugh – everybody does, don't they? When I was eleven, my parents got a clown to come to my birthday party. He was very funny, and I thought, 'I want to do that', so I did!
>
> **Man:** Is it difficult to learn to be a clown?
>
> **Girl:** Learning to juggle is the hardest thing. That took months!
>
> **Man:** What's the best thing about being a clown?
>
> **Girl:** That's easy, I love making people laugh.
>
> **Man:** Do you make much money?
>
> **Girl:** No, not much. I do children's parties for free. It's just something I enjoy doing.
>
> **Man:** What about the future?
>
> **Girl:** I'd like to work in the film industry when I finish school.
>
> **Man:** Well, good luck, and thanks for talking to me.
>
> **Girl:** Thanks. It was fun.

6 Demonstrate this for the students with five sentences of your own to see if they can guess the false one. Set a time limit of one or two minutes for students to write their sentences. Encourage them to start with the false sentence so that if slower students only write four sentences, they can still do the next activity. Monitor and help where necessary.

7 Tell students that, if they did write the false sentence first, they should read them in a different order so that it is more difficult for their partner to guess. When students have finished, ask them if they guessed correctly and elicit some of their true and false sentences.

8 You could allow the students to do this in pairs and ask them to discuss what rule each one is an example of, (1 *like* + *-ing/to* infinitive; 2 preposition + *-ing*; 3 *I'd like* + *to* infinitive ; 4 *want* + *to* infinitive; 5 *stop* + *-ing* form).

> **Answers**
> **2** Thank you **for sending** the letter to me. **3** I'd like **to** know what you had for dinner last night. **4** I want **to invite** you to my house. **5** It soon stopped **raining**.

3 Tell the students that these aren't rules they can apply to all verbs; they just have to remember which verbs are followed by which form. When they record verbs that they learn, they should add this information where appropriate e.g. *enjoy (doing something)*.

> **Answers**
> **1** + *to* infinitive: decide to become, want to do
> **2** + *-ing*: enjoy doing
> **3** preposition + *-ing* form: the best thing about being… ; Thanks for talking to me.
> **4** would (*not*) *like to* : I'd like to work in the film industry.
> **5** adjective + *to* infinitive: difficult to learn
> **6** + *to* infinitive or + *-ing*: love to laugh/love making

4 Allow weaker classes to work in pairs or you might prefer to do the exercise as a class. Some of the answers can be found in the dialogue, some follow rules of adjective + *to* infinitive and preposition + *-ing* form but some are new verbs. Elicit the answers and encourage students to make a list of the new verbs in their notebooks.

Students could do Grammar reference: *-ing* or *to* infinitive after verbs, adjectives and prepositions, Exercises 1– 2, page 121, at this point or for homework.

> **Extension idea**
> If you did the lead-in, ask the students to look at the sentences they wrote. Ask if any of them followed the prompts with verbs and, if so, did they use the correct form, i.e. *I enjoy + -ing, I want + to infinitive, I'd like + to infinitive, The best thing about + -ing*. If they followed the prompts with nouns, e.g. *I enjoy computer games*, ask them to rewrite the sentences using a verb, e.g. *I enjoy playing computer games*. Elicit sentences from different students.

▶ **Grammar reference page 121: *-ing* or *to* infinitive after verbs, adjectives and prepositions**

▶ **Workbook page 37**

Vocabulary SB page 67

Suggesting, accepting and refusing

Lead-in
Ask students to think of a time when they went out with friends. Put students in small groups and set a time limit of two minutes for them to tell each other: who they went with, where they went, whose idea it was and if there were any ideas that other people didn't agree with. Elicit some interesting things that students found out from each other.

1 The students stay in the same groups as for the lead-in. Elicit the answers and write the associated nouns on the board: *suggest – suggestion, accept – acceptance, refuse – refusal*. If they did the lead-in, ask the students to think about what they said and decide together who suggested something, what the suggestion was and what other suggestions were there that some people refused.

Answers
1 b 2 a 3 c

2 Tell the students to underline the suggestions as they find them. Elicit the number and what they were.

Answers
He makes four suggestions.

3 Elicit the three other phrases Carl uses to make suggestions and tell students to write them in the first column. Students then work alone or in pairs to complete the table. Look at the four ways of suggesting and elicit the verb forms following the phrases in bold (*Why don't we* + infinitive without *to*, *How about* + *-ing* form, *Shall we* + infinitive without to, *Would you like* + infinitive with to. Elicit a suggestion from one student using one of the forms and invite other students to make the same suggestion using a different form.

Answers
suggesting: Why don't we …? Good idea; How about …?
Shall we …? Would you like to …?
accepting: Yeah, sure.
refusing: No, thanks; I'd rather not; I don't think so.

4 Encourage Student A to use a different way of making suggestions each time. Monitor and help where necessary. Invite pairs to act out their conversation for the class.

Extension idea
Tell all the students to make a note of two things they would like to do with their friends at the weekend, e.g. *see a film, have a pizza*. When they are ready, divide the class into A and B students. All the A students stay seated. The B students move around and suggest one of their ideas to an A. If it is on A's list, A accepts. If not, A refuses and B tries the other suggestion. If they agree on something they sit together. If not, B tries another Student A. Stop the activity when everyone has found a partner or after a set time.

▶ **Workbook page 36**

Listening Part 2 SB page 67

Lead-in
Ask students: *Have you ever been to a music concert?* This could be a pop singer, a school concert, a concert at a music school or any other kind of concert. Put the students into small groups to discuss the question and share their experiences. Go around the class and note any interesting experiences and elicit these at the end of the activity.

1 Before students look at the poster, ask them to imagine someone asked them: *Do you want to go to a concert?* Elicit questions they might ask. Students then see if the information needed on the poster is the same as information they asked about.

Suggested answers
When is it – date and time? What kind of music is it? How much do tickets cost?

Listening Part 2 (Information completion)
Discuss the advice with the students. Elicit that the first piece of advice prepares students. The second helps them to realise that they have to listen carefully to the exact words the speakers use, e.g. *What time does the concert start? It starts at 8 pm but we should arrive at 7.30. Let's meet at my house at 7.00.* There are three times here but only one is correct.

Exam advice

2 Look at the first piece of information and elicit that the key word is *where*. Elicit that all the headings on the left hand side are key words as they tell us exactly what information is needed. Elicit that the teacher's name will be spelt out and they must spell it correctly. Also look at the other headings and elicit where there might be more than one possible answer, e.g. *concert begins* (there may be more times given or someone may get the time wrong at first) *adult tickets* (there may be a different price for children).

Tell the students you will play the recording twice and that they should use the second listening to check that their answers are correct. Elicit the answers and the spelling of Mr Bagshaw's name.

Answers
1 Saturday **2** rock **3** 7.30 **4** 10 **5** Bagshaw

Track 55
Narrator: For these questions, write the correct answer in each gap. You will hear some information about a concert. Write one word or a number or a date or a time.

Woman: Thank you, everyone. Now it's our school concert in our arts hall at the weekend. I hope you're all practising a lot! I heard a student playing the piano on Monday and it sounded great. Anyway, our concert is on Saturday. Are you all ready?

The music is always varied and this year we have pop, rock and even some jazz – so it'll be different from last year's, which was all classical.

For those of you who are playing, you'll be here all afternoon – I know! But for your parents and friends, the doors open at six thirty and the concert itself starts at seven thirty. The seats are not numbered, so please tell your parents that if they want to be near the front, they should get here by a quarter past six.

Now, as you know, we're selling tickets. They are ten pounds each for adults. Students from this school are free, but students from other schools pay two pounds.

Finally, as there are always questions, please ask your parents to contact Mr Bagshaw – that's B–A–G–S–H–A–W and he will be happy to answer them.

Extension idea
Put the students in pairs or groups of three. Tell the students that they are organising a concert at school. They should think of where it will be, what day, what time it begins, what type of music there will be and how much tickets cost. Set a time limit of two minutes. Groups now join together and ask each other about their ideas. Elicit ideas.

▶ **Workbook page 37**

Grammar SB page 68

The future with the present simple, present continuous and *will*

Lead-in
Tell the students to think of something that they are definitely doing in the future because they or someone else has organised it, e.g. a test, a party, a sports competition, a meeting. They write this down. Write an example for yourself on the board, e.g. *football match on Saturday with friends*. Now ask them to write when this event starts: *3 pm*. Now tell them to think about something unplanned that is likely to happen at this event, e.g. *we lose*. Students share their ideas in pairs.

1 Students read the conversation alone. Elicit the answer and ask why he isn't keen (he thinks it will be boring).

Answer
Yes.

2 For weaker students elicit the form of the present continuous and present simple. Elicit that the exercise asks for examples of these tenses used to talk about the future. There are some examples of the present simple that don't talk about the future. Elicit the answers and elicit that the negative form of *will* is *won't*.

Answer
Francesca: Hey, Daniel. They're having a band competition at Rock City tonight. It starts at 6 o'clock. Do you want to come?
Daniel: I don't know. It'll probably be boring.
Francesca: It won't be boring at all! Come on. It finishes at 10.
Daniel: OK. Let's go. I'll get my coat.
Francesca: Great! I'll ask my dad to take us. The Jacks are playing first, and I don't want to miss them.

3 When the students have completed the rules, check how they are used in the dialogue by asking: *What plans do people have for the future?* (a concert is happening; the Jacks are playing first); *What exact times do we know?* (when the concert starts and finishes); *What do they think will happen?* (the concert will/won't be boring); *What decisions do they make at the time of speaking?* (I'll get my coat, I'll ask my dad).

Answers
1 c **2** a **3** b

4 Look at the first sentence with the class. Elicit the correct form and the reasons why it is correct (it is what the speaker thinks will happen). Students do the same for the other sentences. Elicit the answers and the rules the sentences correspond to. *2 known time 3, 5 what the speaker thinks will happen 4 decision made at time of speaking 6 a plan / what the speaker thinks will happen.*

> **Answers**
> **1** 'll love **2** leaves **3** won't eat **4** 'll close **5** won't like
> **6** 'm playing, 'll be

5 Look at the first question with the students. Elicit the tense used (present continuous) and reason for it (it's asking about your plans). Allow the students to work in pairs to decide which form to use and then alone to write their own answers. Monitor and help where necessary.

6 Pairs ask and answer their questions.

Students could do Grammar reference: The future with the present simple, present continuous and *will* Exercises 3–4 for homework.

Extension idea
If you did the lead-in exercise, ask students to look at the notes they made and ask them to think about the tenses they would use to talk about each piece of information (present continuous to talk about the plan, present simple to talk about the time, *will* to talk about what you think will happen). They then work in small groups and tell each other about their activity. Monitor and check that students are using the correct future forms.

▶ **Grammar reference: The future with the present simple, present simple, present continuous and *will***
▶ **Workbook page 38**

Vocabulary SB page 68

Adjectives

Lead-in
Ask the class what makes a good film, e.g. *story, acting, action.* Talk about a film you have seen and tell the class about it but using only the adjectives *good or bad. I saw … The acting was quite good but the story was really bad. There was no action. It was a love story.*

Tell the students to work in pairs. They should talk together about a film they both know and like and a film they both know and don't like. Students discuss their two films together to see if they agree on what was good and bad.

1 Elicit what a *review* is and where you can read them, (it is someone's opinion about a film, game, hotel, etc; you can read them in newspapers, magazines and online). Students work alone as the first letter is given and there is only one possible answer for each word.

> **Answers**
> **2** interesting **3** boring **4** terrible **5** amazing **6** horrible

2 Students may already know some of the words but ask them to look at the sentence they appear in to help them decide whether they are good or bad. Elicit the answers and that *It never gets old* means it's always good to watch however many times you see it.

Fast finishers
Ask fast finishers to note the words that helped them decide which words were good and which bad: 1 I'm glad they won first prize; 2 but I prefer paintings – the word *but* contrasts the fact that they were good with the fact that she prefers paintings; 3 isn't very good; 4 Everything was bad; 5 third time I've seen this film. Elicit these with the answers.

> **Answers**
> good: awesome, amazing, interesting;
> bad: boring, horrible, terrible

3 Look at the example with the students. Tell them they can use the same questions to ask each other. Encourage them to use a different adjective each time in their answers. Elicit questions and answers from different students.

Extension activity
If the students did the lead-in activity, ask them to discuss the same film but this time using adjectives from the lesson. If they didn't do the lead-in, put the students into pairs and ask them to think of a film they both like and one they both dislike. They then use the vocabulary from the lesson to discuss the story, acting, special effects, etc.

Pairs then join together with a second pair to tell each other about their two films and what they think about them. Invite each group to tell the class about one of the films they talked about.

▶ **Workbook page 37**

Writing Part 7 SB page 69

Lead-in
Write the word *Yesterday* on the board. Tell the students this is the first word of a sentence. Elicit what could come next, e.g. *I*. Keep going, eliciting words and writing them on the board if they are grammatically correct until there is a complete sentence. Put students into small groups and tell them to do the same. Monitor and correct where necessary and then elicit sentences from groups.

1 Allow the students to work in pairs. Tell them that some verbs could match to more than one picture. When they have finished, ask how many regular and irregular verbs there are (three of each). Elicit the past forms and the picture they match to.

> **Answers**
> 1 watched 2 saw 3 arrived 4 went 5 decided 6 ate

2 Students stay in the same pairs to do the matching. To help the class, elicit the answers and ask them to put the verbs and nouns together.

> **Answer**
> A poster, bus stop B cinema C TV, home

Writing Part 7 (a story)
Discuss the advice with the students and elicit why they would use the past simple (because the story happened in the past). Elicit that it is better to choose verbs which they know the past form of. If they are unsure, they can try to find a different verb for the same action, e.g. *They made/had popcorn.* Tell students that by thinking about the nouns and verbs they can use, they make the actual writing much easier.

Exam advice

3 Set a time limit of about five minutes and set a minimum word count of 35 words. Monitor and help where necessary.

Fast finishers
Tell fast finishers to check their work and to pay attention to the 'little' words like articles, prepositions and linking words.

> **Possible answer**
> Kate and Alan saw a poster for a film on a bus stop. They decided to go and see it.
> When they arrived at the cinema it was closed. In the end, they went home and watched a film on TV instead.

Extension idea
Put the students into small groups. The students tell each other their stories and correct any mistakes they hear. They then choose one of the stories and discuss how they could improve it, e.g. by adding adjectives or linking sentences together using *but, so, because* etc. Set a time limit of three minutes and ask students to read out their new, improved story from each group.

▶ **Writing Bank page 141–142: a story**
▶ **Workbook page 38**

Speaking Part 2, Phase 2 SB page 69

Lead-in
Put the students into pairs or small groups. Ask the students to talk about a form of entertainment they have been to, e.g. a concert, a play, a film. The students tell each other who they went with and how they felt. Set a time limit of one minute and elicit ideas from the students.

Exam advice: Speaking, Part 2, Phase 2 (a discussion based on an artwork prompt)
Look at the exam advice with the students. Elicit why the second point is important, e.g. this is how you can show the examiner how good your English is and use a variety of grammatical structures as well as a wide range of vocabulary.

Exam advice

1 When the students have matched the words to the pictures, have a class survey of which forms of entertainment the students have been to. Say: *Put your hand up if you have seen ballet/a play/a rock concert/a classical concert/a film.* When students put their hands up, ask one or two what show/band/film they saw and what they thought about it.

> **Answers**
> 1 D 2 E 3 C 4 A 5 B

2 Again, ask the class to raise their hands to vote for their favourite form of entertainment. Ask students why they like their choice best.

3 When the students have listened, elicit the answers and ask why Mario's answers are better (he gives more details and reasons for his answers).

> **Answers**
> 1 friends, family 2 show

Track 56	
Examiner:	Rita, do you prefer going to shows with your friends or with your family?
Rita:	My family.
Examiner:	Why?
Rita:	I love them.
Examiner:	What about you, Mario. Do you like going to shows with your friends or with your family?
Mario:	I don't go to rock concerts with my family.
Examiner:	Why not?
Mario:	Because my parents don't like rock. They like classical. I always go to rock concerts with my friends.
Examiner:	What kind of show would you like to go and see in the future?
Mario:	I'd like to go to a ballet one day.
Examiner:	Why?
Mario:	I think it's beautiful.
Examiner:	What about you, Rita. What kind of show would you like to go and see in the future?
Rita:	A rock concert.
Examiner:	Why?
Rita:	It will be exciting.

4 Elicit the full sentences from the class and then ask them to write the sentences alone. Monitor and help where necessary.

> **Answers**
> 1 my family because I love them 2 a rock concert because it will be exciting

5 Tell the student answering the questions to close their books so they can concentrate their attention on the other student and try to look at them while they are talking. Students sometimes look down as they are talking because of nerves and this makes it more difficult for the examiner to hear them, so it's good to get into the habit. Monitor and encourage students to look up if they aren't doing it.

> **Extension idea**
> Put students into pairs or small groups. Ask them to think of two more *Yes/No* questions on the topic of entertainment. Set a time limit and monitor and help with ideas where necessary. Each student should make a note of their questions. Put students into new pairs, with students working with someone from a different pair or group who doesn't know their questions. They repeat Exercise 5, remembering to ask their new partner *Why*.

▶ **Speaking bank pages 147–148: Part 2**
▶ **Complete Key for Schools new edition Test Generator Unit 9**

Vocabulary

Entertainment

actor	dancer	play
band	photographer	

Suggesting, accepting and refusing

accept	Shall we …	I don't think so.
refuse	How about …	Yeah, sure.
suggest	Would you like to …	

Adjectives

amazing	boring	interesting
awesome	horrible	terrible

Vocabulary activity 1

Tell the students to think of a film, book, play or an album that they can describe with one of the adjectives in the word list. They then write three choices (e.g. films) A, B and C. One is the one they were thinking about and two are ones which they have different opinions about. They then say their adjective, e.g. *awesome* and the three choices A *Star Wars* B *Kung Fu Panda* C *Pirates of the Caribbean*. Their partner guesses and the first student tells them if they are correct or not, e.g. *Star Wars? No, I hate Star Wars. It's terrible. Pirates of the Caribbean is awesome!* Students repeat the activity with two or three adjectives each.

Vocabulary activity 2

At the end of each unit, write all the words from the word list on small pieces of paper and place these in a box. At the start of the next lesson (and subsequent lessons), choose a few students to take one word each from the box and to give a definition for the other students to guess. The words are placed back in the box. You can use words only from the latest unit or add words from all units together.

10 It's going to be sunny

Topic: weather and places

Listening Part 1: discrete 3-option multiple-choice; listening to identify specific information (times, prices, days of the week, numbers, etc.)

Reading and Writing Part 2: matching: reading for specific information and detailed comprehension

Speaking Part 1, Phase 2: topic-based interview: focus on interactional and social language

Reading and Writing Part 5: open cloze; reading and identifying appropriate word, with focus on grammar

Grammar: *going to*

Vocabulary: What's the weather like?; places

Pronunciation: *going to; must / mustn't*

Starting off SB page 70

Lead-in
Put the students into small groups. Write the letters: J F M A M J J A S O N D vertically on the board one at a time. After each one, ask the groups what comes next. Tell the students that, if they know, they shouldn't say what the letters represent but just give the next letter. When a group realises the pattern (months of the year) and guesses a letter correctly, they stop guessing and let other groups try to work it out. When you have all the letters, elicit the months of the year and leave the letters on the board.

1 Allow students to work in the same groups as in the lead-in. They each choose a photo (if there are three people in the group, they can describe one photo together) and say what they can see, where they think it is, what month of the year they think it is and how the photo makes them feel. Elicit ideas about each photo.

2 When the students have matched the words to the photos, tell students that we use the preposition *in* before seasons; *in spring, in winter*. You could also tell them that they may see the phrase with or without an article (*in spring, in the spring*). Both are correct.

Answers
A summer B spring C autumn D winter

3 Play the recording and elicit the answers. Play it again and ask the students to note down why each person likes the season.

Answers
1 autumn 2 winter 3 summer 4 spring

Track 57
Girl: Where I live, we have amazing autumns! People come from all over the world to see the colours of the leaves on the trees. Autumn is from September to November.

Boy: I live in Canada. Winter here is cold – very cold! It usually snows a lot, which is great because I love skiing! Our winter is from November until February.

Boy: Summer in Australia lasts from December to February. It's great, and not just because of the warm weather. I like it because my birthday is in December, and we usually have a beach party.

Girl: I'm from Spain and my favourite season is spring. There are lots of flowers. It begins in March, and goes on until May. It's the most beautiful time of the year.

4 Look at the first question and ask the students why some countries may be different (some hot countries may not have a real winter, for example). Set a time limit of two minutes and then elicit answers.

Extension idea
Students work in small groups. They imagine someone wants to visit their country but isn't sure when to come. Students should discuss good and bad things about each season. Set a time limit of two minutes and elicit ideas from different groups.

Listening Part 1 SB page 70

Lead-in
Put the students into pairs and ask them to describe a season of the year. Give them an example: *We start the new school year. It is often windy. The sea is quite warm at the start.* (autumn).

Set a time limit of one minute for students to think of their sentences. Students join together in groups of four and tell each other their sentences. The other pair has to guess the season.

Listening Part 1 (multiple-choice)

Elicit how the examiners use distractors, e.g. for a question: *What time of year are they going to visit Spain?* Also, there could be distractors in questions *Are you going in the winter?*; in negative sentences: *We don't want to go in the summer;* and in past forms: *Last year we went in the spring.* Elicit that this is one reason why the second listening is important, so they can check that their answer isn't a distractor.

Exam advice

1 Look at the first question with the students. Elicit that, by looking at the pictures, we can see that *when* is the most important fact because the photos show three different seasons. Students work in pairs to find key words in the other questions and look at the pictures. Elicit the possible answers for question 1 (*winter, spring, autumn*) and give the students 30 seconds to do the same for the other questions.

Suggested answer
1 When, visiting, Japan 2 What, Frances doing, Sunday
3 What time, leave, class 4 How much, book, cost 5 Who, meet, at airport

2 Tell the students they will hear the recording twice and should check their answers on the second listening. Elicit the answers.

Answer
1 A 2 B 3 B 4 B 5 A

Track 58

1

Narrator: You will hear five short conversations. For each question, choose the correct answer.

Narrator: When is Holly visiting her friend in Japan?

Boy: When are you going to Japan? Is it in March?

Girl: No, I'm going after that. In August.

Boy: Oh, lovely. What clothes are you taking?

Girl: Well, it won't be cold and I'll be back before the autumn.

Boy: Summer will be lovely in Japan.

Girl: I know, I can't wait!

2

Narrator: What is Frances doing on Sunday evening?

Frances: Hello?

Dennis: Hi, Frances. It's me. Would you like to come to the new dance class with me on Sunday evening?

Frances: I'd love to but I can't. We've got friends coming for dinner. Do you remember Sally?

Dennis: Yes, her parents are actors, aren't they?

Frances: That's right. Well, they're all coming over on Sunday.

Dennis: OK.

3

Narrator: What time does Lynn need to leave her class?

Lynn: What's the time, Diego?

Diego: It's half past three. Why?

Lynn: I have to leave early today. Mum and I are visiting Auntie Jane. She's in hospital.

Diego: Oh dear.

Lynn: The class finishes at 4.30, doesn't it? I have to go at 4.

Diego: OK. I'll tell you when it's time to go. You don't want to be late for visiting hours.

4

Narrator: How much is the book they buy?

Girl: These are great books for Jack.

Boy: Yes, nice. But is this one £14.30.

Girl: Yes, and the other is more expensive than that. It's £15.50.

Boy: OK. Let's get the cheaper one. Oh, I only have … there … £14.00.

Girl: It's OK, I've got the rest. Jack's going to love it!

5

Narrator: Who will meet Lee at the airport?

Girl: Will someone meet you when you get there, Lee?

Lee: Yes, of course. It's a long way home. I think Mum's working but Dad can pick me up.

Girl: Oh, that's alright then.

Lee: And the best thing is that we're visiting Grandad on the way home. He lives in the city. We're having dinner with him in his new flat.

Extension idea

Put the students into small groups. Play the recording again, stopping after each dialogue, and elicit what the two distractors were and how the students can know they were the wrong answer. You could do question 1 with the class to show them what to do. Elicit that she went to Japan in spring last year and that autumn is lovely but her friend is busy.

▶ Workbook page 40

Vocabulary SB page 71
What's the weather like?

1 When the students have matched the words, elicit what they mean and what type of word they are, i.e. *cold, foggy, windy, hot* (adjectives); *snowing* (verb). Add these words to the board if they weren't used in the lead-in.

> **Answer**
> **1** C **2** E **3** A **4** D **5** B

2 Elicit the meaning of *temperature* (how hot it is) and ask: *What is the temperature today?* Elicit or tell the students that we say, for example, *20 degrees* (20°C). Look at the map with the students and ask which town they think will be the hottest and which the coldest. Play the recording and elicit the answers.

> **Answer**
> Athens 25°C Rome 29°C London 15°C Madrid 32°C
> Copenhagen 5°C

Track 59

Woman: Now it's time for our weather report from Europe. John, what is the weather like today in Greece?

Man: Thanks, Alana. It's sunny today in Athens and the temperature is about 32 degrees.

Woman: That's hot! And what is it going to be like tomorrow?

Man: Tomorrow it's going to be cloudy. It's also going to be cooler – about 25 degrees.

Woman: What about Rome in Italy?

Man: It's cloudy in Rome today, and 24 degrees. But tomorrow it will be sunny all day, and about 29 degrees.

Woman: And what about London?

Man: It's sunny today in London.

Woman: Great. Is it going to stay like that tomorrow?

Man: I'm afraid not. It isn't going to be sunny tomorrow. Tomorrow it will be cloudy all day, and the temperature will be about 15 degrees.

Woman: But it's sunny in Madrid, isn't it?

Man: It is! It's a lovely 32 degrees and tomorrow it's going to be the same.

Woman: OK, and finally, what about Copenhagen? What's the weather like there?

Man: Well, it's cloudy and cold today. 8°C at the moment. And tomorrow it's going to get cooler, probably around 5°C.

Woman: That's still warm for some! OK, now over to Rachel and the news.

3 Look at the questions with the class. Elicit the tenses they will use to answer the questions: 1 *It's*; 2 *It was*; 3 *It's going to be*. Elicit the questions and answers from different pairs.

Extension idea
Re-elicit what kind of words they were in Exercise 1 (*cold, foggy, windy, hot* – adjectives; *snowing* – verb). Tell students there are four more adjectives in the recording. Play the recording again and elicit these words (*cloudy, sunny, cool, warm*) and what they mean. Elicit other related words, e.g. *sun – sunny – to shine, snow – snowy – to snow, fog – foggy, wind – windy – to blow, cloud – cloudy*. You could also add *rain, to rain, rainy*.

▶ **Workbook page 40**

Grammar SB page 72
going to

Lead-in
Put the students into small groups. Tell the students to look back at the previous unit in the Student's Book and find the rules for using *will* on page 68, present continuous and present simple for the future. Elicit these and tell them that they are going to look at a new tense now: *going to*.

1 When the students have found the answers, elicit the answers.

> **Answers**
> **1** Mille and Soraya are going to be there. **2** It's cold and it is going to rain.

2 Students look at the rules in pairs. Ask: *How are the uses of going to and the present continuous similar?* (they can both be used to talk about future plans). Point out that often both forms are possible but we generally use present continuous for things we have planned with someone else and *going to* for things that we have planned alone, e.g. *Juan is going to watch some films*. Now ask: *How are 'going to' and 'will' similar?* (they are both used to make predictions about the future). Elicit that usually we use *will* when it's just our opinion (*the holiday will be great*), and *going to* when it is obvious because we can see something.

> **Answers**
> **1** a **2** b

3 Students look at the examples and discuss them in pairs. Elicit that they are all plans or questions about plans. Ask why Tony uses *will* in the last sentence (it's what he thinks will happen in the future but there's nothing he can see and they don't have any plans).

Answers
b are going to be there
a it's going to rain
b I'm not going to leave
b what are you going to do

Track 61
1 I'm going to be there.
2 Look at the sky. It's going to rain.
3 I'm not going to leave the house today.
4 What are you going to do?
5 I'm going to stay in and watch some films.

4 Point out that we generally use abbreviated forms of the verb *to be* (*I'm, you're, he's, she's, they're*) with *going to*. Monitor and help where necessary. Elicit the answers and point out that, for question 2, students could write *going to go to bed* or just *going to bed*. When the verb is *to go*, we often use the *present continuous* form.

Answers
2 I'm going to (go to) **3** is going to wear **4** isn't going to rain
5 aren't going to walk **6** are going to like

5 Look at the example question and short response. Elicit that the short response is the same as for the verb *to be* and the present continuous. Allow students to work in pairs and monitor and help where necessary.

Fast finishers
Tell fast finishers to write a question starting *Are you going to...?* They then swap questions with another student and answer them.

Answers
2 Is he going to swim in the river? Yes, he is. **3** Is she going to climb a tree? No, she's going to climb a mountain. **4** Are they going to have a picnic? Yes, they are. **5** Is it going to be sunny today? No, it's going to snow.

Students could do the Grammar reference: *be going to* Exercises 1 –2, page 123, at this point or for homework.

/P/ *going to*

6 When the students have repeated the different forms, elicit or tell the students that /gənə/ is a more informal pronunciation. It is often used in songs where two syllables are needed rather than three.

Track 60
goin' ta, goin' ta, gonna, gonna

7 Play the recording and elicit the answers then play it again, stopping after each sentence for students to repeat using the correct pronunciation.

Answer
1 going **2** gonna **3** gonna **4** going **5** gonna

8 Look at the example sentence with the students and elicit that this used the prompts *What – do – after school today*. Write three different prompts on the board, e.g. *Where – meet – this weekend* and elicit a question, e.g. *Where are you going to meet your friends this weekend?*

9 Students ask and answer the questions in pairs. Monitor and help where necessary.

Extension idea
Discuss new year's resolutions with the class. Tell them that, in some countries, people try to start the new year by changing their routines and behaviour. Give two examples: *I'm going to work harder. I'm not going to argue with my brother.* Students work in pairs. Set a time limit of two minutes for them to write their own resolutions, positive and negative. Elicit ideas from different pairs.

▶ **Grammar reference page 123:** *going to*
▶ **Workbook pages 41–42**

Reading Part 2 SB page 73

Lead-in
Talk to the students about days out on holiday – not just lying on the beach but something they have to organise, e.g. *a tour of a castle, a walking tour around a town*. Elicit one or two ideas and then put students into small groups. Ask them to think of holidays they have had and any organised activities they went on or saw others going on. Set a time limit of one or two minutes and elicit ideas.

Reading Part 2 (matching)
Elicit the two ways they can approach this type of activity. One is to read all three texts quickly and underline key words. The other is to read the questions then read one of the texts. They find the answers to this text, cross out the questions and then do the same for the other texts. This means they only have to read each text once. If they can only find one match in a text, they must look again to find a second.

Exam advice

1. Put the students in the same groups as for the lead-in. If students have been on holidays without their parents, e.g. school trips or summer camps, ask them to compare the two. Set a two-minute time limit and elicit ideas from the class.

2. Before the students look at the text, put them in pairs to describe the photos together for one minute then set another 30-second time limit to do the matching.

   Set a time limit of thirty seconds for students to read the questions and underline the key words. Give students seven minutes to do the task. Elicit the answers and the key words in each text that helped them decide (*1 shop after a late breakfast; 2 all year round; 3 I went back ... and had lunch; 4 You can return the bike any time you want; 5 don't forget a warm coat; 6 We had to get up before it got light; 7 Our guide was interesting*).

   Answers
   1 A 2 C 3 A 4 A 5 B 6 B 7 C

Extension idea
For homework, ask the students to write a similar paragraph about an activity they have been on. If they did the lead-in, they have already discussed some ideas and can use them as the basis for their writing. If they didn't, allow them to discuss their ideas in small groups.

▶ Workbook page 41

Vocabulary SB page 74

Places

Lead-in
Draw the outline of a country on the board. Draw one geographical feature on it in the correct place and say: *Here are some* (*mountains*). Students choose a country and do the same in small groups. Set a time limit of two minutes. Monitor and help with vocabulary where necessary.

1. For weaker classes, look at the words in the box and elicit the meanings before they complete the quiz. Tell them not to look at the facts yet. Elicit the answers and then ask the class if they can guess the facts. When students have checked, ask them which they found the most surprising.

   Answers
   1 lake 2 beach 3 mountain 4 islands 5 forest 6 desert

2. If the students are from different countries, arrange the groups so that there are students from different countries if possible. They then tell each other about their country. If they are all from the same country, they discuss what they know in groups. Set a time limit of about three minutes and then elicit ideas from each group.

Extension idea
Tell the class about your favourite beach, island and/or mountain area. Students work in small groups. They each choose one of the places in Exercise 1 and tell the group about their favourite, e.g. beach. Set a time limit of two minutes and elicit ideas from each group.

▶ Workbook page 41

Grammar SB page 74

must / mustn't

Lead-in
Write *have to / don't have to* on the board. Elicit what we use both for: rules, e.g. from parents, at school, and lack of rules. Put students into small groups to think of two sentences for each form. Elicit ideas from different groups

1 Look at the facts with the students and tell them that several people have problems on Snowden each year then ask them to think why (e.g. they go in winter, they wear the wrong shoes, they set off too late and it gets dark). Students then make their lists in small groups. Set a time limit and monitor and give help where necessary, then elicit ideas.

> **Suggested answers**
> check the weather forecast, buy warm clothes, good boots, buy a map, take a phone, take food and water.

2 Tell students to look at the ideas and ask if any were the same as their ideas from Exercise 1. Students then find the information in the text. Elicit the answers and the exact words used (*Plan your day carefully; you must start early; don't forget your phone; decide what path to take; if it's bad, don't go; don't be afraid to turn back*).

> **Answers**
> • plan your day ✓ • choose a good path to take ✓ • do it in any weather ✗ • be afraid to turn back ✗ • leave your phone at home ✗ • wear strong boots ✓ • start late in the day ✗

3 Elicit the rules and compare *must/mustn't* with imperatives. Look at the answers to Exercise 2 and ask students to rewrite them using *must/mustn't*. The last one they should rewrite using an imperative, e.g. *You must plan your day carefully*. Point out that *mustn't* can be used for a formal rule or for strong advice, e.g. *You mustn't talk in an exam; You mustn't wear sandals.*

> **Answers**
> We use *must* and *mustn't* + an infinitive without *to* to talk about obligation or strong advice in a formal way. *You* must *start early*. *You* mustn't *pick one that's too hard for you.*

4 Elicit the answers. As a follow-up, with stronger classes, you could elicit the imperative orders for each sign, e.g. *1 Stop! 2 Don't eat. 3 Don't use your phone. Be careful.*

> **Answers**
> **2** You mustn't eat **3** You mustn't use your phone **4** You must be careful

Students could do the Grammar reference: *must / mustn't* Exercises 1 and 2, page 124 at this point or for homework.

5 Look at one of the places with the class and elicit something you must or mustn't do, e.g. in a hospital *You mustn't make a noise. You must do what the doctor tells you.* Encourage students to think of a variety of rules and advice for the other situations. Set a time limit of three minutes and elicit ideas from different students.

> **Extension idea**
> Put students into pairs. Tell students A to imagine they understand *must/mustn't* but not imperatives. Students B understand imperatives but not *must/mustn't*. Tell them that you are going to give orders but only the student who 'understands' should follow the instructions. Give an example: Say: *Go to the door.* All Students B should go to the door. Then say: *You must sit down in your seat.* All Students A should sit down. Students now work in groups of three and do the same thing, taking it in turns to give orders for the other two students to follow. Monitor and check their use of *must/mustn't.*

▶ **Grammar reference page 124:** *must / mustn't*
▶ **Workbook page 42**

Speaking Part 1, Phase 2 SB page 75

> **Lead-in**
> Put students into pairs. Tell them to imagine an examiner has asked them: *Tell me about your last holiday.* Each student has thirty seconds to tell their partner about their holiday. Elicit what students found out.

> **Speaking Part 1, Phase 2 (topic-based interview)**
> For the first bullet point, tell students it is important for the students to know who they should talk to for each part of the exam. For the second piece of advice, tell them there is nothing wrong with asking the examiner to repeat something and it will help to ensure the students give a correct answer.
>
> **Exam advice**

1 Elicit questions the examiner could ask about these topics, e.g. *What do you do on holiday when the weather is bad? What is your favourite lesson at school? What do you usually do on Saturdays?* Students work in pairs. Set a time limit of about four minutes and make sure both students write the questions. Elicit some ideas from different pairs.

2 Play the recording once for students to see if the examiner asks any of their questions from Exercise 1. They then listen again and complete the questions.

Track 62

Examiner:	Now let's talk about holidays. Clara, what do you like to do on holiday?
Clara:	I like to cycle.
Examiner:	Does everyone in your family like cycling?
Clara:	Sorry, could you repeat that?
Examiner:	Does everyone in your family like to cycle?
Clara:	My mum doesn't, but everyone else does.
Examiner:	Paulo, who do you go on holiday with?
Paulo:	With my family.
Examiner:	Where do you usually go holiday?
Examiner:	Now let's talk about weekends. Paulo, what do you usually do at the weekend?
Paulo:	That's a good question. I always have homework, but I also like to meet my friends.
Examiner:	Where do you meet them?
Paulo:	I meet them in town.
Examiner:	Clara, what do you like to do with your friends at the weekend?
Clara:	I like to go to their houses and play games.
Examiner:	What games do you like?
Clara:	We play a lot of …
Examiner:	Now let's talk about school. Paulo, what is your favourite class in school?
Paulo:	Can you say that again, please?
Examiner:	What is your favourite class in school?
Paulo:	I like English.
Examiner:	Why do you like English?
Paulo:	I have a really good teacher.
Examiner:	Clara, do you have a favourite teacher at school?
Clara:	Um … let me think. Yes, I like my Geography teacher.
Examiner:	Why?
Clara:	Because she's …

3 Play the recording again. Elicit the answers. Elicit that all four phrases are fine to say and point out that just saying the phrase: *let me think* gives you a chance to think of what to say.

Answers
Sorry, could you repeat that? Can you say that again, please? That's a good question … Um … let me think.

4 Encourage students to give as much information as they can. Monitor and listen for interesting answers. Invite pairs to ask and answer their questions for the class.

Extension idea

Tell the students to choose one of their questions from Exercise 4. If there is room in the classroom, ask the students to stand in two circles, one inside the other, or two lines with the students facing each other. If there is an odd number of students, two should work together. The students ask and answer the questions from the person they are facing. One circle or line then all move one place to their left. Students repeat the process with their new partner. You can continue the activity for as long as necessary or until the students who are moving each time return to their starting point.

▶ **Speaking bank pages 146–147: Part 1**

Reading Part 5 SB page 75

Lead-in

Put the students into small groups. Ask the students: *Have you been on holiday and had bad weather?* If students say *Yes* elicit where they were and what the weather was like. Set a time limit of two minutes for students to discuss either what they did when the weather was bad or what they could do if they haven't had bad weather on holiday. Elicit ideas from different groups.

Reading Part 5 (open cloze)
Discuss the advice with the students and ask them why it is a good idea to read the whole text first (to get an understanding of what it is about).

Exam advice

1 Allow weaker classes to work in pairs. Elicit the answers and the tenses of the different sentences, (1 present simple; 2 going to; 3 have got; 4 past simple; (last week); 5 past continuous (when I phoned); 6 present simple).

Answers
2 Are 3 Has 4 Did 5 Were 6 Does

2 Set a time limit of about thirty seconds and elicit the answers.

Answers
It's an email. The writer is giving information about her holiday.

3 Elicit the type of words which are often tested in this sort of activity, e.g. articles, pronouns, prepositions. Set a time limit of seven minutes. Elicit the answers and ask why *Did* and *Are* are the first word in the questions (3 Past simple – last night; 6 Present continuous – are they thinking now).

Fast finishers

Ask fast finishers to look at the gaps and say what kind of words they are and to explain them where necessary, e.g. 6 verb *to be* in the present. We use *are* with *you, we, they*.

Answers
1 the 2 like 3 Did 4 about 5 She 6 Are

Extension idea

Write the second sentence from the text on the board but with one error underlined: *I'm writing from a hotel room.* Ask: *Why is this the wrong word?* (We use *a* when we don't know which one (room) we're talking about. This would mean she just chose any hotel room and started writing there. Students work in pairs, choose a different sentence and write their own wrong word. Students then swap sentences with a different pair who try to explain why it is wrong. Monitor and help where necessary. They then get together with the other pair and explain to them.

▶ **Speaking bank page 146: Part 1, Phase 2**
▶ **Vocabulary and grammar review Units 9 and 10**
▶ **Complete Key for Schools new edition Test Generator Unit 10**

Vocabulary

Seasons

autumn	summer
spring	winter

What's the weather like?

cold	snowing
foggy	windy
hot	

Places

beach	islands
desert	lake
forest	mountain

Vocabulary activity 1

Write the word WINDY on a piece of paper. Don't show the class. Invite two students to come to the front of the class. Show them the word and tell them to stand as if the weather was like this. When they are in position, they stand still. Ask the class if they can guess your secret word. If they say 'wind' use gestures to show they are very close but need a slightly longer word. When they guess the word, put students into small groups to choose a word and discuss how to stand. Invite each group to come to the front of the class for the others to guess the word.

Vocabulary activity 2

Write *code* on the board and elicit what a code is (a different symbol is used in place of letters to hide the word). Tell them your code is very easy. Each number represents a letter. (A = 1, B = 2, etc.). Divide the class into groups and draw a gapped word on the board, e.g. _ _ _ _ _ (beach). Each group takes turns to guess one number at a time. When students say a correct number, write it in the gaps (2, 5, 1, 3, 8). Their group can then have one guess of what the word is. The group who guess the word first win a point.

Vocabulary and grammar review Unit 9

Answers
1 2 Thank you for helping me with this. 3 We decided to buy a new TV. 4 I would like to visit your country. 5 Stefan wants to go to the seaside today. 6 I hope to hear from you soon. 7 We've got a little table for playing cards. 8 After seeing (I see) the film, I will go to the café.

2 2 washing 3 to come 4 walking 5 to drive 6 passing

3 1 It'll be 2 I'll meet 3 won't be 4 starts 5 I'm meeting 6 will need 7 won't have 8 We're going

4 2 Will Susan be at the party? Yes, she will. 3 Will the shops be open on Sunday? No, they won't. 4 Will you go to football practice tomorrow? Yes, I will. 5 Will Daniel win the race next week? No, he won't.

5 1 Why, rather 2 Would, sure 3 How, think 4 Shall, idea

6 2 amazing 3 interesting 4 terrible 5 horrible

Vocabulary and grammar review Unit 10

Answers
1 2 Are you going to fly? 3 No, we aren't going to fly. 4 My dad is going to drive. 5 Where are you going to stay? 6 That's going to be fun.

2 2 mustn't be 3 mustn't talk 4 must go 5 must drink 6 mustn't open 7 must send 8 mustn't ride

3 1 A 2 B 3 B 4 C 5 B 6 A

4 **Across:** 3 mountain 6 island 9 season 10 forest
Down: 1 beach 2 autumn 4 spring 5 river 7 lake 8 desert

11 I like to keep fit

Starting off SB page 78

Lead-in

Discuss a healthy day with the class. Ask what could make it healthy, e.g. food, exercise, go to bed early. Put students in pairs. Tell them to compare what they ate yesterday, what time they went to bed and what they did in the afternoon/evening. When they have asked and answered the questions, elicit from each pair who they think had the healthiest day and why.

1 Look at the photos with the students. Ask: *What are the people doing in each photo? Is the activity healthy or unhealthy? Which of these things do you do?* Set a time limit of 3–4 minutes for students to do the matching and discuss their ideas. Elicit which photo is the odd one out (the fast food – it is the only one which shows something unhealthy). Elicit students' ideas about the statements and reasons for them.

Answers
1 D 2 A 3 B 4 C 5 E

2 When the students have listened, elicit what the speaker said about each point and whether they agree (1 about an hour; 2 nine hours; 3 good sleep and lots of exercise can improve your school work; 4 It's amazing how many people get sick because they don't wash their hands often; 5 fast food can be OK sometimes).

Answers
1 T 2 F 3 T 4 T 5 F

Track 63

Presenter: Today we're talking to Doctor Raymond, an expert on teenage health. Doctor, what's the most important thing for teenagers who want to be healthy?

Doctor: Exercise, and lots of it. A teenager needs about an hour of good exercise every day.

Presenter: That's a lot! Won't they get tired?

Doctor: Not if they get enough sleep. A teenager needs about nine hours a night. Good sleep and lots of exercise can improve your school work, too!

Presenter: Cool! What else?

Doctor: It's amazing how many people get sick because they don't wash their hands often enough. Always wash your hands before a meal and after being outside.

Presenter: What about food?

Doctor: Of course it's important to eat well.

Presenter: So, no fast food.

Doctor: Well, fast food can be okay sometimes, but don't eat it every day!

3 Tell students to think about the five points from Exercise 1 and 2. Put the students in pairs and encourage them to ask each other questions, e.g. *How much exercise do you do every day? How often do you eat fast food?*

Extension idea

Remind the class that we use *must/mustn't* and imperatives for strong advice and elicit that we also use *should/shouldn't* to give advice. Divide the students into small groups so that students are not with their partner from Exercise 3. Students take turns to tell the group their answers from Exercise 3 and the other students give them advice about how to have a healthier lifestyle, e.g. *You should eat more vegetables. You must get more exercise. Don't eat fast food every day.* Elicit advice that students were given.

Reading Part 3 SB page 78

Lead-in
Talk to the students about sports teams. Ask them to think about the people who work for the team, apart from the players. Set a time limit of one minute for students to discuss who else teams need and what they do. Elicit ideas, *e.g. coach/trainer – helps them to keep fit and practise their skills, manager – decides who to buy/sell/pick for the team, physiotherapist/doctor – treats injured players and helps them to get strong again, ball boys/girls – collect the balls when they go out of play and give them back to the players, grounds man/woman – keeps the pitch in good condition.*

1 Put the students into pairs and give them one minute to discuss what they can see in the photo then elicit what they think a personal trainer does and how they are different from a sport trainer (a personal trainer works with one person to help them reach their health and fitness goals).

> **Suggested answers**
> **1** in a gym **2** doing exercise **3** gives exercises to help a person get fit

Reading Part 3 (multiple-choice)
Elicit that, even if they can't guess the exact meaning of a word, reading the words around it could help to decide if it is positive/ negative, for example. Look at the second point and elicit that this is a useful way to check that their choice is correct.

Exam advice

2 Set a time limit of eight minutes. Tell the students to read the text quickly first to give them an overall idea of what it is about. When students have finished, elicit the answers and go over any words they didn't understand.

Fast finishers
Tell students to decide why the two false options in each question are wrong. When you elicit the answers, fast finishers can explain why the other options are incorrect.

> **Answers**
> **1** A **2** C **3** C **4** A **5** B

3 Elicit one or two ideas from the class and then put the students into small groups. Set a time limit of two minutes and then elicit ideas from different groups.

Extension idea
Put the students into pairs. Tell them to write a short dialogue between one of them and a personal trainer. The personal trainer asks about their lifestyle and what they want and then tells them what changes to make to their life and what exercises they think would be good and why. Set a time limit of five minutes and monitor and help where necessary. When the students have finished, invite pairs to act out their dialogues in front of the class.

▶ **Workbook page 44**

Grammar SB page 79
First conditional

Lead-in
Re-elicit how we talk about things that we think will happen in the future but that we don't have any plans for yet (*will*). Elicit some examples, *e.g. I think I'll be a successful businessman. I think I'll go shopping on Saturday.* Students work alone to write three sentences. Put students into small groups to share their ideas. Tell students they will look at these sentences again at the end of the lesson (in the extension activity).

1 Look at the sentences with the class and elicit the answer.

> **Answers**
> **1** the present and the future **2** the future

2 Set a time limit of one minute for students to quickly read the dialogue before they listen so they understand what it is about. Play the recording and elicit the answers.

> **Answers**
> **1** want **2** 'll **3** won't **4** don't

Track 64

Man: Thank you for the interview, Martha. That was very interesting.

Martha: You're welcome.

Man: So, could you be my personal trainer? I need to get fit.

Martha: If you want me to be your personal trainer, I'll be very happy to help you.

Man: I should tell you I'm very lazy, and I don't like to work too hard.

Martha: Ha ha! You won't get fit if you don't work hard!

Man: Oh well, never mind.

3 Tell the students to look at the sentences in the two exercises and choose the correct answers. Elicit the answers and elicit that the two clauses can be written in either order as in the two examples in Exercise 1. Elicit the punctuation difference between the two sentences (when we start with the *if* clause, we separate the two clauses with a comma; when we start with the result clause, we don't use a comma). Elicit the two sentences in reverse order: *My students will sleep, work and play better if I do my job well. 2 If I make enough money to buy my own flat, I will be happy.*

Answers
1 possible 2 present

4 Tell the students to cover the endings and to look at the first beginning: *If you don't exercise,*. Elicit possible endings, e.g. *you'll be unhealthy/you won't get fit*. Make sure students use the *will* future form. Tell the students to work in pairs and think of possible endings for the other beginnings and then to uncover the endings to see how close their ideas were. Students then match the sentences. Check the answers with the class.

Fast finishers
Ask fast finishers to rewrite one or two of the sentences with the two clauses reversed.

Answers
1 e 2 f 3 a 4 d 5 c 6 b

5 Tell the students to look at the first sentence and say what is wrong and why (it has a *will* form in both clauses but (we use the present simple in the *if* clause, so this should be *If I don't keep exercising …*). Allow students to work in pairs and monitor and help where necessary. Elicit the mistakes and the correct answers.

Answers
2 ~~you like~~ you will like 3 ~~will be~~ it will be 4 ~~I'll happy~~ I'll be happy 5 ~~If someone want~~ If someone wants 6 ~~you feel~~ you'll feel

6 Tell the students to work alone. For weaker classes, elicit what tenses they will use to complete each sentence (1, 4, 5, 6 *will/won't* + infinitive; 2, 3, present simple). Elicit some ideas for the first sentence from the class before students start writing alone, e.g. *I won't sleep*. When students have finished, put them in small groups to share their ideas. Elicit the best sentences from each group.

Students could do Grammar reference: First conditional, Exercises 1–2, page 125, at this point or for homework.

/P/ Sentences with *if*

7 When the students have listened and repeated the sentences, elicit how the pause is shown in the sentence (with the comma).

Track 65

Martha: If you want me to be your personal trainer, I'll be happy to help you. You won't get fit if you don't work hard.

8 For weaker classes, elicit that the students will need to use the *will* form for each sentence ending. Set a time limit for the students to complete the sentences. Monitor and help where necessary.

9 When the students have said the sentences in pairs, ask them to reverse the clauses and say them without the pause. Elicit sentences from different pairs.

Extension idea
If you did the lead-in, ask the students to look at the sentences they wrote. Elicit that they can't be sure that these things will happen, so they should think of an *if* clause which will make them come true, e.g. *If I work hard and make the right decisions, I'll be a successful businessman. If I get my pocket money in the morning, I'll go shopping on Saturday.* Students do the same and compare their sentences in small groups. Elicit sentences from each group.

▶ Grammar reference page 125: First conditional
▶ Workbook page 46

Vocabulary SB page 80

Parts of the body

1 If you did the lead-in, some of the words may have come up already. Allow weaker classes to work in pairs. Elicit answers.

Answers
A eye B finger C nose D mouth E stomach F head
G hand H foot I neck J back K arm L leg

2 Look at the first word (*running*) with the students and elicit which parts of the body could be important and which is the most important, e.g. legs, feet, back, arms are all important; legs the most important. Students do the same in pairs for the other activities.

Answers
running – legs; reading – eyes; throwing and catching – arms; eating – mouth

3 Look at the example with students and elicit what part of the body the person asking the first question is thinking of (it must be something plural as it refers to *them*). Elicit that, in the second question, they are thinking of a singular word, probably *mouth*. Monitor and help where necessary. Students may disagree about which parts of the body are used for different activities, so if they aren't sure, they should say *possibly* or *yes, but they aren't very important*, rather than a direct *No*.

Extension idea
Although often used with younger students, *Simon Says*, is a fun way to revise vocabulary for parts of the body. Tell students that, if you tell students to do something using an imperative, they shouldn't do it. If you say: *Simon says ...* first, they should do it. If they do it when Simon doesn't say, they are out and have to sit down. Give instructions quickly to try to catch students out: *Touch your arm, Simon says touch your head, Simon says touch your leg, touch your nose*, etc.

Listening Part 4 SB page 81

Multiple-choice

Listening Part 4 (multiple-choice)
Discuss the advice with the students. Elicit why it is useful, e.g. 1 – the final part of the recording might change the answer. 2 It means they aren't listening for a specific time, price or other piece of information but key words which show which option is correct.

Exam advice

1 Look at the pictures with the students and elicit who the people are, what they are doing and how they feel. Look at the first question with the students and ask which picture it matches and how they know (E – it shows a girl, she's wearing a football kit, she's using a phone). Students match the other questions to the photos alone.

Suggested answers
1 E 2 A 3 B 4 D 5 C

2 Remind the students that they will listen to the recording twice and that they should use the second listening to help them choose the correct answers. When the students listen a second time, ask them to check their answers and note any dialogues where they found the correct option at the end of the conversation. Check answers.

Answers
1 C 2 A 3 A 4 B 5 B

Track 66
1
Narrator: For these questions, choose the correct answer.
Narrator: You will hear a girl leaving a message about a football match. Why is she unhappy?
Girl: Hi Annie – you missed the game! It was two–two, so at least we didn't lose again. I think we played better last week actually, even though we lost that one. I did OK – I got both of our goals, then I had to come off because their goalkeeper kicked my leg. It's better now but I still feel terrible. We should have won!

2

Narrator: You will hear a father talking to his daughter. Where have they been?

Girl: That wasn't so bad. At least we didn't have to wait for hours.

Dad: Yes, it wasn't too busy, was it? How does your foot feel now?

Girl: It still hurts.

Dad: Well, it's good to know that it's not broken. Are you OK to walk to the bus stop?

Girl: Can we get something to eat first?

Dad: Sure, there's a café near here.

3

Narrator: You will hear a mother talking to her son about school. What subject is he getting better at?

Mum: Hi Liam. How was school today?

Boy: OK. I got a good mark in history. We were learning about Spanish kings and queens from the 16th century.

Mum: So, you're improving?

Boy: Yes. Not like in natural science, where we're learning lots of things about the body – it's so difficult for me!

Mum: What about maths? Your teacher said you need to try harder, didn't she?

Boy: I am trying harder, but it isn't getting any easier.

4

Narrator: You will hear a mother talking to her son. What does the boy offer to do?

Mother: Tom, I feel sick today, and there's so much that needs doing.

Boy: I know, Mum. Don't worry. I've already washed the dishes and tidied downstairs.

Mother: That's good – but we really need to think about dinner. There's nothing in the fridge.

Boy: OK – I'll get some food from the market this afternoon.

Mother: Good. I'll cook something when you get home.

5

Narrator: You will hear a boy leaving a message. Why does he want a lift home?

Boy: Hi Dad, it's Fred. Can you come and get me from school? In the car? We've just had a games lesson where we ran about 5 kilometres. It was so hot – Steven had to stop because he had a headache. Not me, I just kept running! But I really don't think I could walk home now. I can't move my legs any more!

Extension idea

Put the students in pairs. Give each pair a copy of one of the audioscripts. They look at the audioscripts and find reasons why the two wrong options are incorrect. Elicit the reasons from different pairs, e.g. *1a she got both goals 1b It was 2–2 / we didn't lose.* Look at the script for 2 with the class. Ask: *Did they mention a hospital, doctor, nurse or anything else which helped to identify the place?* (No). Say that, in this question, it is easier to get the correct answer by deciding that the other two options were wrong than identifying that they were in a hospital.

▶ **Workbook page 45**

Grammar SB page 81

something, anything, nothing, etc.

Lead-in
Students work in small groups. Tell the students to think of a thing or person that they think all the other students in the class like, e.g. *ice cream, football, superhero movies* and a thing or a person that they think all the other students don't like, e.g. *homework, opera, tidying their room.* Elicit ideas from different groups and tell them they will look at their ideas again after Exercise 5 (in the extension activity).

1 Look at the meaning of *concentrate* with the class. Elicit one or two ideas for each question, e.g. 1 *interesting activities* 2 *hot weather.* Set a time limit of one minute for students to think of more ideas, and elicit them.

2 When students have read the article, elicit what they found out and what they think of the idea.

Answer
The children sit on exercise balls instead of chairs.

3 Look at the first underlined word with the class and elicit the sentence it is in (*they don't have to do anything*). Elicit that students will write *anything* in the second column. Students then write the other words in the correct columns alone.

Answers
positive statements: everyone, someone, something
negative statements and questions: anything, nothing, no one, anyone

4 When students have matched the words and meanings, elicit how we can use *no(thing)* with a positive verb and *any(thing)* with a negative one, e.g. *There is nothing I like. = There isn't anything I like.* Dictate another sentence: *I know no one here* and ask students to write it using *anyone (I don't know anyone here).*

Answers
1 b **2** a **3** c

5 Look at the first sentence with the class and elicit what is wrong (we should use *someone* rather than *anyone*) and why (it is a positive statement). Students work in pairs to try to find and correct the mistakes in the other sentences. Tell them that the mistakes aren't only about using the wrong word. Elicit the answers and what the problem is each time. (1 It is a positive sentence, so we use *someone* 2; 6 Indefinite pronouns are followed by the third person singular form, e.g. *everybody is/has, no one likes*; 3 *No one* is written as two separate words; 4 this is a negative sentence, so we use *anywhere*; 5 This is a negative meaning but with a positive verb form, so we use *nothing*).

Answers
2 We are going to get ~~some~~ something to eat and drink.
3 We don't have to bring ~~any thing~~ anything with us.
4 I only paid 100 euros for ~~everythings~~ everything.
5 I love my room because I have ~~all~~ everything I like there.

Extension idea
If you did the lead-in exercise, re-elicit any ideas that they had and how they could write these using *everyone / no one*, e.g. *Everyone likes ice cream. No one likes homework.* Allow students one or two minutes to make new statements using *Everyone/No one*, e.g. *Everyone knows what the capital of France is! No one goes jogging before school!* Elicit sentences from different groups and see if anyone disagrees, e.g. *Everyone likes ice cream. No, they don't! I hate it.* See how many statements are true for everyone.

Students could do Grammar reference: *something, anything, nothing*, etc. Exercises 3–4, page 126, for homework.
▶ **Workbook page 46**

Vocabulary SB page 82

What's the matter?

Lead-in
Talk to the students about a time when they had to stay off school because they were sick/ill. Put them in small groups to tell each other what was wrong. Tell the students to help each other with vocabulary if they can but if they don't know the word for an illness they should explain it or show it through a mime. Monitor to see how well students do this but don't give them any vocabulary yet.

1 Look at the picture with the class. Ask students to describe the people and elicit any vocabulary that students know. Students then do the matching in pairs. Elicit the answers and ask the class if there are any words here that they didn't know and which they needed in the lead-in. Elicit the meaning of each word and point out that we say *I've got a headache but I've got toothache*.

Answers
2 F **3** G **4** D **5** E **6** B **7** C

2 Allow students to complete the sentences in pairs. Monitor and help where necessary. Elicit the answers and point out that we always use *take* when talking about medicine. Draw students' attention to question 4 and elicit how they could say the sentence using *anything*: *There isn't anything you can do, except rest.*

Fast finishers
Tell fast finishers to think of more advice for some of the problems in Exercise 1, e.g. *Go to bed, Eat some dry toast, Don't eat anything, Have a cup of tea.* Elicit these before students do Exercise 3.

Answer key
1 Take **2** down **3** Go **4** nothing **5** Drink **6** Go **7** rest

3 Look at the first problem in Exercise 1 with the class (*I feel sick*). Say: *You are at home. You tell your parents: I feel sick. What do you think they will say?* Elicit some ideas to see what advice the students think their parents would give them. Students then do Exercise 3. They could do the whole exercise as a parent/child role play. Invite pairs to act out one of their conversations for the class.

Extension idea
Put the students into small groups. Tell them they are waiting at the doctors and each have a different problem. Set a time limit of one minute to think of the problems and how they can show them without saying anything. Invite groups to come to the front of the class and sit as if they were in the doctor's waiting room, showing their problem. The other students have to say what is wrong with them.

▶ **Workbook page 45**

Speaking Part 2, Phase 1 SB page 83

Lead-in
Put the students into pairs or small groups. Tell them to look at the five pictures in Exercise 1 and then think of five similar pictures which show an unhealthy lifestyle. They don't have to draw these but should write them on a piece of paper, e.g. *a person playing computer games at midnight, a person eating a burger.* Set a time limit of two minutes and elicit ideas from different groups.

Speaking Part 2, Phase 1 (a discussion based on an artwork prompt)
Elicit that this part of the exam is for the two students to talk to each other and that they should do this as naturally as possible. Tell them to pretend the examiner isn't there for this part of the exam apart from remembering to talk loudly enough for the examiner to hear them.

Exam advice

1 Elicit what the students can see in the pictures and then set a time limit of one minute for them to discuss the questions in pairs. Elicit ideas and reasons from different students.

2 Ask the students to read through all the questions and try to think of how to complete questions 1–7 with one word in each gap. Elicit ideas and then play the recording for students to complete the questions. Elicit the missing words.

> **Answers**
> **2** about **3** long **4** Do **5** Why **6** think **7** Do, like
> **8** about you **9** Why

Track 67
Boy: Do you eat a lot of vegetables?
Girl: I eat vegetables every day. I love them. What about you?
Boy: I don't really like them, but I eat them every day. How long do you sleep for?
Girl: I usually sleep for nine hours. I like it! What about you?
Boy: I sleep for about seven hours. Do you ever go running?
Girl: No, I don't.
Boy: Why not?
Girl: Because I don't like it. It's boring.
Boy: I love running.
Girl: I prefer walking. I like walking in the forest. What do you think about that?
Boy: That's nice. I like that too. Do you like cycling?
Girl: No, I don't have a bike. What about you?
Boy: Yes, I sometimes go cycling at the weekend.
Girl: Why?
Boy: Because I like to keep fit.

3 Look at the questions with the students. Point out that they can't just ask the questions without thinking about them as they might not make sense, e.g. They can only ask *Why not?* if their partner answers *No* to a different question. They then choose appropriate follow-up questions depending on their partner's answers. Monitor and help where necessary. Invite pairs to ask and answer for the class.

Extension idea
Ask the students to think of two questions each, similar to those in Exercise 2 but about unhealthy activities. They then ask and answer as before, adding follow-up questions where appropriate. Monitor and listen to the students.

▶ Speaking bank page 147: Speaking Part 2

Reading and Writing Part 6 SB page 83

Lead-in
Write on the board the following:
1 If I'm late don't worry.
2 Everyone here are very happy.
3 I've got headache.
4 My leg herts.

Tell the class that each sentence has one mistake. You are going to say a word and, if they know which sentence you are talking about, they should put their hands up. Say: Spelling mistake (elicit sentence 4), punctuation (1), missing word (3), grammar (2). Students now write the correct sentences in their notebooks. Elicit the changes needed.

Writing Part 6 (short notes)
Discuss why students should check their work (because everyone makes mistakes and, if we read our work again, we might spot something).

Exam advice

▶ Speaking bank pages 147–148: Part 2, Phase 1
▶ Writing bank page 139: a short message
▶ Workbook page 46
▶ Complete Key for Schools new edition Test Generator Unit 11

1 Elicit the questions and some possible answers in sentence form with a different way of making suggestions each time, e.g. *Let's meet at five o'clock. What about going by bus? We could go to the shopping centre.*

> **Suggested answers**
> What time shall we meet at your house? How are we going to get to the park? What will we do if it rains?

2 Give the students two minutes to read each reply and answer the questions either alone or in pairs. Elicit the answers but don't elicit the actual spelling or grammar mistakes yet.

> **Answers**
> 1 Stefan 2 Mario 3 Stefan 4 Mario 5 Stefan 6 Tony

3 Decide whether you want the students to rewrite the entire emails correctly or just the parts which have mistakes in them and make sure that all the students are doing the same thing. Elicit the answers.

> **Suggested answer**
> Hi Gina, Thanks for the message. Let's meet at 2 o'clock at my house tomorrow. If it rains, we will go to the café near the park.
> Mario
> Hi Gina, Let's meet at my house at 1 o'clock. We can run to the park. If it rains, well take the bus. Stefan

3 Set a time limit of five minutes. The students have had time to think about their email and have lots of ideas to help them so they shouldn't need as long as they get in the exam. Tell them to check their work when they have finished.

> **Extension idea**
> Put the students into small groups. Each group writes one sentence on a piece of paper. It must contain one mistake; of grammar, spelling, punctuation or wrong word. They should try to make it as difficult as possible to spot. Monitor and check that there is one mistake in each sentence. Each group numbers their sentence, which you then put around the room. Students go round the room and try to spot the mistake in each sentence. Set a time limit and collect in the sentences. Read them out and elicit the error in each.

Vocabulary

Keeping fit

exercise	improve
(get) fit	personal trainer
(un) healthy	train

Parts of the body

arm	head
back	leg
eye	mouth
finger	neck
foot	nose
hand	stomach

What's the matter?

drink water	have (got) a temperature
feel sick	have (got) toothache
go to the (doctor/dentist)	(my leg) hurts
have (got) a broken arm	lie down (in bed)
have (got) a cold	rest
have (got) a headache	take (an aspirin)

Vocabulary activity 1

Students work in small groups. Each student writes the words for the parts of the body on small slips of paper. They place these face down on the table so there are three or four copies of each word. The students should rearrange these so that no one knows what word is on each card. Each person in turn takes a card without showing the other students the word. They touch the body part and the other students race to say the word first. The quickest student takes the card. Students can only collect the same word once, so if they already have it, they have to remain silent while the other students race to say the body part first. The first person to collect ten different body part words is the winner (or fewer for a quicker game).

Vocabulary activity 2

Tell everyone in the class to look at the problems in the *What's the matter?* section of the wordlist. They have to go around the classroom miming their problem. They can't speak but they can make noises, e.g. sneezing, coughing, groaning. Students go round looking at each other for about a minute then get into small groups. They then write as many people's problems down as they can remember. Elicit how many each group remembered and see if they were correct.

Have you ever been on a plane?

Topic: travel and transport

Listening Part 2: gap fill: listening and writing down information (including places, days, prices, numbers, etc.)

Reading and Writing Part 1: discrete 3-option multiple-choice: reading for overall understanding of notices, emails and messages

Speaking Part 1, Phase 2: topic-based interview; focus on interactional and social language

Reading and Writing Part 7: story: writing connected text (a short story or narrative) of 35 words +

Grammar: present perfect; *should / shouldn't*

Vocabulary: means of transport; vehicles; travel verbs

Pronunciation: /ʃ/ and /tʃ/

Starting off SB page 84
Means of transport

Lead-in
Put the students into small groups. Set a time limit of one minute for students to think of as many forms of transport as they can. Elicit ideas. Now tell the students to write down the first answer that comes into their heads. Ask: *What's the best form of transport to take:*

... to Tokyo. ... to see beautiful ports in the Mediterranean. ... to get from Madrid to Barcelona. ... to get from your house to school. ... to get from your town to the nearest town.

Elicit ideas from each group, e.g. plane, ship, etc.

1 Students look quickly at the photos and say what each one shows. Play the recording for students to do the matching. Follow up by telling the students to close their books.

Track 68
1 [a boat, blowing its foghorn]
2 [a plane taking off]
3 [a car starting its engine]
4 [a train leaving the station]
5 [a bicycle bell ringing]
6 [a bus arriving at bus stop]

Answers
1 A **2** B **3** E **4** F **5** C **6** D

2 Look at the table and elicit what the students have to do. Tell them that they may have to tick more than one form of transport.

Answers

Name	by car	by boat	by bike	by bus	how long?
John				✓	20 minutes
Karen	✓				30 minutes
Jordan		✓	✓	✓	40 minutes

Track 69
John: My name's John. Last year I cycled to school, because my primary school was near my house. But now I go to a new school, and I get the bus. It takes about 20 minutes.

Karen: I'm Karen. I live in London, and it takes me about half an hour to get to school. It's too far to walk, and I don't like to cycle because there's too much traffic, so my mum drives me there every day.

Jordan: I'm Jordan. I live on an island in Scotland. My school is on another island. Every day I ride my bike, then I take a boat across the water. Then I get off the boat and I get on a bus to school. It takes about 40 minutes.

3 Ask students to note down the sentences the three people used in Exercise 2 to answer the questions. Elicit: *I get the bus, It takes about ..., it takes me about ..., my mum drives me, I ride my bike, I take a boat, I get on a bus.* Write these on the board. Encourage students to use similar sentences.

Extension idea
Put the students into small groups, making sure they are in different groups to their partner from Exercise 3. Tell the groups that they are going to share information and find out whose journey takes the longest, whose takes the shortest time and who uses more than one form of transport. Set a time limit of two or three minutes and elicit information from different groups.

Reading Part 1: SB page 85

Lead-in

Put the students into pairs and tell them to look at the forms of transport in the Starting off section. Tell them to use their imagination to write a sign they may see on one of the forms of public transport, i.e. bus, plane, train, ship or at the bus station, railway station, airport or port. Tell them to try to use 10–15 words in their sign, e.g. *Buy your tickets at the ticket office or pay the driver.* Elicit these from the class.

Exam advice: Reading Part 1 (multiple-choice)

Do an example with the class. Ask them to imagine that they didn't know what the word *half* meant. Look at the first sign with them. They understand *price* and *groups.* Ask: *If there are more people, will the price of a ticket be higher or lower?* (lower). *Why?* (because the boat company can sell more tickets). Elicit that they don't need to know exactly what *half* means, just that it is less than the normal price.

Exam advice

1 Tell the students that there will be a reason for the wrong options being incorrect. This could be that they aren't mentioned or they don't have the same meaning as the question. Students should think about this while they are choosing the correct answers. Elicit the answers.

Answers
1 A 2 C 3 B 4 C 5 B 6 A

▶ Workbook page 48

Grammar SB page 85
Present perfect

Lead-in

Draw a horizontal line on the board. Label this: *My life* and write five places you have visited on the line. Tell the class to do the same with five places they have visited. Put students into small groups and tell them to say when they went to each place and some details, e.g. *I went to France last year with my parents. We went to Paris.*

1 Students can stay in the same groups as in the lead-in to discuss the question. Ask them to tell each other about the longest car journey they have had, where they went and how long the journey took.

2 Look at the photo with the class. Elicit ideas and ask them to guess where the family went in their car and how they felt. Then set a time limit of one minute for students to quickly read the text to see if their ideas were correct, (*went to 75 countries – still travelling – started in 2000 – travelled 320,000 kilometres*).

Suggested answer
a family who went on a long car journey

3 Look at the first paragraph of the article again with the class. Ask: *When did the journey start?* (2000). *When did it finish?* (it didn't). Students then read the sentences and discuss the questions in Exercise 3 in pairs.

Answers
1 yes 2 no

4 Students stay in pairs to discuss the rules. Elicit their ideas and tell the students that the link with the present in rule 1 is either that the activity is still happening, like the journey, or that these things happened at some time in someone's life, which hasn't finished yet.

Ask why we don't say exactly when something happened, (because then we would use the past simple with a past time period – *I went to France in 2015/last year/five years ago*).

Tell the students that past participles can be regular or irregular. Verbs ending in -*ed* in the past simple also have past participles ending in -*ed.* Students will have to learn the irregular forms.

Answers
1 past 2 when 3 *have*

5 Before students start, ask them to look at the verbs in each question and elicit that they are all regular, so all have past participle endings with the same -*ed* form. Elicit that sentence 1 is an example of 'at any time in their life'. Monitor and help where necessary

Answers
2 have never jumped 3 has cooked 4 haven't played
5 has stayed 6 have studied; haven't finished

6 For weaker classes, elicit the base forms of the verbs in the box before they do the exercise. For stronger classes, you could do this after eliciting the answers. Also look at the question forms. *Have you ever ...* is used to ask about any time in your life. In questions, the word order is *Have / Has* + pronoun (+ *ever*) + past participle. Ask students to ask and answer questions 2 and 7 in pairs.

> **Answers**
> **2** driven **3** written **4** been **5** eaten **6** drunk **7** eaten **8** swum

7 Tell the students to read the questions before they listen to the recording. Elicit the answers and then look at how we form and answer *yes/no* questions.

> **Answers**
> **1** A **2** A **3** B **4** A **5** B

Track 70

Interviewer:	Mr Zapp, you've been on the road for over ten years. Have you ever had any problems?
Man:	Yes, we've had some. The car has stopped working a few times, but there is always someone who can fix it.
Interviewer:	Have you ever stayed in a hotel?
Man:	No. Our car is our home, our school, our kitchen and our transport!
Interviewer:	How fast can the car go?
Man:	We have never driven faster than 55 kilometres per hour. That's why we're still going.
Interviewer:	Have the children ever been to school?
Woman:	Yes, they've been to lots of schools in different countries and they learn from the internet. They've also learned a lot about the world around them.
Interviewer:	What kind of things have they learned?
Woman:	They've seen kangaroos and bears in the wild and they've learned words in many languages.
Interviewer:	Have you ever been to Vietnam?
Woman:	No, we haven't. We've been to Japan and South Korea, but not Vietnam.
Interviewer:	Have you ever thought, 'Why are we doing this?'
Man:	No, I haven't. I know why we are doing this. Because this is our dream.

8 Look at the example question and responses. Ask different students the question and elicit the correct answer. Students write the questions and answers alone. Monitor and help where necessary. Elicit the correct question forms but not the responses.

> **Answers**
> **2** Have you ever been on a plane? **3** Have you ever missed a train or bus? **4** Have you ever been on a trip without your parents?

9 Look at the example question and response in Exercise 8 again. Monitor and listen while students ask and answer the questions.

Students could do the Grammar reference: Present perfect Exercises 1–2, page 127 at this point or for homework

> **Extension idea**
> Tell students to look at the information they wrote in the lead-in activity. Look at your own example and say, e.g. *I have been to France.* Ask the class what this means (in my life). Ask: *Can I say 'I have been to France last year?'* (No, because last year is a finished time period, so you need the past simple). Students work in pairs and tell each other the five places they have been to.

▶ **Grammar reference page 127: Present perfect**
▶ **Workbook pages 49–50**

Vocabulary SB page 87

Vehicles

> **Lead-in**
> Tell students to close their books. Write eight gaps on the board to represent the letters in the word *vehicles*. Next to this draw eight steps with a matchstick person standing on the top step. Below the bottom step, draw some water. Elicit letters from the class. If they are in the word vehicles write them in the correct spaces. If not, the person moves one step down. The class have to guess the word before the person falls into the water. When they have found the word, elicit what it means (machines with an engine which carry people or things from one place to another).

1 When students have matched the words, elicit the difference between a *motorbike* and *scooter* (on a motorbike, the engine is part of the frame; on the scooter, it is at the back); a *coach* and a *bus* (a coach travels longer distances and is usually more comfortable); and a *tram*, *train* and *bus*, (trams and trains travel on tracks; trams and buses travel inside a town; trains also travel between towns).

> **Answers**
> **1** motorbike **2** coach **3** tram **4** scooter **5** taxi **6** helicopter

2 Look at the rules box with the students. Elicit other forms of transport we use after *on* (motorbike, train, tram, bus, plane). Look at the four prompts in Exercise 2 and point out that we can also use *go / travel by* with all forms of transport. Tell the class true sentences about yourself using all four prompts. Students then work alone to write their own words. Put students into pairs to tell each other their sentences.

3 Elicit what reasons someone might like or dislike a form of transport , e.g. *Planes are exciting. I like looking out of the window.* When students have discussed their ideas, invite pairs to ask and answer the questions for the class.

Extension idea
Ask: *How do we ask questions in the present perfect?* Elicit the question form: *Have you ever ...?* Students work in pairs to think of three questions about transport using *Have you ever ...?*, e.g. *Have you ever been on a motorbike?* Students then join up with a second pair and ask and answer questions.

▶ **Workbook page 49**

Listening Part 2 SB page 87

Lead-in
Talk to the students about running. Ask them if they like running, if they go running on their own or as part of a club, the longest distance they have ever run and how far they think they could run.

Listening Part 2 (information completion)
Elicit that, in English we often say, e.g. 'double M' when there are two letters the same next to each other, e.g. *summer = S–U–double–M–E–R.* Elicit why the other advice is useful (they know which piece of information they will listen to next and it is quicker to write numbers than words). You could drill the alphabet at this point or ask students to spell their own names.

Exam advice

1 Look at the example answer. Ask students what the person on the recording could say (ten forty-five or quarter to eleven). Elicit the answers.

Answers
2 9.30 3 3.15 4 7.15 5 1.45

Track 71
1   I didn't wake up until 10.45 this morning!
2   The film starts at half past nine. We're going to be late.
3   Let's go home. It's three fifteen.
4   Dinner will be ready at quarter past seven.
5
Man: What time is it?
Woman: Quarter to two.
Man: Thanks.

2 Look at the words in the box and elicit a question from the class, e.g. *What clothes should I wear?* Students work in pairs. Set a time limit of three or four minutes and, if students write a question using each word before the time has finished, ask them to think of one more question for one of the words.

Possible answers
What clothes should I wear? What distance is the run? Where do you meet? What time does it start? Will the run take place if the weather is bad? When should I get there?

3 Allow the students to work in pairs. Elicit ideas and ask if students can guess the words (e.g. 1 10 km 2 warm 3 shorts 4 10 5 Inside the).

Answers
1 a distance 2 an adjective to describe the weather
3 an item of clothing 4 a time 5 a place

4 Tell the students they will hear the recording twice and should use the second listening to check their answers. Elicit the answers and the spelling of the park's name and ask for any distractors the students heard (the last race was 5 km; it's raining now; should get there at 8.30).

Track 72
Narrator: For each question, write the correct answer in the gap. You will hear a teacher talking to her class about a countryside run they are doing. Write one word or a number or a date or a time.
Woman: OK, listen everyone. I've got some information for those of you who are coming on the countryside run on Saturday. Now, I know some of you came to the last one, two weeks ago – that was 5 kilometres, but we're going a bit further this time. It'll be 10 kilometres long, so you need to be quite fit. I know it's raining now, but don't worry I've heard it's going to be dry all weekend. Wear trainers, shorts and a T-shirt as usual and you should be fine. You won't need a sweater. The run starts at 9 o'clock but you should get there early – about half past eight. And make sure you have breakfast at least an hour before that. We're meeting by the lake at Staunton Park. That's S-T-A-U-N-T-O-N Park. I'm sure you know where it is. Tell your parents they'll have to wait about an hour for you to complete the run. You're all pretty fast!

5 Students listen to the recording again and check their answers either alone or in pairs.

> **Answers**
> **1** 10 **2** dry **3** shorts **4** 9 **5** Staunton

> **Extension idea**
> Tell the students to write the name of someone famous from a different country to their own, e.g. a singer, film star, politician. They must know how to spell the person's name. When they are ready, they join together in pairs. They take turns to say their name and then spell it, e.g. *Hello, my name's Daniel Radcliffe. Could you spell that, please? Yes, D–A–N–I–E–L R–A–D–C–L–I–double f–E.* Their partner has to try to write the name while they are listening.

▶ **Workbook page 49**

Grammar SB page 88

should / shouldn't

1 Look at the sentences with the class and elicit the answer. Elicit that *should / shouldn't* is followed by the infinitive of the verb without *to*, the same as *must / mustn't*.

> **Answers**
> *should / shouldn't*

2 Look at the examples with the class. Ask students if they wear bright clothes when cycling or cycle on the pavement. Students complete the sentences in pairs. Elicit the answers.

> **Answers**
> You should look behind you before you turn right or left.
> You should use the bike path – that's the safest place to ride.
> You should turn on your lights at night.
> You shouldn't listen to music – you need to hear what is happening around you.
> You shouldn't ride too close to parked cars – somebody might open a car door in front of you.
> You shouldn't carry passengers– your bike can carry only one person safely.

Students could do the Grammar reference: *should / shouldn't* Exercises 3–4, page 128, at this point or for homework.

/P/ /ʃ/ and /tʃ/

3 Tell students to look at the symbols and ask if anyone knows what sounds they represent. Play the recording and elicit the answer, then play it again to drill the two sounds.

> **Answers**
> /ʃ/ is longer

Track 73
1   /ʃ/
2   /tʃ/

4 Ask students to look at the sentences. Pause the recording after each sentence for students to repeat then ask them to say the sentences in pairs.

Track 74
1   You should check your work.
2   You shouldn't chat during lessons.
3   You should watch this show.
4   You should learn how to catch fish.

5 Students work in pairs to identify where the two sounds are. Tell them that the sounds might appear more than once. (/ʃ/: *should, shouldn't, show, fish* /tʃ/: *check, chat, watch, catch*).

> **Answers**
> **1** You should check your work. **2** You shouldn't chat during lessons. **3** You should watch this show. **4** You should learn how to catch fish.

6 Look at the example sentence with the class and ask the students to think of advice using *shouldn't*, e.g. *You shouldn't use your phone or computer after 9 pm.* Set a time limit of three minutes and monitor and help where necessary. Elicit ideas from different pairs.

> **Extension idea**
> In pairs, students write a problem similar to those in Exercise 6 on a blank piece of paper, which they don't mind sharing with the class. Place these around the room. Students walk round the room and write one piece of advice for each. They should read what other students have written and try to think of different advice. Set a time limit and tell the students to take their piece of paper and read the advice. Ask students for the best advice they were given.

▶ **Grammar reference page 128: *should / shouldn't***
▶ **Workbook page 50**

Vocabulary SB page 88

Travel verbs

Lead-in
Tell students to close their books. Write three verbs on the board: *drive, ride, fly*. Divide the class into two groups. Invite one student from each group to come to the board and ask them to write the past simple form of *drive*. If they don't know it or write it wrongly, another student can take their place. The first group to write the word correctly, wins a point. Continue with the past simple and past participle forms of each verb and make sure no one uses their books or phones to look up the correct forms.

1 Allow the students to discuss their ideas in pairs. Set a time limit of one minute and elicit the answers. Tell students that with most forms of transport, when we are the passenger we use *'travel by/go by'* but we can say *I fly (to America) every summer* if we are the passenger or the pilot.

Answers
1 drive: a bus, a coach, a taxi, a train, a tram **2** fly: a helicopter, a plane **3** ride: a bicycle, a motorbike

2 Look at the first sentence with the students and elicit the correct answer (*ride*) and why. We sit on the scooter like a bike, motorbike, horse, etc. Elicit the other answers.

Answers
2 flies **3** drives **4** rode **5** flew

3 Look at the instructions and give an example: Say: *If you visit London you should fly to Heathrow then travel by train or underground to the centre. At night, you should travel by taxi. If you travel by bus, you should try to sit upstairs to get a good view.* Monitor and help students where necessary. Invite one or two students to give advice to the class.

Extension idea
Re-elicit the past participles of the three verbs; *driven, ridden, flown.* Re-elicit the question *Have you ever ...* and ask the students to ask and answer questions using different forms of transport, e.g. *Have you ever ridden a motorbike?* Elicit the most interesting things students found out.

▶ **Workbook page 49**

Writing Part 7 SB page 89

Lead-in
Put the students into small groups. With books closed, ask them to think of a story together which involves someone using transport and someone giving advice. When they have discussed their ideas, they should think of how to show the story in three pictures. They shouldn't try to draw the pictures but should describe what is happening in each. Set a time limit of five minutes and monitor and help where necessary.

Writing Part 7 (a story)
Discuss the advice with the students and ask them why these are good ideas. 1 It sounds better to say *'Juan went ...'* than *'The boy went ...'.* Also, if there are more characters it becomes confusing if they don't have names. 2 The pictures show what happens in the story. If you don't write about them all, the story won't match the pictures; 3 Students should avoid changing tenses from past to present and stick to one or the other.

Exam advice

1 Allow students to work in pairs. Ask them to think of names for the main character as well. Stronger students could think about what tense they should use for the verbs. Elicit ideas from the students. You could write these on the board to help weaker students.

Suggested answers
Picture 1: Nouns: *breakfast, kitchen, cards, parents*; Verbs: *eating*
Picture 2: Nouns: *bus stop, watch, bag, cars*; Verbs: *look at, look (worried), wait*
Picture 3: Nouns: *bus, friends, banner, sign*; Verbs: *celebrate, arrive, have (a party)*

2 The students may have thought of these words themselves in Exercise 1. Elicit the pictures each word matches and add any new words to the ideas on the board.

Answers
1 breakfast, kitchen, eat, birthday, parents **2** wait, bus stop, watch, worry **3** arrive, bus, friends, music, party

3 Re-elicit that we use the past continuous to set the scene at the beginning of a story, e.g. *Luis was eating breakfast with his parents.*

Possible answer
On his birthday, Philippe ate breakfast in the kitchen with his parents. He had a lot of birthday cards. Then he went to the bus stop, but the bus was late. He looked at his watch. He was worried. Finally, the bus arrived. All his friends were on it. They played music and had a party on the way to school.

Extension idea
Put students in the same groups as for the lead-in. They swap their story ideas with a different group. Together, they look at the other group's picture descriptions and discuss together what they think the story is about. Set a time limit and then ask groups to get together to tell each other their ideas for the story to see if their ideas are the same as the original group's. Elicit story ideas from groups.

▶ **Writing Bank page 141 –142: a story**
▶ **Workbook page 50**

Speaking Part 1, Phase 2 SB page 89

Lead-in
Put students into small groups. Ask them to think of a question they could ask someone who is new to the class.

Tell the students to imagine you are the new student. Elicit a question from one group and say: *I'm sorry. I don't understand.* Encourage someone from a different group to rephrase the question. When they do, give an answer. Do the same with the questions from the other groups.

Speaking, Part 1, Phase 2 (topic-based interview)
Look at the exam advice with the students and ask why it is useful. Elicit that, in this part of the exam, it is the examiner who is asking the questions, so it may be useful for the students to ask them to repeat or rephrase a question. In Part 2 of the exam, when students are talking to each other, it could be useful to be able to rephrase sentences.

Exam advice

1 Look at the example sentence with the class and elicit how you would answer both questions (*I went to …, Yes, I did. I went to …*). Students complete the questions in pairs. Monitor and help where necessary.

Suggested answers
2 Did you get there by plane? **3** Do you go to school by bus every day? **4** Is it far to your school?

2 Elicit the answers and that the examiner started by asking *Have you ever been …?* (at any time in your life) and then started using the past simple (talking about one finished, past holiday).

Answer
Lisa went to the US with her family. She went in the autumn last year, and she travelled by plane.

Track 75

Examiner:	Have you ever been to the US, Lisa?
Lisa:	Yes, I have.
Examiner:	Who did you go with?
Lisa:	Sorry, could you repeat the question please?
Examiner:	Did you go alone?
Lisa:	No, I went with my family.
Examiner:	When did you go there?
Lisa:	I went there in the autumn last year.
Examiner:	How did you get there?
Lisa:	Sorry, I didn't understand the question.
Examiner:	Did you go there by boat?
Lisa:	Oh, no we flew there. On a plane.

3 Elicit one or two ideas from the class, e.g. *Have you ever been to Japan? Do you like travelling by plane?* Weaker classes can work in pairs and then change partners for Exercise 4.

4 Encourage students to pretend they don't understand any of the questions when they first hear them to give students more practice of rephrasing questions. Monitor and listen for interesting answers. Invite pairs to ask and answer their questions for the class.

Extension idea
Tell the students to choose one of their questions from Exercise 3/4. They then mingle and ask as many people as possible their question. They should note down the answers they hear. Set a time limit and ask the students to sit in small groups. They take turns to tell each other what their question was and what they found out.

▶ Speaking bank pages 146–147: Part 1
▶ Vocabulary and grammar review Units 11 and 12
▶ Complete Key for Schools new edition Test Generator Unit 12

Vocabulary

Means of transport

bike	bus	plane
boat	car	train

Vehicles

coach	motorbike	taxi
helicopter	scooter	tram

Travel verbs

drive (a car, a bus, a coach, taxi, a train, a tram)
fly (a plane, a helicopter)
go/travel by/in/on
ride (a bicycle, a motorbike)

Vocabulary activity 1

Write the following letters on the board and tell the students there is a word hidden inside them which is written in the correct order but with other letters mixed up: AHGEFLAMOESTF.

Give students twenty seconds and then say: it's something you wear on your head. Give students another twenty seconds and then start crossing out the extra letters. Keep going until someone guesses HELMET and cross out all unnecessary letters to show the word.

Students now do the same in pairs with a word from the wordlist and join up in groups of four to see which pair can find the word the quickest.

Vocabulary activity 2

Tell students to work in pairs. They have to choose a transport or vehicle word from the word list and write a short paragraph containing the word, e.g. *We flew from Spain to Morocco in a plane. It was great and only took an hour. We had great views from the window.*

When they have finished, they swap with a different pair and see if any other word could replace the word from the wordlist and still make sense, e.g. *We flew from Spain to Morocco in a helicopter*.

Elicit ideas from different groups and elicit the differences between the two words used, e.g. a plane has wings on each side. A helicopter has something (a rotor) above it which goes round very fast to make it fly.

Vocabulary and grammar review Unit 11

Answers

1 2 will be 3 buy 4 go 5 'll get 6 won't have

2 2 What will you do if it's sunny tomorrow? 3 What will your parents do if you pass all your exams? 4 How will you feel if you eat too much chocolate? 5 Where will you go if it rains this weekend? 6 Who will you ask if you need help with your homework.

3 2 some 3 every 4 Every 5 No 6 No 7 any 8 some

4 Across: 3 foot 4 nose 6 hand 7 back 8 arm 9 head
Down: 1 mouth 2 stomach 3 fingers 4 neck 5 eyes

5 2 toothache 3 temperature 4 hurt 5 cold 6 sick

Vocabulary and grammar review Unit 12

Answers

1 2 bought 3 read 4 eaten 5 been/gone

2 2 He hasn't made sandwiches 3 He's cleaned the tent. 4 He hasn't bought a map. 5 He's washed his clothes. 6 He's invited Maria. 7 He hasn't found a cooking pot.

3 2 I have never eaten sushi. 3 My best friend has read lots of books. 4 My brother has eaten too much chocolate. 5 Have they ever been to Spain? 6 My dad has bought a new car.

4 2 He should practise more often. 3 You should go to sleep. 4 You shouldn't wear small shoes. / You should wear bigger shoes. 5 You shouldn't use your tablet much. 6 He shouldn't eat vegetable soup.

5 2 bus 3 boat 4 plane 5 tram 6 scooter 7 helicopter 8 motorbike

6 2 A 3 B 4 C 5 A 6 B

13 What's your hobby?

Topic: hobbies

Listening Part 3: 3-option multiple-choice: listening to identify specific information, feelings and opinions

Reading and Writing Part 3: 3-option multiple-choice; reading for detailed understanding and main ideas

Speaking Part 2, Phases 1 and 2: discussion based on an artwork prompt: focus on organising a larger unit of discourse; comparing, describing, expressing opinions

Reading and Writing Part 6: short message: writing a communicative note or email of 25 words +

Grammar: present perfect with *for* and *since*; *may / might*

Vocabulary: hobbies; adverbs; jobs

Pronunciation: /w/ /v/ /b/

Starting off SB page 92

Lead-in
Before the students open their books, write *free time* on the board. Elicit what this means (time when you have nothing to do). Ask the students to work in pairs and tell each other how much free time they have on a school day and at the weekend. They should say what they are doing when they aren't free, e.g. *On a weekday, I don't have any free time in the morning because I have to get ready for school.*

1 Look at the photos with the class. Elicit what the people are doing. Elicit how we ask about things people have done at any time in their life (*Have you ever ...?*) and how we can respond (*Yes, I have / No, I haven't*). Students ask each other if they have ever done any of the things in the photos. Students then look at the rubric and ask each other.

2 When the students have done the matching, ask them which of these they enjoy, which they have never done but would like to do and which they aren't interested in.

Answers
1 D 2 B 3 E 4 A 5 C

3 Look at the questions with the class. Elicit that they ask about the past, present and future. Elicit the answers and ask students about hobbies they did when they were younger that they don't do now.

Answers
1 playing computer games 2 climbing and snowboarding
3 sailing

Track 76
Teacher: So, Natasha, tell me about your hobbies. Do you like computer games, for example?
Natasha: I played a lot of computer games until I was about 10. But I haven't played any for a long time.
Teacher: What do you do now?
Natasha: I prefer doing things outside. Activities like climbing and snowboarding.
Teacher: Is there anything you haven't tried, but would like to?
Natasha: I'd love to go sailing. But dad says it's very expensive.

4 Tell students to work in pairs and take turns to ask and answer the questions. Set a time limit of two minutes. Monitor and listen for any interesting ideas. Elicit ideas from different students.

Extension idea
Put students into small groups. Tell them to try to find an activity that they all like doing. When they have done this, tell them they are going to try to persuade the rest of the class that it's a good way to spend their free time. Set a time limit of two minutes. Invite groups to present their hobby to the class and have a vote on the best presentation.

Listening Part 3 SB page 93

Lead-in
Ask the class: *Do you prefer to do a free-time activity alone or with friends? Do you prefer to have lessons and get better at the activity or just have fun?* Elicit after-school lessons that the students go to. Elicit adjectives to describe the lessons.

Listening Part 3 (multiple-choice)

Elicit that often, words from the options will appear in the text as distractors. Ask how the students can know how to choose the correct option, e.g. by listening carefully to the context, by using the second listening to check.

Exam advice

1 Put the students into pairs and give them two minutes to discuss their ideas. Tell them there is more than one way to paraphrase the sentences. After two minutes, ask if students have rewritten every sentence. If not, tell them that the words on the board might help and give them an extra minute. Elicit ideas from different students.

Suggested answers
2 The bus was too crowded. **3** The puzzle took me just over ten minutes to do. **4** I watched a film. **5** I'll teach you how to ride. **6** My helmet was too small. **7** I'm improving at snowboarding.

2 Play the recording to see if any of the students' ideas were used. Play it again for them to do the matching. Elicit the sentences used in the recording.

Answers
2 c 3 g 4 f 5 a 6 e 7 b

Track 77
A   I'll teach you to ride.
B   My snowboarding is improving.
C   The bus was full.
D   I'll send you a message.
E   My helmet was too small.
F   I saw a film.
G   The puzzle took me about 15 minutes to complete.

3 Look at the first question with the students and elicit that *start* is the key word as there may be distractors based on when he first wanted lessons, booked the lessons or had his most recent lesson. Students work together to underline key words in other sentences. Elicit ideas and reasons for them.

Answers
1 start 2 thought, first 3 borrow, first 4 teacher 5 plan, future

4 Elicit that students should listen for paraphrasing of the three options and also decide which one answers the question.

Answers
1 B 2 A 3 C 4 A 5 B

Track 78
Narrator: For each question, choose the correct answer. You will hear Rich talking to his friend Jess about horse riding.
Girl: Hi Rich, I hear you're having horse-riding lessons.
Boy: Yes. We'll be able to go riding together!
Girl: Great! When did you start?
Boy: I saw an advert about a month ago. So Mum phoned the place and we visited last week, but I only had my first lesson this morning.
Girl: How was it?
Boy: All we did was brush the horses. It wasn't difficult but I wanted to ride. I hope the next lesson will be more interesting.
Girl: I remember my first lesson. I got a riding hat as a birthday present, plus boots and trousers, then my friend's mum had to lend me her jacket because it was so cold that day!
Boy: What was your teacher like?
Girl: She won a lot of prizes for horse-riding, but I don't think she really knew how to teach us and she wasn't always fun. But I kept going, and now I love riding!
Boy: That's my plan. My friend wants me to start tennis lessons, but I like this better and I want to ride with you one day, so …

▶ Workbook page 52

Grammar SB page 93

Present perfect with *for* and *since*

Lead-in
Give students three examples from your life of things which are true about you now, e.g. *I am a teacher; I live in (the town you live in now); I am married; I have got a car.* Tell the students to do the same using *I am …, I have got …* or other verbs. Now tell students when these things started, e.g. *I became a teacher in …/… years ago. I got married in …/… years ago. I bought my car in …/… years ago.* Students make similar sentences in pairs.

13

1 Put the students into pairs and ask them to describe one photo each saying what the people are doing and how they are feeling. Elicit ideas and ask the class the second question.

Answers
They are climbing; They are kayaking

2 Set a time limit of two minutes for the students to read the text. Elicit the answer and ask when and where he started climbing (last year in France). Ask the students if there is anywhere like Adventure Zone in their town and, if there is, if any of the students go.

Answers
indoor climbing

3 Look at the two examples with the students. Elicit that when we follow *since* with a verb, the verb is in the past simple.

Answers
1 a 2 b

4 Tell the students to work alone and to use the rules to help them. Elicit the answers and what the sentence endings would be if you changed *for* with *since* and vice versa, i.e. if you use *since* in sentence 1. For stronger classes, tell students how we use the past simple and present perfect to give similar information in different ways. Write on the board: *I got/bought my sailing boat in 2005/14 years ago.* (past simple, a finished activity); *I have had my sailing boat since 2005/for 14 years.* (present perfect, an unfinished activity or situation).

Answers
2 since 3 for 4 since 5 for

Students could do Grammar reference: Present perfect with *for* and *since*, Exercises 1–2, page 129, at this point or for homework.

5 Look at the first sentence with the class. Ask: *Can you finish this with 'three years'?* (yes). *Can you finish this with 'my first year at secondary school'?* (No, that is when it started, so needs *since*). Students work alone. Monitor and help where necessary.

6 Look at the example sentence with the students. Elicit that the question form they need for all the questions is: *How long have you + past participle ...?*

You could review comparatives when eliciting answers. Ask pairs: *Who has known their best friend longer? Whose family has lived here longer?*

Extension idea
Write three facts about yourself on the board, e.g. *I am a teacher, I live in (the town you live in now), I am married. I have got a car.* If you did the lead-in, you can use the facts you used then. Elicit questions from the class using *How long have you ...?* and answer them using *for* and *since. I have been a teacher for ...; I have lived in this town since ...; I have been married for ...; I have had a car since ... .* Students write their own facts alone then work in pairs. They take turns to ask each other *How long have you ...?* questions to respond using *for* or *since.* Monitor and help where necessary.

▶ **Grammar reference page 129: Present perfect with *for* and *since***
▶ **Workbook pages 53–54**

Vocabulary SB page 94

Adverbs

Lead-in
Tell the students one thing you are good at, e.g. teaching, one thing you are careful with, e.g. marking tests and one thing you are bad at, e.g. singing. Tell the students to do the same and write down the three things in their notebooks. Put students into pairs and ask them to guess what their partner wrote. Elicit ideas from different students.

1 Elicit what a noun is (a person or thing) and what a verb is (an action). Students look at the two example sentences. Elicit the noun in the first sentence (parts) and the verb in the second sentence (climb). Elicit that *easy* is an adjective and *easily* is an adverb. Ask: *Where is each word in the sentence?* (the adjective is before the noun and the adverb is at the end of the sentence).

Answers
noun – easy verb – easily

2 Tell students that if they aren't sure which word to choose they should decide what it is describing. Look at 1 with the class. Ask: *Is the word describing the experience or the verb* to have? (the experience). Elicit that they need the adjective. Students do the same with the rest of the exercise in pairs. Elicit the answers and what the words are describing. (*1 the experience 2 to fall 3 to get better 4 it 5 you 6 to get hurt 7 to plan 8 teacher 9 to teach*)

> **Answers**
> **1** bad **2** badly **3** quickly **4** easy **5** careful **6** easily
> **7** carefully **8** good **9** well

3 Tell students to look at the examples in the dialogue to find the correct forms. Elicit that, for regular adverbs we add -*ly*. Even when the word ends in an -*l* we add a second -*l*, e.g. *carefully*. Elicit that for adjectives ending in -*y*, we change the *y* to an *i* before we add -*ly*. Look at the irregular adverb with the class and elicit one or two sentences using it, e.g. *I don't feel well. Harry Potter is a well-known character.*

> **Answers**
> Adjectives: regular: bad, careful, slow, quick, *easy*, happy; irregular: good
> Adverbs: regular: carefully, slowly, quickly, easily, happily; irregular: well

4 Elicit the answers and the spelling of easily. Tell fast finishers to choose one or two of the adjectives in the box and write new sentences using them as an adverb. Elicit their ideas when everyone has finished the activity.

> **Answers**
> **2** slowly **3** well **4** badly **5** easily **6** sadly

5 Look at the activities with students. Encourage stronger students to use more adverbs, e.g. *I cycle well but slowly. I sing badly but happily.* When they have finished, you could put the pairs together in groups of four and ask students to guess what the other pair said.

Extension idea
Tell students to choose four adverbs from the lesson and one activity they do in each manner, e.g. read – slowly, talk – quickly, play basketball – well. Students then work in small groups and take turns to tell each other an activity. The other students have to guess the correct adverb. Elicit interesting facts from groups.

▶ **Workbook page 52**

Reading Part 3 SB page 95

> **Lead-in**
> Talk to the students about board games, card games and computer games. Elicit some names, e.g. chess, bridge, Monopoly. Put students into small groups and set a time limit of one minute for them to use comparative sentences about them, e.g. *Board games are more relaxing than computer games.* Elicit sentences from different groups.

> **Reading and Writing Part 3 (multiple-choice)**
> Discuss the advice with the students. Tell students that the advice relates to all multiple-choice tasks; reading and listening. Look at the second point and elicit that, if they do see the same word in the text as in one of the options, they should read the information around the word carefully to see if it is the correct option or not.
>
> **Exam advice**

> **Background information**
> *Go* is possibly the world's oldest board game. It is popular all over the Far East. The idea is to take the other player's pieces by surrounding them with yours. It has far more possible moves than chess and it was very difficult to develop an artificial *Go* programme. However, Google DeepMind created AlphaGo which, in 2017, beat the world champion in three games out of three. You can see *Go* in films such as *A Beautiful Mind* and *Tron: Legacy* as well as in Japanese manga and anime.

1 Put the students into pairs or small groups and ask them to think of all kinds of games; board games, card games and computer games. If they did the lead-in, they will already have some ideas. Elicit students' opinions and ask how often they play and who they play with.

2 Look at the photo with the students and ask if they know the game. Give them the information from the background information box as well and explain how the game is played.

3 Before the students start doing the exercise, ask what they should do first. Elicit that they should look through the questions and options and underline key words then read the whole text quickly to get a general understanding. Give them two minutes to do this and then tell them they have another six minutes to complete the task.

> **Answers**
> 1 A 2 C 3 B 4 A 5 C

4 Talk to the students about similar board games, e.g. chess, draughts. Elicit good and bad things about these games. Students then discuss the questions in pairs. Set a time limit of one minute and elicit ideas.

> **Extension idea**
> Put the students in small groups. The groups try to find a game that they all know. They then plan a presentation of the game saying the kind of game it is, how many people can play and a brief description of how to play it. Set a time limit of 3 or 4 minutes and then allow each group to present.

▶ **Workbook page 53**

Grammar SB page 96

may/might

> **Lead-in**
> Elicit when we use *will* for future (for predictions that are just our opinion; not based on evidence and decisions made at the time of speaking). Elicit one or two predictions using *will*, e.g. *I think it will rain at the weekend. The end of year exams won't be easy.* Put students in pairs and ask them to write two sentences of their own, one positive and one negative. Elicit ideas from different pairs and ask them to say how sure they are on a scale of 0% – 100%.

1 Look at the sentences with the students. Ask: *When is he talking about?* (the future); *Will he definitely be the world's number one player?* (No); *Will he definitely become a doctor?* (No); *Is he definitely going to stay at home this evening?* (No). Elicit the correct option for the gap (not sure). If you did the lead-in activity, re-elicit the predictions on the board but tell students to use *may / might* instead of *will*.

> **Answers**
> not sure

2 Look at the first sentence with the students. Elicit that it is a prediction about the future. Look at the second sentence and tell students we can also use *may / might not* to say we aren't sure about the present. Point out that both *might* or *may* can be used with no difference in meaning. Elicit the answers and whether they refer to the future or present. Follow up by looking at the sentence grammar: *May / Might* are followed by the infinitive without *to*. Point out that we don't generally use the abbreviated *n't* form with *may* or *might* and that they should use the full form *not* as a separate word.

> **Suggested answers**
> 2 may / might be (a police officer) 3 may / might be sick
> 4 may / might not like me anymore 5 may / might win

Students could do Grammar reference: *may / might* Exercises 3–4, page 129, at this point or for homework.

> **Extension idea**
> Elicit or write a mini dialogue in which someone is worrying about the future and makes a prediction using *will*. The second person tries to make them feel better using *may/might*, e.g.
> – *I think it will rain at the weekend.*
> – *Don't worry. It might be sunny.*
> Students work in the same pairs. Monitor and help where necessary. Elicit dialogues from different pairs.

▶ **Grammar reference page 129: *may/might***
▶ **Workbook page 54**

Vocabulary SB page 96

Jobs

> **Lead-in**
> Put the students into small groups. Set a time limit of one minute for them to brainstorm as many jobs in English as they can. Find out how many jobs each group wrote and elicit these, starting with the group who had the fewest.

1 Look at the photos with the class. Ask them to describe the people and elicit any vocabulary that students know. Students then answer the questions in pairs. Elicit the answers and ask the students if they enjoy these activities.

Answers
1 cook / chef **2** doctor / nurse / carer **3** vet / farmer / zoo keeper

2 Look at the job titles and elicit what these people do. Elicit that a coach can also be called a *trainer*. Model and drill *mechanic* for the pronunciation on the *-ch* sound and *photographer* for the word stress. In stronger classes, when students have done the matching, you could elicit other jobs that these people could do, e.g. *1 engineer, flight attendant; 4 PE teacher; 5 blogger; 6 doctor.*

Answers
2 vet **3** photographer **4** coach **5** journalist **6** nurse
7 mechanic

/P/ /w/ /v/ /b/

3 Tell the students to say the words in pairs before they listen to the recording then repeat them when they have heard them. Depending on pronunciation problems the students have, you could look at international words such as *Wikipedia* and drill how it is said in English (with a /w/ sound, not a /v/ sound as in many countries). You could also use famous people: *Brad Pitt, Will Smith, Justin Bieber, Emma Watson* or geographical places: *Washington, Vesuvius, Vietnam, Barcelona.*

Answers
business /b/; vet /v/; waiter /w/

Track 79
business
vet
waiter

4 Tell students to work in pairs and take turns saying the three words. Their partner looks at their mouth and they then complete the rules together. When students have completed the rules, model and drill the three sounds showing clearly how the mouth and lips look when saying each letter sound.

Answers
For the /b/ sound, the mouth is closed at first.
For the /w/ sound, the mouth is slightly open.
For the /v/ sound, the bottom lip touches the top teeth.

5 Play the recording once all the way through, then line by line for the students to repeat. Students then practise the dialogues in pairs, using the rules in Exercise 4 to help them. Invite pairs to read out one dialogue each.

Track 80
1
A: Would you like to work in a bank?
B: No. That would be very boring. I want to be a vet.
2
A: Vicky was a window cleaner. Now she's a very rich businesswoman.
B: Wow!
3
A: Victor makes videos for bands. They're wonderful!
B: Yes, he does them very well.

6 Look at the example sentence with the class. Elicit ideas for the second sentence, e.g. *I wouldn't like to be a mechanic because I don't like mending things.* Elicit that, as well as *I like / don't like* they could use the phrases *I'm good at / not very good at* for their reasons. Set a time limit of two minutes and then elicit ideas and reasons.

Extension idea
Put students into small groups. Each groups needs a piece of A4 paper. Give each group a letter: *v, w, b*. They should look back in their books at the vocabulary lists and find words starting with or containing their letter. They then design a poster including some of the words, pictures representing some of the words and, if they like, a picture of a mouth when saying their sound. When the students have finished, display the posters in the classroom.

▶ **Workbook page 52**

Writing Part 6 SB page 97

Lead-in
Tell the class to close their Student's Books. Dictate the following:

Hi,

Would you like to come to the cinema on Friday? Let's meet at seven o'clock outside the shopping centre. If it rains, I'll wait in the Chinese Dragon café. I love their green tea. Let me know what you think.

Tell the students to swap texts with a different student. They start with 100 points. Tell them to take away one point for each mistake. Write the message one word at a time and tell students to check that the text includes the correct spelling and punctuation. Underline these to make sure they notice, e.g *Would ... on Friday? If it rains,* Elicit how many points students got.

Writing Part 6 (short notes)

Discuss the advice with the students and elicit the sort of things they should check (grammar, spelling, punctuation). Elicit that, if they don't respond to all three points, they will lose marks for not completing the task.

Exam advice

1 Set a time limit of one minute and then ask students to compare answers in pairs. Elicit the answers and ask how easy or difficult the errors were to find.

> **Answers**
> Hi Maddy,
> Would you like to come shopping with me on Saturday**?** L**e**t's meet at 10 o'clock outside the **library**. I hope **we have** a very nice time.
> See you,
> Frederico
> Not answered: say what she should bring

2 Tell students they have about 8–10 minutes for each of the writing tasks in the exam and, as this is the shortest, they should try to do it slightly more quickly. Set a time limit of seven minutes. Tell students to spend the first minute thinking about what to say and any useful vocabulary or grammar they can use and the last minute to check their work. That leaves five minutes for the writing. While the students are writing, monitor and note any mistakes. Don't make it obvious that you are doing this.

> **Possible answer**
> Hi Bobbie,
> Would you like to come sailing with me on Saturday? I'd like to sail to Trudy Island if the weather is good. Don't forget to bring some lunch!
> See you,

Extension idea

Write some of the mistakes you noticed in Exercise 2 on the board, one at a time. For each one, elicit what the error is and what it should be. Don't mention who wrote them as they may have corrected them when they checked their writing.

▶ **Writing Bank page 139: Writing Part 6**
▶ **Workbook page 54**

Speaking Part 2 SB page 97

Lead-in

Put the students into pairs or small groups. Elicit different structures the students have learned in this unit and previous units, e.g. *may/might*, First conditional, adverbs, present perfect with ever, *never, for and since*. Tell the students to imagine that they are in a speaking exam. In small groups or pairs, they should think of ways of using some of the different structures to answer questions about hobbies and free time, e.g. *If the weather is nice this weekend, I'll go sailing. I love sailing.* Set a time limit of two minutes and elicit ideas from different groups.

Speaking Part 2 (a discussion based on an artwork prompt)

Elicit that although students talk together, not to the examiner, the examiner is still listening and needs to hear what they are saying. Point out that, if they can invent a hobby and talk about it, the examiner isn't going to check that they told the truth. It's better than saying that you don't have any hobbies.

Exam advice

1 Elicit the answers and the structures that the students used in their answers (a present perfect; *may/might*; b *maybe + will*; c *may/might*.

> **Answers**
> 1 c 2 b 3 a

2 Look at the task and remind students that they should speak for two minutes and talk about all the photos. They should also ask each other questions and take turns. Elicit some useful phrases for taking turns, e.g. *What do you think about …? Do you like …? Have you ever tried …?* Set a time limit of two minutes and tell students to try to keep talking until you tell them to stop. Give feedback on the useful phrases you heard when students have finished.

3 Elicit that, after the students have discussed the pictures, the examiner will ask them more questions on the same topic. Tell them that the questions here aren't about free time but a different topic. Elicit the answers and the meanings of the words *indoor* and *outdoor* and the examples the examiner gave.

> **Answers**
> **1** indoor job, outdoor job **2** job

Track 81

Examiner: Sonya, when you're older, would you prefer to do an indoor job or an outdoor job?

Sonya: I'm sorry, I don't understand the question.

Examiner: Do you think jobs people do inside, like a doctor, are better than jobs people do outside, like a football coach or police officer?

Sonya: Oh, I think outdoor jobs are better.

Examiner: Why?

Sonya: Because I don't like to spend too much time indoors.

Examiner: What about you, Stefan. Would you prefer to do an indoor job or an outdoor job?

Stefan: Indoor job.

Examiner: Why?

Stefan: I like computers.

Examiner: What job do you think you might like to do?

Stefan: I'd like to work with computers.

Examiner: Why?

Stefan: They're interesting.

Examiner: What about you, Sonya, what job do you think you might like to do?

Sonya: I haven't decided. I think I might like to be a swimming teacher.

Examiner: Why?

Sonya: Because I love swimming, and I want to teach.

Examiner: Thank you, that's the end of the test.

4 Play the recording again and ask students to think of reasons for their answers. Elicit the answers and why Sonya's answer was better.

Answers
Sonya gives fuller answers.

5 Set a time limit of two minutes. Monitor and listen to how well the students answer the questions. Give feedback on some good phrases and interesting information you heard.

Extension idea
Put the pairs into groups of four. Two students play the roles of examiners and two play the parts of students. One examiner asks the students the questions in Exercise 1 and the other notes down the structures and linking words each student uses. When they have both answered all three questions, the pairs swap roles and, when the second pair have finished, they give each other feedback on the language they used.

▶ **Speaking Bank page 147: Speaking Part 2**
▶ **Complete Key for Schools new edition Test Generator Unit 13**

Vocabulary

Hobbies
doing puzzles   snowboarding
making jewellery   sailing
playing computer games

Adverbs
bad – badly   happy – happily
careful – carefully   quick – quickly
easy – easily   sad – sadly
good – well   slow – slowly

Jobs
coach   photographer
journalist   pilot
mechanic   vet
nurse

Vocabulary activity 1
Write on the board: *Now, open your books to page 35 and do Exercise 6.* Ask the class who would say this (a teacher). Students work alone. They choose a job from the job wordlist and write a sentence that the person might say while at work. It should be clear from the sentence what their job is. Students then mingle and say their sentences to each other. The other student should make a note of their name and job. If they don't know, they can't ask. They just have to write a question mark. Students then work in small groups and compare what they wrote to see if they all had the same answers. Elicit what each person's job was and what they said.

Vocabulary activity 2
Write on the board: *I can sing ... .* Ask the students to guess the missing adverb. Tell them to do the same. They should choose an adverb from the list and write a sentence about one thing they do in this manner. Students then join together in small groups. The students take turns to say the beginning of the sentence, without the adverb. The other students guess which adverb is correct. Elicit ideas from each group for other groups to guess the adverb.

14 Keep in touch!

Unit objectives

Topic: communication

Listening Part 5: matching: listening to identify specific information

Reading and Writing Part 4: 3-option multiple-choice cloze: reading and identifying the appropriate word

Speaking Parts 1 and 2: individual personal questions: focus on interactional and social language and topic based interview

Reading and Writing Part 5: open cloze: reading and identifying appropriate word, with focus on grammar

Grammar: the passive: present perfect with *just, already* and *yet*

Vocabulary: communication verbs; *-ed / -ing* adjectives

Pronunciation: sentence stress

Starting off SB page 98

1 Set a time limit of two minutes for students to discuss the questions together. Elicit ideas from different pairs. Other ways of communicating could include writing a letter, using smoke signals, etc.

Listening Part 5 SB page 98

Lead-in
Put students into small groups. Tell them to imagine they want to set up a website together. They have to decide what the website would be about and how they would design the home page. Set a time limit of two minutes and elicit ideas from different groups.

1 Students could stay in the same groups as for the lead-in or work in pairs. Each person tells their group or partner about the website they like. Ask each group to choose one website to present to the class.

2 Tell the students to discuss all five features, saying why they are or are not important, then give their opinions with reasons and try to come to an agreement. Set a time limit of two minutes and elicit students' ideas.

Listening Part 5 (matching)
Look at the information with the class. Tell the students to look at Exercise 4 for an example of this sort of matching. If students are sure of the answers while they are listening, they can cross the options in the second column out so there are fewer options to choose from. Remind them to use the second listening to check their answers.

Exam advice

3 When the students have done the matching, elicit other words or phrases which could paraphrase each adjective, e.g. *modern – new, clear – simple, funny – makes us laugh, slow – not fast, terrible – awful.*

Answers
1 c 2 d 3 a 4 e 5 b

4 Allow the students 45 seconds to look at the names and the adjectives and think of words they might hear in the recording. Don't elicit any answers yet.

Track 82
Narrator: For these questions, choose the correct answer. You will hear Billy talking to Sian about a new school website. What was each person's opinion about the website?

Sian: You went to the meeting about the new school website, didn't you?

Billy: Yes, I did.

Sian: What did people think of it? Did Rose like it?

Billy: Not really. She didn't think it was very interesting – too much like every other school website.

Sian: Oh dear, what about Jeremy?

Billy: He thought it was ok, except that it needed brighter colours. He thought there was too much black and grey.

Sian: I know what he means. Did Alex like it?

Billy: Yes, and she disagreed with Jeremy. She liked the way it looked – she said it was 'very 21st century'.

Sian: Did David have anything to say about it?

Billy: Not much, just that it was easy to understand and to find what he was looking for.

Sian: That's good. What about Sandra?

Billy: She said something quite useful. She said it took a long time for everything to download – there were too many big pictures.

Sian:	OK, we'll make them smaller. What about Ruth?
Billy:	This is strange: she said it didn't work for her at all – she couldn't get off the home page.
Sian:	That's strange.

5 Play the recording again and tell the students to try to note down the words and phrases used in the recording which helped them to do the matching. Elicit the answers and these words, (*Rose – not very interesting, Jeremy – needed brighter colours, too much black and grey, Alex – very 21st century, David – easy to understand, Sandra – took a long time for everything to download, Ruth – didn't work at all*).

> **Answers**
> **1** D **2** E **3** C **4** F **5** B

▶ **Workbook page 56**

Grammar SB page 99

The passive

> **Lead-in**
> With books closed, put students into small groups and tell them you are going to give them a quiz. Ask the students questions about the information in Exercise 1, e.g. *How many languages are there in the world? Which letter is used most often in English?* Elicit ideas then ask students to open their books and look at Exercise 1.

> **Background information**
> Mandarin Chinese has the most native speakers in the world – 1.2 billion. Taushiro, a Peruvian language, had just one fluent speaker in 2008.
>
> One new word added to English in 2018 was *hangry* meaning 'angry' because you are 'hungry'. The letter E is also used more often than any other in Czech, Spanish, French, German and other languages. There are about 1.1 billion speakers of English as a second language in the world. Esperanto has Latin, German and Slavic influences. The text message was sent from a computer to the director of Vodafone. *Emoji,* is a combination of the Japanese words for; picture – e – and character – moji.

1 Tell students to read the information and decide which is the most surprising. Give them more information from the background information box.

2 Tell students to look at the questions in pairs. Elicit the answers and tell students that the sentences in the information box are in a form called 'the passive'.

> **Answers**
> **1** no **2** no **3** no **4** yes **5** The last three facts are in the past tense, all the others are in the present tense.

3 Look at the options with the class. Elicit the answers and sentences in the language facts box which illustrate each, e.g. the first sentence is one where we don't know exactly who speaks each language. In the sixth and seventh sentences, it isn't important (in these sentences). For the third rule, elicit the forms of the verb *to be* in the 8 sentences (*are, is, is, is, is, was, was, was*).

> **Answers**
> **1** don't know **2** by **3** to be

4 Ask how the students can tell if the sentences are passive, (the verb form is verb *to be* + past participle). Look at the example sentence. Elicit the verb form *was made* and ask: *Did the phone make anything?* (no). Students look at the other sentences in pairs. Elicit the answers and, if anyone has a wrong answer, use the questions above to show them why the answer is wrong.

> **Answers**
> 1, 3, 5

5 Look at the instructions with the students and elicit that all the gaps are passive. Tell weaker classes they just have to decide if they are past or present and write the correct form of the verb *to be* and the past participle. Monitor and help where necessary.

> **Answers**
> **1** are called **2** was made **3** are shown **4** was discovered **5** are used **6** aren't understood **7** was surprised

Students could do Grammar reference: The passive Exercises 1–2 , page 130, at this point or for homework.

6 Tell the students to work alone and set a time limit of one minute for them to guess. They then compare answers in pairs. They can check their answers on page 150.

> **Answers**
> **1** 20, **2** 3,200, **3** 1971, **4** Papua New Guinea **5** because (beautiful is 2nd, tomorrow 3rd) **6** checking the time

Extension idea

Tell students to look at the question in Exercise 4, number 5 (*Who was this book written by?*). Elicit similar questions students could ask, e.g. *Who were the Harry Potter books written by?* Students could also ask questions ending in *sung by / painted by / directed by*, etc. Students work in small groups. Give them two minutes to think of questions to ask the class. Invite groups to ask their questions and see if other students can answer them.

▶ **Grammar Reference page 130: The passive**

▶ **Workbook page 57**

Vocabulary SB page 100

Communication verbs

Lead-in

Put the students into small groups. Tell them to discuss how people communicate in different situations, e.g. a parent whose child is late home, (shout); a teacher who wants to tell parents about a school trip next month, (send a letter / email).

Set a time limit of two minutes and elicit ideas from different groups.

1 Students can work in pairs or the same groups as for the lead-in. Look at the first sentence and elicit who the two people and the speaker might be, e.g. *a teenager talking to younger brother and sister.*

Fast finishers

Tell students to imagine who may be speaking to who in sentences 3, 5, 6, 7, 8. Elicit their ideas after you elicit the answers to the exercise.

Answers
1 b 2 e 3 c 4 h 5 f 6 a 7 d 8 g

2 Play the recording once for students to do the matching. After eliciting the answers, you could play it again, pausing after each section to elicit what the situation is and who is speaking, e.g. 1 It is an announcement at a railway station. The speaker works for the railway.

Answers
b persuade **c** describe **d** chat **e** explain **f** discuss **g** shout
h argue

Track 83

A

Announcer: Platform three for the 9.30 to London. Platform three for the 9.30 to London.

B

Boy: Oh, please come to my party. You'll enjoy it. Lots of your friends will be there – and I've cooked some delicious food!

C

Girl: He's really friendly. He's quite tall, with brown eyes and short blonde hair. I think he's about 14 years old.

D

Man: Hello. What a lovely day!

Woman: It is, isn't it?

Man: How are you? I haven't seen you for a long time.

Woman: I'm fine, thank you. How are you?

E

Teacher: We use the present perfect with *for* to say how long the action has been going on. And we use it with *since* to say when the action started.

F

Girl: I enjoyed the film. The acting was very good.

Boy: I agree. The acting was excellent. But I thought the film was too long.

Girl: Yes, I think you are right.

G

Boy: Hey, Dan! Over here!

H

Girl: That's not right!

Boy: Yes, it is. I know it is.

Girl: You don't know anything!

Boy: I know more than you do!

3 Allow the students to do this in pairs. Elicit the answers and elicit what the words mean using the definitions in Exercise 1, e.g. 1 *Let's talk about this book and share our ideas and opinions about it.*

Answers
2 explain 3 shouts 4 persuade 5 chat 6 repeat 7 describe
8 argued

4 Encourage students to give details in their answers, e.g. for 1 they could say what they chat about, where, when and how (face to face, texting) and give an example of a recent conversation. Set a time limit of three minutes, then invite feedback.

Extension idea
Students work in pairs and write a short dialogue similar to those in the recording to illustrate one of the verbs. Set a time limit of three minutes and then invite students to act out their dialogues in front of the class. The other students say what communication verb the dialogue showed.

▶ Workbook page 56

Reading Part 4 SB page 100

Lead-in
Before the students look at their books, put them in small groups. Ask them to think of adverts they have seen on TV or at the cinema and ask them to discuss the ones they like and dislike most, giving reasons. Set a time limit of two minutes.

Background information
An early example of skywriting happened in 1922 over Times Square in New York. A skywriter wrote a giant hotel phone number and operators at the hotel said they received more than 47,000 calls in under three hours. Skywriting is popular again thanks to social media. An interesting message is uploaded and seen all over the world. These can be adverts, messages and jokes.

1 The students can work in pairs or the same groups as for the lead-in. Ask them to describe each photo before they look at the questions. Elicit what they can see and then set a time limit of two minutes for students to answer the questions. Elicit ideas and reasons for their answers.

Reading Part 4 (multiple-choice gap fill)
Elicit that the three options will all be the same kind of word, e.g. past simple verb forms, so this is testing their understanding of meaning or words that go together. The second piece of advice is useful because, even if students aren't sure of the correct answer, there is often one option which sounds correct.

Exam advice

2 Set an overall time limit of eight minutes. Tell the students to read the text quickly to get an overall understanding of the text. Next, tell students to cover the choices and see if they can guess any of the missing words. Finally, tell them to uncover the options.

Answers
1 A 2 B 3 C 4 A 5 C 6 A

Extension idea
Put the students into small groups. Tell them to think of a book, game, film or other form of entertainment that they all like. Students discuss the best way to advertise it (e.g. social media) and how they would do it, e.g. for a game: ask a famous online gamer to play it and comment on it. Set a time limit of three minutes and invite groups to present.

▶ Workbook page 57

Grammar SB page 101

Present perfect with *just, already* and *yet*

Lead-in
With books closed, put the students into small groups. Tell them to think back about the present perfect and discuss how it is formed and what we use it for. Set a time limit of two minutes and invite groups to present one part to the class.

1 Before the students look at the questions ask them to look at the pictures and say what they show (a girl with an envelope, a stamp on an envelope, a girl walking in the street with a letter looking for a letter box). Students now discuss the question in pairs. Ask the class when the last time they wrote a letter was.

2 Look at the pictures again. Look at the first and ask when she finished the letter (probably very recently). Now ask when she bought the stamp (we don't know). Look at the third picture and ask if she is going to post the letter (yes). Students now complete the rules. Elicit these and tell the students that we usually add *already* to emphasise that something has happened, e.g. *'Are you going to buy a stamp?'* Eva would probably respond *'No, I've already bought one.'*

Answers
2 yet 3 just

14

3 Tell the students to work in pairs. Elicit the answers and why they are correct, e.g. 1 it happened a very short time ago; 2 they have seen it before; 3 she's still working; 4 the train started leaving a very short time ago; 5 The father is emphasising how quickly something happened; 6 She is asking if something has happened or not.

Students could do the Grammar reference: Present perfect with *just*, *already* and *yet* Exercises 3–4, page 131, at this point or for homework.

> **Answers**
> 1 just 2 already 3 yet 4 just 5 already 6 yet

/P/ Sentence stress

4 Play the recording for students to mark the stress. Elicit the answers and play the recording again and ask the students to repeat the three sentences.

> **Answers**
> 1 just 2 already, done 3 made

Track 84

Woman: Have you had lunch yet?
Boy: Yes, I've just finished.
Man: Do your homework!
Girl: I've already done it!
Boy: What's for dinner?
Woman: I haven't made it yet.

5 Look at the example and ask a confident pair to model it for the class. The rest of the class continue in the same way with the words in the box.

> **Extension idea**
> Write on the board: *planned my summer holidays.* Ask the class whether they think you have just done it, already done it or haven't done it yet. Elicit guesses and then tell them the correct answer. Students then do the same in pairs with different activities.

▶ **Grammar reference page 131: Present perfect with *just*, *already* and *yet***

▶ **Workbook page 58**

Vocabulary SB page 102

-ed / -ing adjectives

> **Lead-in**
> Tell students to imagine they are watching a film. Put them into two groups, A and B. Tell all the A students they are going to ask other students the question: *How do you feel?* Tell all the B students they are going to ask other students the question: *How's the film?* They should try to reply with one word. Students mingle. Set a time limit and monitor to see how students answer the questions. When the students have finished, elicit responses to both questions.

1 Look at the photos with the class and elicit what they can see and why they think the people look like this. When they have done the matching activity, ask if they ever have any of these feelings. If so, when.

> **Answers**
> A tired B surprised C worried D interested E bored
> F excited

2 Play the recording and elicit who was talking and to whom (the boy in the car to the father).

> **Answers**
> E

Track 85

Boy: Are we there yet, Dad? We're bored!
Man: Not yet. We'll be there in an hour.
Girl: This is so boring!

3 Play the recording again and elicit the answers. Ask: *Why are the children bored?* (they are on a long journey); *What can you do to make a car journey more interesting?* (listen to music, play games, read).

> **Answers**
> 1 the children 2 the car journey

4 Elicit the answers and, if you did the lead-in activity and some people used *-ed* or *-ing* adjectives, elicit whether these talked about a feeling or a thing.

> **Answers**
> 1 *-ed* 2 *-ing*

5 Before the students listen, ask them to read the sentences and guess the missing words, e.g. a long walk could be tiring or boring. Play the recording and elicit the answers.

118

Track 86

1

Nicky: I can't believe I won. I'm so surprised!

Dad: Well done, Nicky. It was a great tennis match.

2

Boy: This is such a long walk. I just want to go to bed.

Girl: Me too. We'll be home soon.

3

Mum: What's the matter, Jamie?

Jamie: I've got a maths exam tomorrow. I think I'm going to fail!

Mum: Don't worry about it.

4

Suzie: It's my birthday today! I can't wait to see what presents I've got!

Man: Happy birthday, Suzie.

5

Paula: Jack, look at this book. It's about unusual animals.

Jack: Oh, yes! Let's buy it. I'd like to read it when you've finished.

6 Before the students do the exercise, elicit some more adjectives that have -ed / -ing adjectives that they might need, e.g. *confused, amazed, frightened, pleased, shocked*. Check the meaning of each. Monitor and help where necessary. Elicit answers and ask why students would feel like this, e.g. 1 *because he might be lost or ill*.

Fast finishers
Students could look at the situations and think of alternative answers and reasons for them, e.g. *2 I'm surprised – I'm usually really slow. I'm tired – 10 km is a long way.*

Answers
2 It's exciting. I'm excited. 3 It's frightening. I'm frightened. 4 I'm surprised. It's surprising. 5 It's annoying. I'm annoyed.

Extension idea
Read out a list of -ing adjectives. Students write the adjectives and one thing that each could describe. Students then work in pairs and, without showing each other their lists, read out one noun they wrote. Their partner has to guess which adjective it matches. Read out: *interesting, surprising, exciting, boring, tiring, worrying*.

▶ **Workbook page 56**

Reading Part 5 SB page 102

Lead-in
Elicit some prepositions, e.g. *in, on*. Put the students in small groups and tell them to think of as many phrases as they can which include prepositions. This can be phrasal verbs, e.g. *wake up*, adjectives followed by prepositions, e.g. *interested in*, prepositions of time, prepositions of place. Set a time limit of one minute and elicit ideas from groups.

Reading Part 5 (open cloze)
Look at the exam advice with the students. Elicit other words which can be tested in open cloze tasks, e.g. articles, quantifiers, pronouns, auxiliary verbs. Elicit that they should always check the meaning and spelling in any type of task where they have to write a word.

Exam advice

1 Tell the students to work alone and then check in pairs. If they have different answers they should try to agree on which answer is correct.

Answers
1 by 2 at 3 to 4 in 5 at 6 on 7 for 8 of

2 Ask the first question to the class. Tell students who haven't been on a summer camp to think about other holidays. Look at the second question and the meaning of *keep in touch*. Set a time limit of one minute for students to discuss their ideas.

3 Elicit what students should do first (read the text quickly to find out what it is about). Set a time limit of five minutes for students to do the gap fill and check their answers.

Answers
1 much 2 It 3 to 4 about/of 5 Have 6 in

Extension idea
Elicit other people that we keep in touch with, e.g. people who have moved town. Students work in small groups and discuss who they keep in touch with and how, and why they like their method of keeping in touch. Set a time limit of three minutes and elicit ideas from different groups.

▶ **Workbook page 58**

Speaking Parts 1 and 2 SB page 103

Lead-in
Ask the students what they can remember about the speaking test. Can they remember what order it comes in? Elicit that it starts with a few personal questions to each student about their home country, age, etc. There are then some questions about one topic, e.g. school, home, free time. The next stage is where the students talk together about some pictures and finally there are some more questions on the topic of the pictures.

Speaking Parts 1 and 2
Elicit that this advice is important so that you don't answer the wrong question. There is nothing wrong with doing this once or twice during the test.

Exam advice

1 Allow weaker classes to work in pairs. Don't elicit the questions yet as students will listen to check in the next exercise.

2 Play the recording once for students to check their questions. Students then ask and answer in pairs. Encourage the students answering the questions to close their book and look at the questioner as if they were in an exam.

> **Answers**
> **1** What's your name? **2** How old are you?
> **3** Where are you from? **4** Where do you live?

Track 87

Examiner:	What's your name?
Examiner:	How old are you?
Examiner:	Where are you from?
Examiner:	Where do you live?

3 Monitor and help where necessary and encourage stronger classes to use a variety of tenses.

Fast finishers
Ask students to think of a third question for one or two of the topics.

4 If students wrote the questions in pairs, put them in different pairs now so that they don't know what questions they will be asked. Remind students of the exam advice for what to do if they don't understand or hear the questions at first. Monitor but don't interrupt at this stage. Make notes of errors for correction later.

5 Ask the class what the topic of the questions is (communication). Put the students in pairs to think of the question that might be asked. Elicit these before playing the recording. Elicit if anyone's question was asked. If not, elicit what the question was.

> **Answers**
> Do you like these different ways of keeping in touch?

Track 88
Examiner: Now, in this part of the test you are going to talk together. Here are some pictures that show different ways of keeping in touch. Do you like these different ways of keeping in touch? Say why or why not. I'll say that again.

6 Tell students that they have about two minutes for this part of the test. Tell them to start talking as soon as the recording finishes and stop them after two minutes. Monitor and check for errors.

7 Tell the students to read through the text first to see if they can guess the missing words but say that this is not a Reading and Writing exam-style task. In some gaps lots of different words are possible. Set a time limit of one or two minutes and then play the recording. You could warn students that one gap needs two words. Elicit the answers and ask students how many they guessed correctly.

> **Answers**
> **1** meeting **2** summer **3** swim **4** different **5** usually
> **6** grandma **7** nice **8** meeting **9** get out

Track 89

Examiner:	Martin, do you prefer meeting your friends at your home or in a café?
Martin:	I like meeting my friends at my house.
Examiner:	Why?
Martin:	Sometimes they come to my house and sometimes I go to where they live. In the summer it's good because we can swim at my friend's house.
Examiner:	Mina, is it better to write a message or talk on the phone?
Mina:	It's different. Sometimes it's better to talk on the phone. But I usually send a message on Whatsapp or text my

friends. We have a group and we can talk there. But I talk to my grandma on the phone. That's nice.

Examiner: Do you prefer meeting your friends at your home or in a café?

Mina: In a café, usually.

Examiner: Why?

Mina: Because I like to get out of the house sometimes. All my friends do, too.

Examiner: Thank you. That is the end of the test.

8 Encourage the students who are answering the questions not to look at their books while they are doing so. They should concentrate on listening to the questions and practise talking to the examiner while looking at them.

Extension idea

Divide the class into four groups of A–D. In pairs, students from group A look back through the Student's Book to find examples of the Speaking Test Part 1, Phase 1, group B Part 1, Phase 2, group C Part 2, Phase 1 and group D Part 2, phase 2. They each find questions from their section of the test and group C also find pictures to discuss.

Students now get into groups of four with one student from each group. They take turns to ask their questions to the other three students.

▶ Speaking Bank page 146: Speaking Parts 1 and 2
▶ Vocabulary and grammar review Units 13 and 14
▶ Complete Key for Schools new edition Test Generator Unit 14

Vocabulary

Communication verbs

argue
chat
describe
discuss

explain
persuade
repeat
shout

-ed / -ing adjectives

bored – boring
excited – exciting
interested – interesting

surprised – surprising
tired – tiring
worried – worrying

Vocabulary activity 1

Put the students into pairs. Tell them to choose a communication verb, e.g. *argue*. They then have three minutes to make up a short dialogue showing their form of communication. Invite students to act out their dialogues and other students to guess which verb they chose.

Vocabulary activity 2

Put students into small groups. Tell the groups to look at one unit in the book so that they are all looking at different units if possible. Tell the students to choose one or two words that they don't think other students will remember. They use a dictionary or look online to find a definition for their word and also make up a second incorrect definition. They then tell the class their word and read out their two definitions – one true and one false. The other groups have to guess which one is correct. Teams who choose the right definition win a point.

Vocabulary and grammar review Unit 13

Answers

1 **2** have lived here since **3** has known Chloe for **4** haven't seen the sea since **5** have had this laptop for **6** have been at school since **7** hasn't rained for **8** have loved this cartoon since

2 **2** might **3** might not **4** might **5** might not **6** might **7** might not **8** might not

3
```
P H O T O G R A P H E R
D O C B E N S W E T U X
G C V E T U P P C L R N
J O U R N A L I S T S U
I A E W K T E L A C E R
B C E A L E W O N M X S
C H E V N E R T I M C E
F D M E C H A N I C M K
R T O T R G U I D E G D
```
2 mechanic **3** journalist **4** nurse **5** photographer **6** vet **7** pilot

4 **2** well **3** badly **4** slowly **5** fast **6** carefully **7** easily **8** happily

Vocabulary and grammar review Unit 14

Answers

1 **1** cleaned **2** cooked **3** invited **4** built **5** given **6** hurt

2 **2** This picture was painted by my grandfather. **3** This book was written by our teacher. **4** Good pizzas are made by Italians. **5** The noise was heard by nobody / wasn't heard by anybody. **6** I was laughed at by my friends. **7** You are loved by everybody.

3 **2** just **3** already **4** just **5** already **6** just **7** yet

4 **2** C **3** A **4** B **5** C **6** B **7** A

5 **2** exciting **3** interesting **4** interested **5** tiring **6** tired **7** surprised **8** surprising

Grammar reference Answer key

Unit 1

1
2 isn't   3 I'm not   4 aren't; We're   5 She's

2
1 is/'s   2 am/'m   3 are   4 Is; isn't; is/'s   5 Are; am

3
1 plays   2 get up   3 likes   4 live   5 goes

4
1 Paul doesn't play the piano every evening.
2 I don't get up at 6 o'clock every day.
3 My brother doesn't like football.
4 My friends don't live near me.
5 Hannah doesn't go to school by bus.

5
1 My father **works** in London
2 Tom **doesn't** play the piano.
3 I **play** football every weekend.
4 Does she **start** work at 9 o'clock every morning?
5 My parents **don't** watch TV in the afternoon.

6
1 I never go to school in the evening.
2 My parents sometimes help me with my homework.
3 My brother and I walk to school every day.
4 I am sometimes late for school.
5 I always work hard at school.

7
Students' own answers.

Unit 2

1
1 are not/aren't watching; are/'re listening
2 am/'m writing
3 Are you doing?; 'm not; am/'m playing
4 is/'s running
5 isn't washing

2
1 reading   2 putting   3 cooking   4 sitting   5 dancing

3
1 hasn't   2 have   3 have   4 Have; haven't   5 have

4
1 've got   2 haven't got   3 has got   4 Have (you) got; haven't.
5 haven't got

Unit 3

1
Countable nouns: baby, box, child, knife, man, person, school, strawberry, student, teacher
Uncountable nouns: bread, coffee, juice, milk, money, rice, tea, water

2
babies, boxes, children, knives, men, people, schools, strawberries, students, teachers

3
1 an   2 any   3 Some   4 some   5 any   6 a

4
1 How much   2 How many   3 a lot of   4 a few
5 a lot of   6 no   7 a little   8 a few

Unit 4

1
1 go   2 is doing   3 love   4 is starting   5 play   6 have

2
1 we usually get (*not* ~~we are usually getting~~)
2 I'm listening or I am listening (*not* ~~Listen~~)
3 hates (*not* ~~is hating~~)
4 has (*not* ~~is having~~)
5 Jon is having (*not* ~~Jon has~~)
6 Do you understand (*not* ~~Are you understanding~~)

3
2 Tom's coat isn't big enough.
3 This exercise isn't easy enough.
4 My tea isn't hot enough.
5 I'm not old enough to drive.
6 Those jeans aren't cheap enough for me.

4
1 The sea is too cold for a swim.
2 That bag is too heavy for me.
3 Those plates are too dirty.
4 My computer is too slow.
5 I'm too short for basketball.

Unit 5

1
1 bigger   **2** more interesting   **3** heavier   **4** warmer
5 worse   **6** larger

2
1 I am the **best** footballer in my class.
2 Anna is **happier** than she was this morning.
3 I want to be **fitter**, so I do lots of exercise.
4 What is the **most** expensive thing you have?
5 Ben's apartment is **larger** than mine.
6 Tom is taller **than** his father.

3
1 on   **2** at   **3** on   **4** in   **5** in   **6** at

4
1 on Tuesday evenings
2 at the end of the year
3 in 2013
4 at breakfast time
5 in the afternoon
6 at night

Unit 6

1
1 have to help   **2** do you have to do   **3** I have to tidy
4 Does she have to tidy   **5** she does   **6** has to wash
7 don't have to do

2
1 have to   **2** don't have to   **3** don't have to   **4** have to
5 have to

3
2 She's phoning him.
3 They go to school with us.
4 I'm watching them.
5 He's reading to you.
6 I'm helping her.

4
1 them   **2** him   **3** her   **4** We; them   **5** He; it

Unit 7

1
1 were; broke; walked
2 did (you) have; ate; drank
3 did (you) get; got; gave
4 Did (you) go; did; went
5 Did (you) watch; didn't; took; was
6 came; weren't; was

2
1 left
2 won; felt
3 made
4 met; bought
5 began

3
1 Don't use
2 Don't shout; Talk
3 Don't run; Walk
4 Don't come; Use

4
2 Wash them.
3 Don't forget to buy her a present.
4 Turn it off.
5 Go to bed.

Unit 8

1
1 were having; we were listening
2 was sleeping; phoned
3 was doing
4 woke up; was raining
5 were you doing

2
2 were travelling
3 were reading
4 were listening
5 saw
6 was standing
7 was telling
8 stopped
9 was coming
10 was

3
1 can't
2 can; can
3 can't
4 couldn't; could
5 Can; can't

4
2 Could you swim when you were three?
　Yes, I could. / No, I couldn't.
3 Can you speak more than two languages?
　Yes, I can. / No, I can't.
4 Can you play basketball?
　Yes, I can. / No, I can't.
5 Can both of your parents drive?
　Yes, they can. / No, they can't.

Unit 9

1
1 to tell
2 to help
3 playing
4 watching
5 playing
6 helping

2
1 My friends and I always enjoy **meeting** in town on Saturdays.
2 I hope **to visit** Brazil one day.
3 I'm sorry **to hear** you're ill.
4 All my friends enjoy **watching** football.
5 Do you mind **waiting** a little longer?

3
1 won't have
2 will go
3 Will (you) be; won't
4 won't pass; will be
5 will meet

4
1 We'll probably go to Spain for our holiday next year.
2 I think it will be colder tomorrow.
3 Perhaps we'll have a new teacher next term.
4 Are you sure you'll be OK?
5 He probably won't come to our party.

Unit 10

1
1 It's nearly 8 o'clock. **You're going to miss** your bus.
2 Tomorrow morning, **we're going to ride** our bikes to school.
3 **I'm going to do** more exercise in future.
4 **We aren't going to need** our coats. The sun is coming out.
5 **We are going to visit** our grandparents at the weekend.

2
2 A: What are you going do this evening?
　B: I'm going to play a video game.
3 A: Is it going to rain tomorrow?
　B: No. Look at the red sky. It's going to be sunny all day.
4 A: What are you going to do when you leave school?
　B: I'm going to look for a good job.
5 A: Is your team going to win the match?
　B: No, the other team is much better. We're going to lose.

3
1 going to eat　　　**2** catching　　　**3** seeing
4 going to do; going to phone　　　**5** having

4
1 mustn't be　　　**2** must wear　　　**3** mustn't run
4 mustn't talk　　　**5** mustn't use　　　**6** must finish

5
1 **You must visit / go to** the museum. It's really interesting!
2 **You mustn't use** the taxis. They're very expensive.
　Use the metro.
3 **You must try** the pizza restaurant. They have fantastic food.
4 **You mustn't lose** your passport. Keep it somewhere safe!
5 **You must see / visit** the cathedral. It's a beautiful building

Unit 11

1
1 If I **see** my brother, **I'll tell / I will** him to text you.
2 You'll / You will hurt yourself if you **fall over** on the ice.
3 If we don't catch the 10 o'clock bus, **we'll / we will have** to wait for an hour.
4 You'll / You will be late for school if you **don't leave** soon.
5 If the music **is** loud, **it'll / it will wake** the baby.

2
1 If I get a holiday job, I'll earn money.
2 I'll buy a bike if I have enough money.
3 If I have a bike, I'll use it to go to school.
4 I'll get fit if I ride my bike to school.
5 If I don't have enough money for a bike, I'll go to school by bus.
6 I won't get fit if I go to school by bus.

3
1 Everyone in my class enjoys football.
2 There is nobody here.
3 That is someone I know.
4 There is nothing in my bag.
5 Did you phone anyone this morning?
6 Where is everybody?

4
1 Nothing **worries** me.
2 Everything in the garden **is** beautiful.
3 Nobody **came** to see us yesterday.
4 Correct
5 Everyone **loves** summer holidays.

Unit 12

1
1 has met   **2** have never been   **3** Have (you ever) travelled
4 has won   **5** has never swum

2
1 didn't see   **2** Have you ever been   **3** haven't   **4** have been
5 have been

3
You should …
go to bed early. ask parents or friends to help you.
You shouldn't …
work late the day before. spend too much time alone. worry.

4
1 should drink   **2** should wear   **3** shouldn't eat
4 shouldn't ride   **5** should get   **6** shouldn't arrive

Unit 13

1

for	*since*
24 hours	6 o'clock
400 years	last November
ten minutes	my birthday
three weeks	October 12th
12 months	the end of May
	yesterday

2
1 two weeks   **2** 14 years   **3** last weekend
4 January   **5** 23 years   **6** the age of nine
3 Tom and Julie are going. The others are not sure.
4 1 e   **2** f   **3** a   **4** b   **5** c   **6** d

Unit 14

1
1 is grown   **2** are sold   **3** are shown
4 is made   **5** is closed

2
1 was built   **2** were told   **3** was closed
4 was given   **5** were taken   **6** was sent

3
1 Have you tidied your bedroom yet?
2 They've already finished their school project.
3 I'm really hot. I've just run home from college.
4 I don't want to watch that programme. I've already seen it twice.
5 Tania doesn't want to go to bed yet. She isn't tired.

4
1 I haven't worn my new shoes yet.
2 We've just finished eating.
3 I've already texted all my friends.
4 Have you finished reading that book yet?
5 I've just phoned my older brother.

Answer key
Phrasal verbs builder

Getting about

1
get back = return
take off = leave the ground (a plane)
come round = visit someone's house
come in = enter a place
pick (someone) up = collect someone from somewhere

2
1 takes off   **2** get back   **3** picked me up
4 come in   **5** came round

In the morning

1
take something off = stop wearing
wake up = stop sleeping
get up = get out of bed
go out = leave
put something on = start wearing

2
1 wake up   **2** get up   **3** take off
4 put (my school uniform) on   **5** go out

People and communication

1
grow up = become an adult
call someone back = return a phone call
find out = get information about
look after = take care of
get on with someone = be friendly with someone

2
1 look after   **2** get on   **3** find out   **4** call (you) back
5 grew up

Other phrasal verbs

1
lie down = usually something you do before you go to sleep
turn off = stop a machine or light from working
fill in = write information on a form
give back = give something to the person who gave it to you
try on = put on clothes to see if they fit

2
1 lie down   **2** turn off   **3** try (shoes) on   **4** fill in   **5** give back

Answer key
Writing bank

How to make your writing better

1
1b There was a <u>comfortable</u> chair in the corner of the room.
2b We had lunch in a <u>small</u>, <u>friendly</u> restaurant.
3b A <u>kind</u> woman showed me the way home.
4b I knew I had made a <u>big</u> mistake.

2
1 true   **2** false   **3** true

3
1 heavy   **2** important   **3** modern/lovely   **4** lovely   **5** expensive

4
1 exciting, funny   **2** beautiful, lovely   **3** brilliant, great
4 friendly, kind   **5** sunny, pleasant   **6** great, excellent

5
1 wonderful   **2** terrible   **3** amazing
4 horrible   **5** awful   **6** fantastic

very good	very bad
wonderful	terrible
amazing	horrible
fantastic	awful

How to make your writing better: adverbs and interesting verbs

1
1b I <u>quickly</u> ran home.
2b The children were playing <u>happily</u> in the garden.
3b I read the invitation <u>carefully</u>.
4b She opened the letter <u>slowly</u>.
5b I couldn't see <u>well</u> because it was cloudy.

2
1 true   **2** true   **3** false   **4** true

3
1 loudly   **2** hungrily   **3** clearly   **4** fast
5 carefully   **6** easily   **7** well   **8** beautifully

4
1 The police officer spoke to me angrily.
2 I quickly read the letter.
3 She closed the door quietly.
4 He carefully carried the hot drinks into the sitting room.
5 We walked slowly through the park.
6 Mark didn't sleep well last night.

5
1 hurried   **2** shouting   **3** relaxing
4 jumped   **5** threw   **6** cried

6
1 ran   **2** shouted   **3** relaxed
4 jumped   **5** threw

Use verb forms correctly to talk about the past, present and future

1
Hi Jo,
I go swimming next Saturday. My cousin are here at the moment, and he love swimming. Are you want to come too? There's a swimming pool on Wood Road. We can to get the bus. I meet you at the bus stop.
Sam

2
Hi Jo,
I will go swimming next Saturday. My cousin is here at the moment, and he loves swimming. Do you want to come too? There's a swimming pool on Wood Road. We can get the bus. I will meet you at the bus stop.
Sam

3
| **1** 'm going | **2** is | **3** loves | **4** Do you want |
| **5** 've never been | **6** went | **7** get | **8** can meet |

4
1 'm going   **2** went   **3** 've never been   **4** We can get, I can meet

5
| **1** 'm going | **2** bought | **3** will start / starts |
| **4** to come | **5** have met | **6** go |

6 Possible answer
Hi Max,
I'm going to a water park next Saturday. Would you like to come? My friend Paul is coming too. He went there last month and loved it. We can get there by train. I think it will be amazing!
Stan

Use linking words and relative pronouns to make sentences longer

1
10 sentences

2
Dan woke up and got out of bed. He didn't look at his clock. He opened the fridge, but it was almost empty. He was hungry, so he decided to go out for some food. He went to a café, but it was closed because it was only 6.30 in the morning!

3
| **1** but | **2** and | **3** so | **4** because | **5** but | **6** so |

4
| **1** which | **2** who | **3** who | **4** that |

5
| **1** who | **2** which |

6
| **1** who | **2** which | **3** which | **4** who |

Writing Part 6: A short message

1
Write about three things. Write 25 words or more.

2
1 don't   **2** could   **3** Shall   **4** Let's   **5** Why

3
1 c   **2** a   **3** d   **4** e   **5** b

4
2 I'm afraid I can't come to your party.
3 I'm sorry, but I'll be a bit late.
4 Guess what! I won the competition!

5
Hi Joe,
My cousin Beth is coming to visit on Saturday, and I am (I'm) really excited. She is (She's) very good at computer games I have (I've) got a new game and we are (we're) going to play some games together. Do you want to come too? I will (I'll) call you later.
Sam

6
You should say that you can't go to the concert, give a reason why you can't go and suggest another time when you can go

8
Hi Laura,
I'm sorry, but I can't go to the concert on Saturday. I have to stay at home because my grandparents are coming to visit. Why don't we meet on Sunday and go to the cinema?
See you soon,
Ana

Writing Part 7: A story

1
35 words or more

2
| **1** was feeling | **2** was raining | **3** arrived |
| **4** was carrying | **5** ate | **6** played |

3
1 First   **2** Next   **3** Finally   **4** Suddenly   **5** Then   **6** Finally

4
1 tall   **2** empty   **3** pleased   **4** quick   **5** high   **6** ready

6
Alice wanted to watch TV, but her TV was broken. She told her mum. They looked on their computer and quickly found a big, new TV online. It wasn't expensive, so Alice's mum bought it. The next day, the new TV arrived, and Alice felt really happy.

Answer key
Speaking bank

Giving personal information

1

very good	Paul	Lucia
Age	13	14
From	Madrid	Milan

2
1 b   **2** c   **3** d   **4** a

Track 90

Paul: Hello. My name's Pablo and I'm 13 years old. I'm Spanish and I come from Madrid.

Lucia: Hi. My name's Lucia. I'm fourteen years old, and I'm Italian. I live in Milan.

Talking about habits, likes and dislikes

1
doing homework, meeting friends, playing tennis, watching TV

2
1 always get up   **2** 'm never   **3** usually do
4 often watch   **5** on Saturdays   **6** sometimes mee

Track 91

Girl: I always get up early on school days, and I'm never late for school. I usually do my homework when I get home from school. I don't often watch TV. I usually play tennis on Saturdays, and I sometimes meet my friends at the weekend too.

3
basketball

4 1 like   **2** don't   **3** listening   **4** prefer   **5** favourite

---
Track 92

Boy: I like maths and science, but I don't like art. I enjoy listening to music, but I don't like singing because I'm not a very good singer. I love sport! I like tennis, but I prefer football to tennis. Basketball is my favourite sport because it's very exciting.

Giving opinions and reasons

1
cycling

2
1 Do   **2** do   **3** about   **4** don't   **5** think
6 going   **7** What   **8** prefer   **9** fun   **10** love

---
Track 93

Girl: Do you like swimming?

Boy: Yes, I do. It's fun. What about you?

Girl: No, I don't like swimming. I think it's boring. But I love going to the cinema. It's really interesting. What do you think?

Boy: No, I think going to the cinema is expensive. I prefer to watch films at home. My favourite activity is cycling. Do you think cycling is fun?

Girl: Yes, I do. I love cycling!

3
1 b   **2** a   **3** a

Track 94

Narrator: One

Boy: I often travel to other countries with my family. I like travelling because you visit interesting places and you learn about different countries.

Narrator: Two

Girl: My brother loves skateboarding, but I don't like it because I think it's dangerous. You can fall down and hurt yourself.

Narrator: Three

Boy: [sound of gaming] This is my new computer game. I play it a lot. I'm not very good at it, but I love it because it's exciting. [sound of a player being zapped or failing] Oh, no!

4

Track 95

Narrator: One

Girl: I like reading because it's relaxing and you can learn about a lot of different things.

Narrator: Two

Boy: I love football because it's an exciting game, and you feel really good when you win.

Narrator: Three

Boy: I don't like shopping because there aren't any good shops here.

Agreeing and disagreeing

1
1

2
1 not sure about   **2** That's true   **3** agree with you   **4** Yes, but

---
Track 96

Girl: Do you play any musical instruments?

Boy: Yes, I'm learning to play the guitar. What about you?

Girl: I'm learning the piano. I think it's very difficult to learn an instrument.

Boy: I'm not sure about that. The guitar isn't very difficult, but it's important to practise every day.

Girl: That's true. I agree with you that it's important to practise so that you can get better. I think that lessons are very expensive, too.

Boy: Yes, but you can watch lessons online and teach yourself. That isn't expensive.

Dealing with problems

1
1 Could you repeat
2 Can you repeat
3 say that again

2
1 Could you repeat that <u>again</u>, please?
2 Can you repeat ~~me~~ the question, please?
3 Could you say <u>that</u> again, please?

Track 97

Narrator: One
Teacher: Don't forget the school trip tomorrow. We're meeting at 9.45.
Girl: Could you repeat that, please?
Teacher: Yes. It's 9.45 tomorrow morning.
Girl: Thank you.

Narrator: Two
Teacher: Do you think swimming in the sea is dangerous?
Boy: Can you repeat the question, please?
Teacher: Of course. Do you think swimming in the sea is dangerous?
Boy: Yes, I think that sometimes it can be dangerous, especially in bad weather.

Narrator: Three
Girl: I'm glad you can come to my party. It's at my house. I live at 29, West Street.
Boy: Could you say that again, please? I need to write it down.
Girl: Sure. It's 29 West Street. It isn't far from here.

3
1 c   2 a   3 b

4
1 not, word   2 what, called   3 know, is

Track 98

Boy: I'm not sure what the word is, but you often play this on the beach, with your friends. You have a ball, and you hit the ball with your hand.
Girl: I'm not sure what this is called, but it's something you wear around your neck in winter, when it's very cold.
Boy: I'm don't know what the word is, but it's something you eat. It's sweet, and very cold, and you often eat it in the summer.

Speaking Part 1

1
Yes, she does.

3
1 or   2 because   3 because

Track 99

Examiner: Now, let's talk about weekends. What do you do at weekends?
Ana: I often go shopping, or I sometimes go to the cinema.
Examiner: And who do you like spending your weekends with?
Ana: I like spending my weekends with friends, because we laugh and have fun together.
Examiner: Now, let's talk about shopping. Where do you like going shopping?
Ana: I like going shopping in London because there are lots of good shops.
Examiner: And what do you like buying?
Ana: I like buying clothes and shoes because I'm interested in fashion.

4
1 love   2 buy   3 bought   4 liked   5 'm going to take

Track 100

Examiner: Now, please tell me something about presents that you buy for other people.
Ana: Well, I love buying presents for people. I usually buy presents for people, when it's their birthday. For example, last month I bought a T-shirt for my brother and he really liked it. It's my friend's birthday next week, and I'm going to take her to the cinema as a present.

5
1 b   2 a   3 b   4 a   5 b   6 b

6
1 have – present   2 'm going to meet – future   3 watch - present
4 cooked – past   5 'm going to play – future   6 bought - past

7
1 c   2 d   3 e   4 b   5 a

Track 101

Examiner: Tell me something about what you like doing at home.
Ana: I like watching films, and I enjoy playing video games. I've just got a new game, so I'm quite excited about that.
Examiner: Tell me something about what you like to eat with friends.
Ana: I sometimes go to restaurants with my friends, and I prefer Italian food. We went to a pizza restaurant last weekend, and it was very nice.
Examiner: Tell me something about the clothes you like to buy.
Ana: I love buying new clothes, and my favourite thing to buy is jeans, because I like wearing them. I bought some really nice jeans last week, so I was happy.
Examiner: Tell me something about the places you like to visit.
Ana: I don't like going to big cities because there's too much traffic. I like visiting places that are near the sea. I love swimming when the weather's hot.
Examiner: Tell me something about the sports you like to do.
Ana: I like playing football. I play for a team, and we have a game every Saturday. My team doesn't often win, but it's still fun.

Speaking Part 2

1

Yes, they do

Track 102

Girl: So, do you like playing video games?

Boy: Yes, I do. I've got a lot of video games, and I often play with my friends. I think they're exciting. What do you think?

Girl: I'm not sure about that. I sometimes play video games, but I think they're a bit boring.

Boy: What about taking photos? Do you like taking photos?

Girl: I often take photos when I'm with my friends, but I don't have a camera. I take photos on my phone. What about you?

Boy: I like taking photos, too. I have got a camera, and I love taking photos of animals and the countryside.

Girl: What about cycling? I love cycling because it's fun, and it's healthy. I always go cycling at weekends. What do you think about it?

Boy: I agree with you that it's fun and it's also good exercise. What about music? Do you play any instruments?

Girl: No, I don't. But I enjoy listening to music. What about you? Do you play an instrument?

Boy: I'm learning to play the drums. I'd like to be in a band one day.

Girl: And what about reading books? Do you like reading?

Boy: Yes, I like reading books, for example adventure books. But I prefer films to books.

Girl: Yes, I agree with you. I think films are more exciting than books.

2

Yes, she does.

3

1 think   **2** sure   **3** like   **4** about   **5** do   **6** agree

Track 103

Examiner: So, which of these hobbies do you like best?

Girl: I like cycling the best because I enjoy being active and I like spending time outside, and I think that cycling keeps you fit and healthy.

4 **1** d   **2** a   **3** e   **4** b   **5** c

Track 104

Boy: I think video games are exciting. What do you think?

Girl: I'm not sure about that.

Boy: What about taking photos? Do you like taking photos?

Girl: I often take photos when I'm with my friends.

Girl: I take photos on my phone. What about you?

Boy: I like taking photos, too. I've got a camera.

Girl: I always go cycling at weekends. What do you think about it?

Boy: I agree with you that it's fun.

5

Track 105

Boy: Well, I love music festivals because I'm a music fan. I think they're great. What about you?

Girl: I agree with you. I like going to music festivals with my friends. And do you like going to the beach?

Boy: Yes, I do. I like swimming in the sea and playing football on the beach. What about you?

Girl: Yes, I agree. Going to the beach is fun, when the weather's hot. And what about walking in the mountains? I don't like that because it's really difficult. What do you think?

Boy: I'm not sure. I like it because you can see the beautiful countryside. I like camping, too because it's fun and you're outside. Do you agree?

Girl: No, I don't agree. I hate camping because I prefer to sleep in a comfortable bed! But I like picnics. I often go for picnics with my friends in the summer. Do you like picnics?

Boy: Yes, I do. When it's sunny, it's lovely to eat outside in a nice place, for example near a river.

6

Track 106

Examiner: Which of these activities do you like the best?

Student: I like going to music festivals because you can listen to some exciting bands and also spend time with your friends and have fun.

Examiner: Do you prefer to go on holiday to the beach or the countryside?

Student: I prefer to go to the beach because in the countryside it's sometimes a bit boring, because there aren't many people and there are no restaurants or cafés. At the beach there are lots of people, so it's more exciting.

Examiner: Do you prefer swimming in the sea or in a swimming pool?

Student: I prefer swimming in the sea. It's more interesting because you can see different things around you, but in the swimming pool you just have to go up and down all the time, so I think it's a bit boring.

Photocopiable audioscripts

Unit 1, Student's Book p 9, Listening Part 1, Exercises 5 and 7

Track 6

Narrator: Unit 1, Listening Part 1, Exercise 5. Choose the correct answer.

1

Narrator: Where does Thiago live?

Girl: There's a boy called Thiago in our class. He lives in our street.

Man: Really? In the blue house? Number 42?

Girl: No, Number 40. And my other friend, Stevie, lives at number 25.

Man: It's great that you have friends in the street.

Track 7

Narrator: Unit 1, Listening Part 1, Exercise 7. For these questions, choose the correct answer.

2

Narrator: Which is Lucy's family?

Man: So, can you tell me about your family, Lucy.

Girl: Yes, of course. There's me, my mum and my dad. We live in a house in a village.

Man: Have you got any brothers or sisters?

Girl: Yes, I've got one brother and one sister. There are five of us.

3

Narrator: How much is the bag?

Boy: Excuse me, how much is this bag? Is it £30?

Girl: I don't think so. Let me look. Ah, yes - today it's £13.

Boy: It's a beautiful bag. Oh, but look. It says here it's £31!

Girl: I know, but today it's on offer.

4

Narrator: Which is the girl's bus?

Girl: Are you catching the bus home?

Boy: Yes. Look, that's my bus, over there.

Girl: Is it the number 50?

Boy: No, that's not the one I need. My bus is the 55.

Girl: Oh, yes. Well, I think my bus is the 15! See you tomorrow!

5

Narrator: Which is Charlotte's favourite photo?

Boy: I like this photo. Is that your dad?

Girl: Yes, it is. But I don't like that photo at all. Look at this one. What do you think?

Boy: Hmm – I don't like it. You don't look happy. This one's nice!

Girl: Yes! That's the best one. It's me and my best friend!

Unit 2, Student's Book p 15, Listening Part 3, Exercise 3

Track 11

Narrator: Unit 2, Listening Part 3, Exercise 3. For these questions, choose the correct answer. You will hear Jarred talking to his friend.

Gemma: Hi Jarred!

Jarred: Hi Gemma.

Gemma: I'm excited about Jake's party. Are you?

Jarred: Yes. I don't usually like parties. I worry that I'm not going to know anyone there. But this is a surprise party and I think it'll be fun.

Gemma: What time does it start? Is it at 2?

Jarred: Here, look at the invitation. It's at 3 o'clock. So I'm leaving here at 2:30.

Gemma: Do you know who's going?

Jarred: It's family and friends - so Jake's brother, my cousin Martin. Oh, and Rachel, your friend from swimming. She's going too.

Gemma: Is the party at their new house - number 14 Green Street?

Jarred: I'm not sure - I thought it was 24.

Gemma: Oh, no look here. It says 40 on the invitation.

Jarred: Oh, yes! Haha! So, are you taking any food?

Gemma: No, I'm taking music.

Jarred: Oh cool, is it hip hop? Jake really likes hip hop.

Gemma: No, I haven't got any. I'm bringing mainly pop. I think that's best - I've got lots of rock, but not everyone likes that.

Jarred: That's true. You need to bring something everyone will enjoy.

Unit 3, Student's Book p 25, Listening Part 2, Exercise 3

Track 20

Narrator: Unit 3, Listening Part 2, Exercise 3. For these questions, write the correct answer in each gap. You will hear a teacher talking to her class about a cake competition.. Write one word or a number or a date or a time.

Woman: At cooking club next week, we're having a cake competition. You can make the cake at home over the weekend and bring it to school.

Here's the information. It's on Monday the third of May. School starts at 9 o'clock as usual, and all cakes need to be on their plates and ready at 9.45 – that's when the head teacher will look at them and decide which one is best.

The competition will be in the room next to the school kitchen, that's room 425. All cakes must include flour, eggs, butter and sugar. You can include other things too, like fruit or chocolate, if you want.

If you have any questions, ask Mrs. Pallister – that's P-A-double-L-I-S-T-E-R. When you arrive, she will give you a number and ask for your name. Put the number next to your cake.

Last year's prize was a scooter, but this year we're giving the winner a camera – so we're hoping for some really good cakes!

Unit 4, Student's Book p 29, Listening Part 5, Exercise 3

Track 25

Narrator: Unit 4, Listening Part 5, Exercise 3. For these questions, choose the correct answer. You will hear Pip and Sara talking. What is each person wearing?

Sara: Hi Pip - nice hat! Are you having fun?

Pip: Oh, hi Sara. Yes, I'm really enjoying this fashion show. That's a lovely dress!

Sara: Thanks. It's fun being a model.

Pip: It is, isn't it?

Sara: Have you seen Ben?

Pip: No - is he wearing a jacket with jeans?

Sara: No. He's in a really nice blue sweater.

Pip: Oh yes, I see him. Is that Amy with him, in the yellow dress?

Sara: I don't think so. Amy's wearing trousers with an interesting belt tonight.

Pip: Look! Is that George? It is! He looks great in smart trousers and a jacket doesn't he!

Sara: It's a bit different from his usual jeans and boots, isn't it!

Pip: It's a shame he hasn't got a tie.

Sara: True. Alice looks amazing, doesn't she? She looks like Taylor Swift!

Pip: Her boots are too high! I hope she doesn't fall.

Sara: She'll be fine. But look at Katy - she doesn't look comfortable. Why doesn't she take off that heavy coat?

Pip: That's not Katy. That's her sister. Katy's over there.

Sara: Oh yes, of course. She's wearing a T-shirt and jeans! And looks very comfortable!

Unit 5, Student's Book p 39, Listening Part 3, Exercises 3 and 4

Track 35

Narrator: Unit 5, Listening Part 3, Exercise 3.

1

Narrator: You will hear a girl talking to her friend about a pair of shoes. Why does she buy them?

Girl: Hey, Pedro. Look – what do you think of these shoes?

Boy: They look comfortable. But that colour is horrible.

Girl: Oh, it's not too bad. Anyway, they're for training – not for school, or going to parties.

Boy: Well, if you want them for training, they're fine. The colour isn't important.

Girl: You're right. I'm buying them!

Track 36

Narrator: Unit 5, Listening Part 3, Exercise 4. For these questions, choose the correct answer.

2

Narrator: You will hear a football manager talking to his team at half-time. What does he want them to do?

Man: OK, you are playing really well – and that's good. I just want you to think a bit more about what you're doing. It's great to see you trying to get the ball. When you get it, try to keep it for a while. Don't give it to somebody else immediately, and don't just run towards the goal. Play a slower game.

3

Narrator: You will hear a woman talking to her son. Why doesn't she want him to go out?

Woman: Are you going out on your bike now, John?

Boy: Yes – I'm training for the race on Saturday. It's not raining.

Woman: I know, but it's very early. You just had breakfast, and it's still dark!

Boy: That's OK – the roads are quiet

Woman: I don't like you going out when people can't see you properly.

Boy: I've got lights, Mum.

Woman: I don't think that's enough.

4

Narrator: You will hear a woman talking about surfing. What advice does she give to someone who wants to start the sport?

Woman: Well, the first thing I'd say is get the best board you can. The cheap ones are no good. Then be ready to make a lot of mistakes – it takes time and practice to be a good surfer. You can do it without a teacher, though – there are plenty of good lessons available on the internet.

5

Narrator: You will hear a girl talking about running.While she's training, what does she think about?

Girl: When I'm training, I feel like I'm in my own little world. I don't worry about winning the next big race, or trying to run faster than before. That's only for the competitions. I just enjoy the beautiful countryside and the clean air. I might think about what to have for dinner, or what's on TV that night – anything, really.

Unit 6, Student's Book p 43, Listening Part 3, Exercise 3

Track 38

Narrator: Unit 6, Listening Part 3, Exercise 3. For these questions, choose the correct answer. You will hear Louis and Rachel talking about their new schools.

Rachel: Hey Louis, how's your new school?

Louis: Hi, Rachel – I love it. What's your new school like?

Rachel: It's great. But I don't like the uniform!

Louis: I don't have that problem, because there isn't one! I usually go in trousers and a T-shirt. The school rules are that I can't wear jeans or trainers, that's all.

Rachel: What time does your school start?

Louis: I catch the eight-thirty bus, which gets me to school at about quarter to nine. Lessons don't start until nine o'clock, so that gives me plenty of time to talk to my friends. What are the teachers like at your school?

Rachel: Great – especially my Maths teacher. She's from the US and she uses different words for some things. But she speaks slowly. She isn't funny, but she's kind. I think the best thing about her is that she tells us how to do things really clearly, you know, so we understand!

Louis: What about English?

Rachel: It's fine. We have homework for tomorrow. We have to write about a famous person. I talked about it with my family. My dad said I should write about a famous actor, but I think I want to write about a football player. What sports do you play at school?

Louis: It's different each term. At the moment, it's basketball. Next term I think it's hockey or football. And of course, I have badminton on Fridays at my mum's club.

Unit 7, Student's Book p 53, Listening Part 4, Exercise 2

Track 46

Narrator: Unit 7, Listening Part 4, Exercise 2. For these questions, choose the correct answer.

1

Narrator: You will hear two friends talking about a place they visited. What did they think of it?

Boy: That museum trip was great, wasn't it?

Girl: Yes. It's a pity we only had a little time to spend there.

Boy: Oh, I thought two hours was enough. I'm glad mum paid for the tickets though!

Girl: Yes, twenty pounds is a lot, isn't it?

Boy: I didn't like the long train journey, though.

Girl: Me neither. That wasn't much fun.

2

Narrator: You will hear a teacher talking to her class about a trip. Where did they go?

Teacher: For your homework, I'd like you to write about today's trip. Think about the people who lived in that building, what sort of food they cooked, what they did in their spare time, and their work. We didn't have time to visit the factory nearby, but we do know what they made there. How were their lives different from ours today?

3

Narrator: You will hear two friends talking about their town. Why do they both like it?

Girl: Our town's great. Especially our museums. Lots of people come and visit them.

Boy: I guess they're interesting – but I don't go to them very often.

Girl: Nor me. I prefer going to the football.

Boy: We haven't got a great team, though. What I like is that we're so near the beach.

Girl: Yeah, it's great for surfing, isn't it?

Boy: The best!

4

Narrator: You will hear a father asking his daughter about what she did last night. What did she do?

Girl: I had a lovely time last night.

Man: You went to the cinema, didn't you?

Girl: No, I was at Olivia's house. The film was on Thursday.

Man: Oh, right.

Girl: Last night we played games on the internet. I won all of them!

Man: Well done. Did you have dinner?

Girl: Yes, Olivia's dad cooked it. He's a really good chef.

5

Narrator: You will hear a boy leaving a message for his friend. Where does he want to meet?

Dave: Hi Dan, it's Dave. The match starts at three, and I've got your ticket. We should meet either at the stadium or somewhere in town. Actually, I need to do some shopping and post a letter before the game, so let's not meet in town. I'm too busy. Meet me at the main entrance at two forty-five. Don't be late!

Unit 8, Student's Book p 57, Listening Part 5, Exercise 3

Track 49

Narrator: Unit 8, Listening Part 5, Exercise 3. For these questions, choose the correct answer. You will hear Marta talking to her dad about what she and her friends bought at the computer fair. Write two things that are mentioned for each person.

Dad: How was your trip to the computer fair, Marta? Did you get the game you wanted?

Marta: Yes, I did.

Dad: What about Ollie, did he get a new laptop?

Marta: No, he's still saving money for that. But he did buy a mouse. Everybody bought something, actually.

Dad: What did they get?

Marta: Well, Susie's parents gave her a smartphone for her birthday, and she's worried about breaking it.

Dad: She's always dropping things!

Marta: I know - so she bought a phone case for it.

Dad: Good idea! What did Anna buy?

Marta: She bought a memory card for the old camera her dad gave her.

Dad: She likes taking photos doesn't she?

Marta: Yes, she does - and you know how Pedro always copies Anna?

Dad: Did Pedro buy a memory card too?

Marta: No! He bought a camera. It was really expensive!

Dad: Miguel was looking for a present for his sister's birthday, wasn't he?

Marta: Yes, he was thinking about getting her a mouse like the one I bought, but he changed his mind. I think she'll like the nice keyboard he bought for her.

Dad: I'm sure she will.

Unit 9, Student's Book p 67, Listening Part 2, Exercise 5

Track 55

Narrator: Unit 9, Listening Part 2, Exercise 2. For these questions, write the correct answer in each gap. You will hear some information about a concert. Write one word or a number or a date or a time.

Woman: Thank you everyone. Now it's our school concert in our Arts hall at the weekend. I hope you're all practising a lot! I heard a student playing the piano on Monday and it sounded great. Anyway, our concert is on Saturday. Are you all ready?

The music is always varied and this year we have pop, rock and even some jazz – so it'll be different from last year's, which was all classical.

For those of you who are playing, you'll be here all afternoon, I know! But for your parents and friends, the doors open at six thirty and the concert itself starts at seven thirty. The seats are not numbered so please tell your parents that if they want to be near the front, they should get here by a quarter past six.

Now, as you know we're selling tickets. They are ten pounds each for adults. Students from this school are free, but students from other schools pay two pounds.

Finally, as there are always questions, please ask your parents to contact Mr Bagshaw – that's B-a-g-s-h-a-w and he will be happy to answer them.

Unit 10, Student's Book p 71, Listening Part 1, Exercise 2

Track 58

Narrator: Unit 10, Listening Part 1, Exercise 2. You will hear five short conversations. For each question, choose the correct answer.

1

Narrator: When is Holly visiting her friend in Japan?

Boy: When are you going to Japan? Is it in March?

Girl: No, I'm going after that. In August.

Boy: Oh, lovely. What clothes are you taking?

Girl: Well, it won't be cold and I'll be back before the autumn.

Boy: Summer will be lovely in Japan.

Girl: I know, I can't wait!

2

Narrator: What is Frances doing on Sunday evening?

Frances: Hello?

Dennis: Hi Frances. It's me. Would you like to come to the new dance class with me on Sunday evening?

Frances: I'd love to but I can't. We've got friends coming for dinner. Do you remember Sally?

Dennis: Yes, her parents are actors, aren't they?

Frances: That's right. Well, they're all coming over on Sunday.

Dennis: OK.

3

Narrator: What time does Lynn need to leave her class?

Lynn: What's the time, Diego?

Diego: It's half past three. Why?

Lynn: I have to leave early today. Mum and I are visiting Auntie Jane. She's in hospital.

Diego: Oh dear.

Lynn: The class finishes at 4.30, doesn't it? I have to go at 4.

Diego: OK. I'll tell you when it's time to go. You don't want to be late for visiting hours.

4

Narrator: How much is the book they buy?

Girl: These are great books for Jack.

Boy: Yes, nice. But this one is £14.30.

Girl: Yes, and the other is more expensive than that. It's £15.50.

Boy: OK. Let's get the cheaper one. Oh, I only have … [sound of coins being counted] there … £14.

Girl: It's OK, I've got the rest. Jack's going to love it!

5

Narrator: Who will meet Lee at the airport?

Girl: Will someone meet you at the airport when you get there, Lee?

Lee: Yes, of course. It's a long way home. I think Mum's working but dad can pick me up.

Girl: Oh that's alright then.

Lee: And the best thing is that we're visiting Grandad on the way home. He lives in the city. We're having dinner with him in his new flat.

Unit 11, Student's Book p 81, Listening Part 4, Exercise 2

Track 66

Narrator: Unit 11, Listening Part 4, Exercise 2. For these questions, choose the correct answer.

1

Narrator: You will hear a girl leaving a message about a football match, Why is she unhappy?

Girl: Hi Annie - you missed the game! It was two-two, so at least we didn't lose again. I think we played better last week actually, even though we lost that one. I did OK - I got both of our goals, then I had to come off because their goalkeeper kicked my leg. It's better now but I still feel terrible. We should have won!

2

Narrator: You will hear a father talking to his daughter. Where have they been?

Girl: That wasn't so bad. At least we didn't have to wait for hours.

Dad: Yes, it wasn't too busy, was it? How does your foot feel now?

Girl: It still hurts.

Dad: Well, it's good to know that it's not broken. Are you OK to walk to the bus stop?

Girl: Can we get something to eat first?

Dad: Sure, there's a cafe near here.

3

Narrator: You will hear a mother talking to her son about school. Which subject is he getting better at?

Mum: Hi Liam. How was school today?

Boy: OK. I got a good mark in history. We were learning about Spanish kings and queens from the 16th century.

Mum: So, you're improving?

Boy: Yes. Not like in natural science, where we're learning lots of things about the body – it's so difficult for me!

Mum: What about maths? Your teacher said you need to try harder, didn't she?

Boy: I am trying harder, but it isn't getting any easier.

4

Narrator: You will hear a mother talking to her son. What does the boy offer to do?

Mother: Tom, I feel sick today, and there's so much that needs doing.

Boy: I know, Mum. Don't worry. I've already washed the dishes and tidied downstairs.

Mother: That's good - but we really need to think about dinner. There's nothing in the fridge.

Boy: OK - I'll get some food from the market this afternoon.

Mother: Good. I'll cook something when you get home.

5

Narrator: You will hear a boy leaving a message. Why does he want a lift home?

Boy: Hi Dad, it's Fred. Can you come and get me from school? In the car? We've just had a games lesson where we ran about 5 kilometres. It was so hot - Steven had to stop because he had a headache. Not me - I just kept running! But I really don't think I could walk home now. I can't move my legs any more!

Unit 12, Student's Book p 87, Listening Part 2, Exercise 4

Track 72

Narrator: Unit 12, Listening Part 2, Exercise 4. For each question, write the correct answer in the gap. You will hear a teacher talking to her class about a countryside run they are doing. Write one word or a number or a date or a time.

Woman: OK, listen everyone. I've got some information for those of you who are coming on the countryside run on Saturday. Now, I know some of you came to the last one, two weeks ago - that was 5 kilometers, but we're going a bit further this time. It'll be 10 kilometers long, so you need to be quite fit. I know it's raining now, but don't worry I've heard it's going to be dry all weekend. Wear trainers, shorts and a T-shirt as usual and you should be fine. You won't need a sweater. The run starts at 9 o'clock but you should get there early - about half past eight. And make sure you have breakfast at least an hour before that. We're meeting by the lake at Staunton Park. That's S-T-A-U-N-T-O-N Park. I'm sure you know where it is. Tell your parents they'll have to wait about an hour for you to complete the run. You're all pretty fast!

Unit 13, Student's Book p 87, Listening Part 3, Exercise 4

Track 78

Narrator: Unit 13, Listening Part 3, Exercise 4. For each question, choose the correct answer. You will hear Rich talking to his friend Jess about horse riding.

Girl: Hi Rich, I hear you're having horse-riding lessons.

Boy: Yes. We'll be able to go riding together!

Girl: Great! When did you start?

Boy: I saw an advert about a month ago. So Mum phoned the place and we visited last week. But I only had my first lesson this morning.

Girl: How was it?

Boy: All we did was brush the horses. It wasn't difficult but I wanted to ride. I hope the next lesson will be more interesting.

Girl: I remember my first lesson. I got a riding-hat as a birthday present, plus boots and trousers, then my friend's mum had to lend me her jacket because it was so cold that day!

Boy: What was your teacher like?

Girl: She won a lot of prizes for horse-riding, but I don't think she really knew how to teach us, and she wasn't always fun. But I kept going, and now I love riding!

Boy: That's my plan. My friend wants me to start tennis lessons, but I like this better and I want to ride with you one day, so...

Unit 14, Student's Book p 99, Listening Part 5, Exercise 4

Track 82

Narrator: Unit 14, Listening Part 5, Exercise 4. For these questions, choose the correct answer. You will hear Billy talking to Sian about a new school website. What was each person's opinion about the website?

Girl: You went to the meeting about the new school website, didn't you?

Boy: Yes, I did

Girl: What did people think of it? Did Rose like it?

Boy: Not really. She didn't think it was very interesting - too much like every other school website.

Girl: Oh dear, what about Jeremy?

Boy: He thought it was ok, except that it needed brighter colours. He thought there was too much black and grey.

Girl: I know what he means. Did Alex like it?

Boy: Yes - and she disagreed with Jeremy. She liked the way it looked - she said it was 'very 21st century'.

Girl: Did David have anything to say about it?

Boy: Not much - just that it was easy to understand and to find what he was looking for.

Girl: That's good. What about Sandra?

Boy: She said something quite useful. She said it took a long time for everything to download - there were too many big pictures.

Girl: OK, we'll make them smaller. What about Ruth?

Boy: This is strange: She said it didn't work for her at all – she couldn't get off the home page.

Girl: That's strange.

Workbook answer key and audioscripts

Unit 1
Listening Part 1

1
1 B   2 C   3 A   4 C   5 A

1
Boy:	Where's your brother today, Sarah? I usually see him in the school library at around this time.
Sarah:	Yeah, that's right, but he's got a doctor's appointment today, at two o'clock.
Boy:	Oh really? But it's only twelve thirty.
Sarah:	Is it? Oh, I remember now … he went home to get something to eat first.

2
Girl:	Great baseball boots, Jon!
Jon:	Thanks! Grandma gave me thirty-five pounds for my birthday, so Dad and I went into town to spend it.
Girl:	So did you buy your boots at the new sports shop?
Jon:	No, they were too expensive – forty-two pounds. We found these in another shop, for twenty-nine pounds. That was a great price!
Girl:	You're lucky!

3
Boy:	Is this a photo of your brother and sister, Marta?
Marta:	Yes, that's right. My little sister and I still live at home with mum and dad.
Boy:	And is that your brother?
Marta:	Yes, that's Jerry. He's older than me. He's twenty and he lives in Paris. But he's coming to visit us soon.
Boy:	That's cool!

4
Boy:	What do you do on Saturdays, Holly?
Holly:	Well, I always spend the day with my friends. We don't often have enough money to go shopping, so we just have to go to someone's house and watch films instead.
Boy:	Well, that's cheaper than going to a café or somewhere and spending money, isn't it?
Holly:	It certainly is!

5
Sam:	Do you want to go out on Friday, Kasia?
Kasia:	I can't, Sam. My family's having a big party because my baby brother will be two that day!
Sam:	Cool!
Kasia:	Yes, we're going to have a great time. Even my grandfather is coming. My dad's going to collect him from the airport.
Sam:	Well, I hope you have a lovely day!

Grammar

Present simple

1
2 do   3 don't   4 does   5 doesn't   6 do   7 don't   8 does

2
2 get up	3 am	4 don't live	5 is
6 teaches	7 have	8 has	9 doesn't teach
10 finish	11 drives	12 watches	13 play 14 isn't

3
3 Are, I'm not   4 Does, she doesn't   5 Is, it isn't.   6 Do, I do

Adverbs of frequency

4
2 always	3 often	4 always
5 sometimes	6 never	

5
2 watch often → often watch
3 always can buy → can always buy
4 stay often → often stay
5 has sometimes → sometimes has
6 go usually → usually go

Vocabulary

Family members

1
2 husband	3 uncle	4 cousin	5 grandma
6 daughter	7 brother	8 auntie	

Reading Part 2

1
1 C   2 A   3 B   4 A   5 C   6 B   7 C

Writing Part 6

1
What time shall we go? How shall we get there? What do you want to do in town?

2
1 Hi Jade; See you on Saturday! Zoe   2 Yes she does. Yes, it is.

3 *Sample answer:*
Dear Alex,
Come to my house at 2 pm. I live at 28 Green Street, near the park.
We can go and play football and then watch some films at home.
See you soon!
Best wishes,

Vocabulary Extra

Daily life
1a
a Henry   **b** Agnes   **c** Richard   **d** Stella   **e** Michael
f Connie   **g** Dan   **h** Maria   **i** Ben

1b
2 husband   **3** uncle   **4** wife   **5** son   **6** sister
7 daughter   **8** cousin

2
2 e   **3** a   **4** j   **5** g   **6** b   **7** c   **8** h   **9** i   **10** f

3
Across: 3 three   **4** eleven   **6** fourteen   **7** forty
Down: 2 twelve   **5** ninety

Unit 2
Listening Part 3

1
1 C   **2** A   **3** B   **4** B   **5** A

Ava:	So Jake, what do you think of the new house Mum and Dad have decided to buy?
Jake:	I like it, Ava! The kitchen isn't as large as in our old one, but I'm happy the living room isn't cold and it's much more comfortable! But we need to tidy the garden.
Ava:	I know. Anyway, the house is in a good place! I probably won't use the library near us to do my schoolwork, but my room's got great views of the park. I'm just sorry we're so far from the river.
Jake:	Me too. But at least the house is easy to find – it's so unusual! I know it's not the only one in the street painted white…
Ava:	… and they're all made of wood.
Jake:	But they haven't got red roofs!
Ava:	True!
Jake:	So, will Mum buy you anything for your room? She's getting me a new bookshelf.
Ava:	Well, she's already got me a nice armchair. But I need an alarm clock for the mornings …
Jake:	Right! Well, about getting to school every day – Mum's offered to drive us, but I think we should cycle.
Ava:	Hmm. The bus stop is quite far from here, so … OK!

Grammar

Present continuous
1
2 's/is sleeping   **3** isn't/is not raining   **4** 're/are washing
5 isn't/is not riding   **6** 'm/am writing

2
2 comming → coming   **3** goeing → going   **4** listenning → listening
5 swiming → swimming   **6** enjoing → enjoying

have got
3
2 has got   **3** has got   **4** hasn't got   **5** have got
6 haven't got   **7** Have, got

4
2 Have you <u>got</u> a special dress to wear for the party?
3 We haven't <u>got</u> a pet in our family.
4 I've <u>got</u> some friends who play in a rock band.
5 Olivia has <u>got</u> a lot of presents for her birthday.
6 Have you <u>got</u> any money in your bag?

Reading Part 1

1
1 C   **2** C   **3** A   **4** B   **5** B   **6** A

Vocabulary

Rooms
1
2 garage   **3** stairs   **4** kitchen   **5** window   **6** floor
7 bedroom   **8** garden   **9** lift   **10** swimming pool

Furniture
2
2 b   **3** a   **4** c   **5** e   **6** d

Writing Part 7

2 *Sample answer:*
Ben and his parents are driving a lorry. They stop outside their new house. They carry their furniture inside. The dog plays on the grass. Later, they sit on the sofa and have pizza. They're happy! They can open the boxes tomorrow!

Vocabulary Extra

At home
1a
2 watching, living room   **3** listening, bedroom   **4** repairing, garage
5 brushing, bathroom   **6** riding, garden   **7** talking, hall

1b
cooker **14**   cupboard **11**   curtains **4**   flowers **16**   fridge **12**
garage **1**   gate **15**   lamp **2**   plate **13**   pillow **3**
roof **5**   shelf **6**   shower **7**   stairs **10**   toilet **8**
TV **9**

2
2 carpet (not in the garden)   **3** furniture (not a room)
4 chair (not electrical)   **5** cooker (not in a bedroom)
6 bookshelf (can only be inside)   **7** garage (you can't live in it)

Unit 3
Reading Part 3

1
1 B   **2** A   **3** C   **4** A   **5** B

Vocabulary

Food phrases
1
2 g   **3** a   **4** f   **5** e   **6** c   **7** d   **8** b

2
2 box   **3** can   **4** glass   **5** bottle   **6** piece   **7** cup

School lunches
3
2 cheese sandwiches   **3** fish and chips   **4** chicken salad
5 apples   **6** bananas   **7** ice cream
8 orange juice   **9** lemonade

Listing Part 2

1
1 17 July / 17th of July   **2** Summer
3 half past two / 2.30 (pm)   **4** 150   **5** pasta

Speaker:	Now, news of a big event coming to the city soon! It's called the International Festival – and it's about food from all over the world! So, put the date in your diaries – the school year ends on the sixteenth of July, and this'll be on the day after, the seventeenth.
	You might remember last year there was an event like this in King's Park. Well, this year it's going to be bigger, so it'll be in Summer Park – that's opposite the shopping centre.
	They're expecting lots of people to go and it'll be open from half past two till seven pm. So, get there early if you want to try different things to eat from all over the world – there will be at least 75 different countries selling things! And you'll get a free gift if you're one of the first hundred and fifty visitors!
	There will be a cook at the festival making pasta – and you can make some, too! You can also buy some delicious cakes to take home. So, see you there!

Grammar

Countable and uncountable nouns
1
2 isn't any   **3** aren't any   **4** are some   **5** is an
6 isn't any   **7** is some   **8** is a

How much / many; a few, a little, a lot of
2
2 How many, Only a few.
3 How much, Just a little,
4 How much, A lot,
5 How much, Only a little.
6 How many, None.

3
2 a lot of   **3** a few   **4** How much   **5** any   **6** some

Writing Part 5

1
1 the   **2** for   **3** Would   **4** me   **5** your   **6** if

Vocabulary Extra

Food
1
2 orange juice   **3** apples   **4** biscuits   **5** cake
6 pizza   **7** chicken   **8** sandwiches

2
FRUIT: bananas, grapes, lemons
VEGETABLES: carrots, onions, potatoes
MEAT: chicken, burgers, steak
DRINKS: coffee, milk, tea

3
2 box   **3** piece   **4** slice   **5** bowl

4
2 knives   **3** plates   **4** bowls   **5** lunch   **6** sandwiches
7 fork   **8** cake   **9** boxes   **10** tomatoes

Unit 4
Listening Part 5

1
1 E   **2** F   **3** B   **4** D   **5** A

Girl:	Did you go to that new department store with your family, Tom?
Tom:	Yes, I finally got the jeans I wanted!
Girl:	Cool! What about your sister? She loves buying bags, doesn't she?
Tom:	Mm – but she saw some great shoes, and got those instead. They look good with her favourite party dress.
Girl:	How about your dad?
Tom:	Oh, he looked for some T-shirts for our beach holiday, but the store didn't have any nice ones. But at least he got a suit for work.
Girl:	And your mum?
Tom:	We're going to a family wedding soon, so she needed something special to wear. She got a great dress, but she didn't find any shoes she liked.
Girl:	That's a shame. And did your brother buy anything?
Tom:	He wanted a new watch, but he didn't like any of the ones we saw! Anyway, he also needed a new shirt, so he got a nice blue one.
Girl:	And what about your grandma?
Tom:	She bought a cool bag for when she's swimming at the beach – she can put her clothes and her watch in it, to keep them dry!
Girl:	Great!

Grammar

Present continuous and present simple
1
2 are you doing   **3** have   **4** is watching   **5** want
6 is waiting   **7** doesn't understand   **8** Do you know

2
2 are playing   **3** are/'re having   **4** play   **5** come
6 is/'s cooking   **7** doesn't cook   **8** gets   **9** is/'s travelling

3
2 am wanting → want
3 not needing → don't need
4 'm having → have
5 'm loving → love
6 isn't liking → doesn't like
7 Are you knowing → Do you know

too* and *enough
4
2 too young, old enough
3 too heavy, strong enough
4 too small, big enough

Reading Part 4

1
1 B   **2** A   **3** C   **4** B   **5** A   **6** C

Vocabulary

Shops

1

2 supermarket   **3** department store   **4** bookshop   **5** chemist

Adjectives

2

1 clean   **2** expensive, cheap   **3** long, short

4 small, large   **5** new, old   **6** light, dark

Writing Part 7

1

Tom goes into a clothes shop because he wants to buy a new jumper. **H**e finds a nice one that he likes. **H**e tries on the jumper, but it's too small. **H**e's very unhappy.

2 *Sample answer:*

Tessa goes into a clothes shop because she wants to buy a dress. She finds a beautiful dress and she looks at the price. It's only £**10**! It's very cheap, so she's happy. She takes the dress to the desk and she pays for it.

Vocabulary Extra

Clothes and adjectives

1

2 jeans   **3** boots   **4** hat   **5** sunglasses   **6** dress

7 belt   **8** jacket   **9** trainers **10** bag   **11** suit

12 shirt   **13** tie   **14** watch   **15** umbrella

2

2 c   **3** d   **4** b   **5** c   **6** a   **7** b   **8** e

3

2 change out of, change into   **3** take off   **4** put on

4

2 crowded   **3** dark   **4** low   **5** dirty   **6** high

Unit 5

Reading Part 3

1

1 A   **2** B   **3** A   **4** B   **5** C

Grammar

Comparatives and superlatives

1a

2 heavier, the heaviest

3 harder, the hardest

4 more exciting, the most exciting

5 cheaper, the cheapest

6 more expensive, the most expensive

7 better, the best

8 worse, the worst

1b

2 the most expensive   **3** better   **4** harder

5 the cheapest   **6** more exciting

Prepositions of time *at, in, on*

2

3 in   **4** at   **5** at   **6** in   **7** –   **8** on   **9** at   **10** –

3

2 in Monday → on Monday

3 6.30 pm → at 6.30 pm

4 in 5 o'clock → at 5 o'clock

5 in my birthday → on my birthday

6 At the first day → On the first day

Listening Part 4

1

1 C   **2** A   **3** B   **4** A   **5** C

1

Girl: What happened on sports day?

Boy: Well, I was in the running race. I wasn't expecting to come first or anything, but then I injured my knee, so I couldn't finish. It meant I missed doing the cycling race too, which I like the best, so I was upset.

Girl: How annoying! At least your mum got you the new sports shirt you wanted.

Boy: True!

2

Boy: Great tennis racket! It looks like it cost a lot.

Girl: Well, I saw the perfect racket in a shop, but I couldn't afford that one. But my sister had this one that she never uses, so she offered it to me. I paid her, but not much. It's a bit heavy, really, but I've needed one for ages.

Boy: Lucky you!

Girl: I know.

3

Girl: So, how was your holiday?

Boy: Great! I did some snowboarding and skiing. Mum and Dad also took us walking in the mountains, although that wasn't very interesting, really.

Girl: So, did you spend most of your time skiing?

Boy: Actually, I got quite good at snowboarding and preferred that to skiing.

4

Girl: Hi Mum! I'm just calling to say I'll be late home. I'm meeting Tina for a walk soon, but I had some free time, so I came to do an exercise class here before I go. I've had a shower, so I'm just drying my hair, then I'll set off. It'll take a while to get to the park, so I'd better hurry! Hope you enjoyed your swim. See you soon!

5

Boy: Hi Jason! Just calling about tomorrow's match. I think we could easily beat the other team! I know they won last time we played them, but we've really improved since then, because of all the time we've spent with our coach. OK, some members of their team are fantastic, but I've got a good feeling about this match!

Vocabulary

do, play and go with sports

1

2 go climbing　**3** play hockey　**4** do judo　**5** play football
6 do gymnastics　**7** play badminton

2

2 does　**3** play　**4** 'm going　**5** goes　**6** do

Nationalities

3

2 Portuguese　**3** Indian　**4** Swedish　**5** Japanese
6 Greek　**7** Australian　**8** American

Writing Part 6

1

1 on　**2** Would　**3** to　**4** at　**5** afternoon　**6** Let　**7** See

2 *Sample answer:*

Hi Olivia,
Would you like to come with me to the new sports centre in town?
We can go there on Saturday afternoon. We can play tennis there,
and go swimming, too. It'll be fun!
Let me know!
See you soon!

Vocabulary Extra

Sport

1a

climbing **2**　cricket **6**　running **3**　tennis **4**
sailing **5**　skateboarding **1**

1b

b skateboarding　**c** climbing　**d** sailing　**e** running
f cricket

2

S	T	A	D	I	U	M	M
K	E	R	U	G	B	Y	A
A	N	A	G	O	L	F	T
T	N	C	B	A	T	M	C
I	I	E	G	L	B	N	H
N	S	K	I	I	N	G	P
G	R	A	C	K	E	T	O
S	U	R	F	I	N	G	M

3

1 89p　**2** £300　**3** £45.50　**4** £15.97

Unit 6
Listening Part 3

1

1 C　**2** A　**3** C　**4** B　**5** A

Jamie:	Hi Amelia! How was your day?
Amelia:	Hi Jamie. It was fine, thanks, although my school bus was late. It usually leaves at seven forty-five but today it came at eight.
Jamie:	So what time did you get to school?
Amelia:	Half past – but my classes started at eight fifteen.
Jamie:	That's not good!
Amelia:	I know! And my timetable's changed. Last year, my first class was maths, but this morning it was physics, followed by biology. That'll be every week now.
Jamie:	Sounds interesting. Mine's quite simple, so at least I won't forget it. Not like last year! And we get free time for study now, so that'll make things easier than last year.
Amelia:	True …
Jamie:	Anyway, it was a good day. I liked seeing my friends again.
Amelia:	Yeah. And I chatted to new students I didn't know – that was really cool! But I miss my old classroom.
Jamie:	Me too.
Amelia:	Your football boots were in the kitchen this morning. Did you forget them?
Jamie:	I didn't need them. But I left my lunch in the fridge. I forgot to put it in my school bag, so I went to the café instead.
Amelia:	Oh no!

Vocabulary

Classroom objects

1

2 ruler　**3** notebook　**4** dictionary　**5** pencil
6 timetable　**7** library　**8** uniform

Education verbs

2

2 take　**3** learn　**4** passes　**5** study　**6** fail

Reading Part 2

1

1 A　**2** C　**3** B　**4** A　**5** C　**6** B　**7** C

Grammar

have to

1

2 don't have to　**3** have to　**4** doesn't have to
5 has to　**6** doesn't have to　**7** has to

2

2 Do, have to, d
3 Do, have to, f
4 Do, have to, b
5 Does, have to, c
6 Do, have to, e

Object pronouns

3

2 us　**3** him　**4** We　**5** it　**6** They
7 us　**8** They　**9** I　**10** them　**11** It

Writing Part 5

1
2 than   **3** They   **4** with   **5** It   **6** a   **7** to

Vocabulary Extra

School and education
1
2 biology, g   **3** physics, h   **4** geography, e
5 chemistry, c   **6** history, a   **7** languages, f
8 mathematics, i   **9** sport, d

2
2 leave   **3** fail   **4** study   **5** teaches   **6** collects   **7** writes

3
Across: 5 dictionary   **6** lunch   **8** break   **9** test
Down:1 timetable   **2** diploma   **3** university   **4** late   **7** course

Unit 7
Reading Part 1

1
1 B   **2** C   **3** C   **4** A   **5** A   **6** B

Vocabulary

Buildings
1
2 train station   **3** factory   **4** hospital   **5** stadium
6 church   **7** cinema   **8** mosque

Directions
2
2 straight   **3** turning   **4** bridge   **5** roundabout
6 traffic   **7** crossing   **8** square

Listening Part 4

1
1 A   **2** C   **3** B   **4** A   **5** C

1
Girl: How was the film?
Boy: Well, I've read the book, so I was really interested to see how they told the story. But it wasn't what I expected. They played rock music all the way through it, and that was what I liked most.
Girl: How about the actors in it?
Boy: I didn't recognise any of them and they weren't that great, really.

2
Girl: Grandma, thanks for my birthday present! I thought you'd sent me one of your lovely scarves, so I was really surprised when I opened it. We had them after dinner last night – delicious! I love anything with chocolate in it! I hope you enjoyed the story Markus sent you as well – he wants to be a famous writer one day. Thanks again!

3
Girl: So, how was the gallery?
Boy: Well, we saw some of the paintings our teacher showed us in class. Some weren't as good as I'd remembered, but I really liked one of them, so I did a drawing of it in my notebook. That was fun!
Girl: And how was your picture?
Boy: Not very good! Maybe I need to join a class and learn how to do it properly!

4
Boy: How was your journey, Naomi?
Naomi: Not easy! I didn't have a big bag, and someone put it on to the train for me. The train was full, but I got a seat.
Boy: It was raining when you left, though.
Naomi: Yes. Dad gave me a lift to the station but I still got really wet – horrible. But luckily Auntie Jane met me when I arrived!

5
Boy: I love our garden. It's not like our neighbour's – that's full of flowers and has got more colour than ours. And he has a cat, too, so he doesn't get as many birds as we do, especially ones from the forest nearby. We love hearing them sing, so we put out lots of food, and they come flying down to eat. They're beautiful!

Grammar

Past simple
1
2 threw, caught   **3** slept, left   **4** drove, give   **5** heard, saw

2
2 enjoied → enjoyed   **3** choosed → chose   **4** gived → gave
5 buied → bought   **6** drinked → drank

3
2 didn't go   **3** didn't buy   **4** didn't keep
5 didn't drive   **6** wasn't

4
2 were you, e
3 did you go, f
4 did you get, a
5 Were you, b
6 Did you have, d

Imperatives
5
2 Don't get   **3** Don't eat   **4** Buy
5 Don't forget   **6** Don't travel

Writing Part 6

1
How are you? ✓
Best wishes,
Dear Harry, ✓
See you soon.
Thanks for your email. ✓
It was nice to hear from you. ✓
Bye for now.
Yours,

Vocabulary Extra

Town and city
1a

garage **2**	library **5**	post office **8**	police station **7**
restaurant **4**	supermarket **3**	theatre **1**	

1b

b theatre	**C** post office	**d** supermarket	**e** police station
f castle	**g** restaurant	**h** garage	

2

2 from	**3** straight	**4** turn	**5** over
6 is	**7** turning	**8** across	**9** opposite
10 Where	**11** past	**12** next	

Unit 8
Vocabulary

Technology verbs
1
2 check your social media
3 email a friend
4 send a message

2 *Sample answers:*
2 I often check my social media when I wake up.
3 I never email my friends.
4 I take selfies with my friends every day and then we upload them.
5 I sometimes download music from the internet but I never download films.

Music
3a

2 opera	**3** pop	**4** electronic	**5** classical	**6** rock	**7** R&B

3b

2 jazz	**3** rock	**4** classical	**5** pop	**6** R&B	**7** opera

Listening Part 5

1
1 F   **2** H   **3** E   **4** A   **5** B

Girl: Hi, Max! What did you do on Saturday?
Max: I stayed at home because I wasn't feeling well. At least I finished that book for school.
Girl: Oh no, really? So you didn't go with Josh to the football match?
Max: No, he went without me, but he was happy because his team won.
Girl: That's great! I didn't see Matt on Saturday. Did you?
Max: No, he was busy playing tennis and he won! He's such a good player!
Girl: Cool! Oh, and guess what? I saw Elise on Saturday on her way to the cinema with her sister.
Max: Oh really? But I thought it was her cousin's party on Saturday.
Girl: No, that was Sunday. And didn't Susie have a party at her house?

Max: Well, it was her birthday but they went out. They went to eat some delicious Italian food at a new place that's supposed to be amazing!
Girl: What about Nick?
Max: He's mad about video games and couldn't wait to try his new one.

Grammar

Past continuous
1

2 was watching	**3** were playing	**4** was raining	**5** was
your brother doing	**6** was uploading		

2

2 started	**3** decided	**4** was downloading
5 called	**6** wanted	**7** was waiting
8 was listening	**9** saw	**10** took

3
2 Lily was wearing her new dress when I met her.
3 We were watching a scary film when we heard a strange noise.
4 When you called me I was having dinner.
5 When my dad got home my sister was listening to music.

can / can't, could / couldn't
4
2 can listening → can listen
3 could met → could meet
4 could to go → could go
5 can going → can go

5
2 can't download   **3** can't play   **4** couldn't ride   **5** can speak

Reading Part 2

1
1 A   **2** C   **3** A   **4** A   **5** B   **6** C   **7** B

Writing Part 5

1

1 were	**2** for	**3** the	**4** than	**5** lot	**6** Did

Vocabulary Extra

Technology and music
1a
2 h   **3** g   **4** e   **5** a   **6** b   **7** f   **8** d

1b
One word: website, laptop, keyboard
Two words: mobile phone, computer game, digital camera

2

2 check	**3** send	**4** download	**5** email	**6** go

Sample answers:
2 I always check my phone for messages before I do my homework.
3 I usually send messages to my friends five times a day.
4 I sometimes download music from the internet.
5 When I'm on holiday I don't email my friends but I sometimes message them.
6 I go online at least four times a day.

3

2 left	**3** go	**4** spent	**5** hear	**6** bought

4a

2 D	**3** B	**4** F	**5** A	**6** E

4b

b 5	**c** 6	**d** 4	**e** 1	**f** 2

Unit 9
Reading Part 4

1

1 B	**2** B	**3** C	**4** C	**5** B	**6** A

Vocabulary

Suggesting, accepting and refusing

1

2 R	**3** S	**4** A	**5** S	**6** A

2

2 How about	**3** OK	**4** Would you like to	**5** thanks	**6** Shall

Adjectives

3

2 amazing	**3** boring	**4** horrible	**5** interesting
6 awesome			

Listening Part 2

1

1 month	**2** (£)5.75	**3** exhibitions	**4** laptop	**5** haylee / Haylee

Speaker: Before tonight's show, listen carefully for some interesting news about our new magazine for young people. It's called *What's On?* and it will be available for you to buy once a month. This magazine has got a very special price of five pounds seventy-five. That's less than an eight-pound cinema ticket.

And now for the exciting part. We're looking for young people like you to write articles about the things that you're interested in. We don't need any articles about films, music or computer games, but we do want to hear about exhibtions you have seen recently.

There are some amazing prizes for every article we include, for example cinema or concert tickets, but the writer of the best article will win a laptop. If you would like to write for us then send an email to haylee@whatson.co.uk, that's H-A-Y-L-double E. We hope to hear from you soon!

Grammar

Verbs with *-ing* and *to* infinitive

1

2 to be	**3** going	**4** to work	**5** playing
6 to buy	**7** downloading	**8** to dance	**9** singing

2

2 to get	**3** to see	**4** to be	**5** singing (or dancing)
6 dancing (or singing)	**7** going	**8** to hear	

3 *Sample answers:*
2 to tidy my bedroom
3 riding his bike
4 doing my homework
5 to work in an office
6 to speak English

The future with the present simple, present continuous and *will*

4

2 'll call	**3** leaves	**4** 's coming	**5** 'll have	**6** ends

5 *Sample answers:*
2 I'm going shopping with my mum.
3 No, I think it'll be boring.
4 It finishes at half past three.
5 I'll have pizza, please.
6 School finishes on 4 April.

Writing Part 7

1 *Suggested answers:*
Picture 1: nothing to do; rain a lot
Picture 2: make a poster; write invitations, have a good idea
Picture 3: sing together, play the piano, have fun

2 *Sample answer:*
It was raining a lot and three friends were feeling bored because they had nothing to do. Then Jake had a good idea. Let's have a concert! They made a poster and wrote invitations. Jake played the piano and they sang together. Everybody had a good time.

Vocabulary Extra

Entertainment and media

1

actor **4**	cinema **7**	concert **1**	photographer **2**
picture **8**	programme **9**	screen **6**	stage **5**
theatre **3**	ticket **10**		

2

2 dancer	**3** group	**4** play	**5** disco
6 exhibition	**7** instrument	**8** musician	

3

2 G	**3** B	**4** G	**5** G	**6** G

Unit 10
Listening Part 1

1

1 B	**2** A	**3** A	**4** C	**5** B

1

Mum: Sophie, where are you? Are you on your phone again?

Sophie: No, Mum! I've just done my homework. Maths was quite easy.

Mum: Well done! If you're not studying, can you help me with the dinner?

Sophie: OK. I'll finish downloading this film and then I'll come and help.

2

Boy: Are you doing anything tomorrow? Would you like to go to the History Museum?

Girl: If it's sunny like today, why don't we go to the beach? Mum could give us a lift.

Boy: But it says on my mobile that it's going to rain.

Girl: Are you sure?

Boy: Yes! Look at my phone screen and at all those grey clouds outside!

3

Boy: Lucy! Where are you?

Lucy: Here! What time is it?

Boy: It's five o'clock. We're late and you're playing on the computer.

Lucy: But Harriet's party starts at six o'clock, doesn't it?

Boy: No! It starts now. Let's take the bus! We'll be there by half past five.

4

Matt: I'm so sorry I can't come to your party tonight. I'm playing in a concert with my band.

Girl: Really? Is it still the three of you in your group?

Matt: Well, it was me and my two brothers until last week but Gemma's just joined the band so there are four of us now. She's got a wonderful voice. You'll have to come and watch us!

Girl: I'd love to!

5

Girl: It's Owen's birthday on Saturday. Shall we get him a football scarf?

Boy: I'm not sure. He had one on yesterday.

Girl: Really? Where did you see him? Was he wearing that baseball cap again?

Boy: No, he wasn't. He was indoors at the shopping centre with his mum. He wanted to buy some new football boots but they didn't have his size.

Vocabulary

What's the weather like?
1
2 windy   **3** snowing   **4** foggy   **5** cold   **6** raining

Places
2
2 forest   **3** mountain   **4** island   **5** beach   **6** desert

Reading Part 2

1
1 C   **2** B   **3** A   **4** B   **5** C   **6** B   **7** A

Grammar

going to
1
2 I'm not going to have a good time.
3 I'm going to be cold.
4 It's not going to rain.
5 We're not going to fail.
6 She's going to cry.

2
2 are (you and) your family going to have
3 are you going to wake up
4 is the weather going to be like
5 is your teacher going to give
6 are you going to see

must / mustn't
3
2 to learn → learn   **3** going → go   **4** visiting → visit
5 musn't → mustn't   **6** mustn't → don't have to

4
2 mustn't climb   **3** mustn't play   **4** must take
5 mustn't light   **6** mustn't swim   **7** must use
8 must leave

Writing Part 5

1
1 is   **2** in / during   **3** a   **4** must / should   **5** about   **6** you

Vocabulary Extra

The natural world
1a
B winter   **C** autumn   **D** spring

1b
2 B   **3** C   **4** A

2a
2 mountain   **3** desert   **4** lake   **5** river   **6** forest
7 path   **8** beach   **9** sea   **10** island

2b
2 sky   **3** path   **4** forest   **5** Lake   **6** island   **7** beach

Unit 11

Reading Part 3

1
1 C   **2** C   **3** B   **4** B   **5** A

Vocabulary

Parts of the body
1

H	B	A	C	K	H	R	M	O	G
Y	C	B	M	J	V	E	C	S	K
F	Q	A	V	F	Z	G	S	C	I
Z	O	D	M	H	L	N	G	O	G
I	L	O	T	Q	I	H	M	N
K	G	U	T	P	T	F	A	R	U
J	O	K	C	E	N	S	N	A	E
M	I	Y	E	E	H	F	D	Y	L
Z	H	E	A	D	J	E	E	L	E
C	M	U	M	Y	K	B	W	N	G

What's the matter?
2a
2 e   **3** a   **4** f   **5** b   **6** d

2b
2 feel sick   **3** drink some water   **4** go to the dentist
5 lie down in bed   **6** have got a temperature

Listening Part 4

1
1 A   **2** B   **3** C   **4** C   **5** A

1
Boy: I'm sorry I missed class this morning. It was icy and I fell over on my way to school.
Teacher: I'm sorry to hear that. I thought you were at the dentist.
Boy: That was yesterday. I went to the school nurse this morning and I couldn't move my fingers, so she called mum who took me to the doctor.
Teacher: Oh dear. I hope you feel better soon.
2
Tennis coach: What's the matter? You look worried.
Girl: I am! Yesterday the sky was completely blue but look at it today! It's so grey! If it rains then, I won't be able to play the match.
Tennis coach: Don't worry. The weather forecast says the temperature is going to go down but it isn't going to rain until the weekend.
3
Boy: What are you listening to?
Girl: It's a band from Italy. I'm downloading it for Hannah.
Boy: For Hannah? Why?
Girl: Because it's her birthday party this weekend. We're all going to her house on Saturday, remember? I bought her a scarf to go with her dress. I hope she likes it.

4
Teacher: Great work today class! Don't forget that we're meeting tomorrow outside the main entrance to the park at half past nine. Please wear comfortable shoes as it's a five-kilometre walk to the lake. And remember we'll be walking around it taking photos and not going in it. There's no need to bring your swimming things or anything valuable.
5
Girl: What did you think of the show then? We both laughed a lot at the beginning, but when the singer sang …
Boy: Yes, his voice was awful. And the guitar player was only a little bit better. It was so embarrassing!
Girl: I agree with you about that! And I thought the ending was slow and boring. I wanted to leave.
Boy: Me too!

Grammar

First conditional
1
2 won't wear   **3** doesn't rain   **4** don't listen
5 are   **6** 'll pass

2
2 is   **3** rains   **4** will visit   **5** will you do
6 don't hear   **7** am   **8** won't catch
9 Will your mum drive   **10** miss

3 *Sample answers:*
2 If I go shopping this afternoon, I'll buy some new trainers.
3 If I don't go to school tomorrow, my friends won't worry.
4 I'll go to the beach if it's sunny on Saturday.
5 I'll play football with my friends if I meet them at the weekend.

something, anything, nothing, etc.
4
2 something   **3** everyone   **4** Nobody
5 something   **6** someone   **7** anything

5 *Sample answers:*
2 No, I've got nothing to eat in my bag. / No, I haven't got anything to eat in my bag.
3 Yes, somebody in my family goes running every week.
4 Yes, everyone in my class can speak English.
5 No, I did nothing interesting last night / No, I didn't do anything interesting last night.

Writing Part 6

1 What time would like to meet? Where shall we go? Where do you want to have lunch afterwards?

2 *Sample answer:*
Hi Alex
Why don't we meet at 10.30? We could go to the skate park if you like. My mum says we can have lunch at my house.
Best wishes,
Jon

Vocabulary Extra

Health, medicine and exercise
1

ear **2**	eye **4**	face **3**	forehead **9**	hair **1**
head **10**	mouth **6**	nose **5**	tooth **7**	

2

b shoulder	**c** arm	**d** hand	**e** finger	**f** thumb
g back	**h** stomach	**i** leg	**j** knee	**k** ankle
l foot				

3a
2 She's got toothache.
3 You've got a temperature.
4 You've got a broken leg.
5 He's got a headache.
6 You feel sick. / You've got stomach ache.

3b
b Don't go to school. Lie down in bed. **3**
c Drink some water. **6**
d Call an ambulance and go to hospital. **4**
e Take an aspirin. **5**
f Go to the dentist. **2**

4

2nd – second	3rd – third	4th – fourth
5th – fifth	9th – ninth	15th – fifteenth
19th – nineteenth	20th – twentieth	21st – twenty-first
30th – thirtieth	31st – thirty-first	

Unit 12
Reading Part 1

1
1 B   **2** C   **3** C   **4** A   **5** A   **6** B

Vocabulary

Means of transport
1

1 bus	**2** coach	**3** motorbike	**4** boat	**5** tram
6 plane	**7** train			

Secret word: scooter

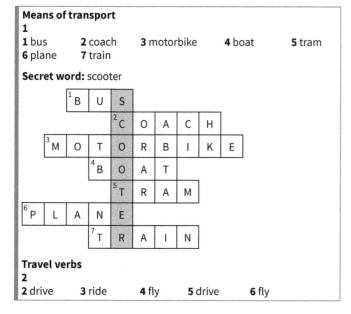

Travel verbs
2

2 drive	**3** ride	**4** fly	**5** drive	**6** fly

Listening Part 2

1
1 4th   **2** 9:30   **3** bus   **4** trainers   **5** bryant

> **Speaker:** Now I'd like to give you some information about your school trip to Lisbon. As 50 of you are now going, the final cost will be £225 and not £250. I know we wanted you to pay for the trip by the sixth of April, but we need the money by the fourth of April instead. Remember the coach leaves from outside the school at a quarter to ten so please be there by half past nine. There has been a change to the programme. On the first day, we planned to take you on one of the city's famous yellow trams, but we're going on a bus tour instead so we can see more of the city. We won't have time to go to the beach, so leave your swimsuits at home, but you need trainers because you'll be doing a lot of walking. If you or your parents need any more information, you can email me at bryant@school.com. I'll spell 'bryant'. It's B-R-Y-A-N-T. I hope everyone has a fantastic time!

Grammar

Present perfect
1a

2 drink	**3** eaten	**4** swum	**5** visit	**6** written

1b

2 haven't written	**3** has swum	**4** haven't drunk
5 has driven	**6** hasn't visited	

2

2 drove → drive	**3** ate → eaten	**4** swum → swam
5 bouth → bought	**6** drank → drunk	

3
2 Have, read   No, I haven't.
3 Has, driven   Yes, he has.
4 Have, travelled   Yes, they have.
5 Have, missed   Yes, I have.
6 Have, been   No, we haven't.

should / shouldn't
4

2 should	**3** should	**4** shouldn't	**5** should	**6** shouldn't

5

2 should take off	**3** shouldn't go	**4** shouldn't eat
5 should see	**6** shouldn't have	

Writing Part 7

1
intresting → interesting; beatiful → beautiful; to → too;
becouse → because

2 *Sample answer:*
It was raining a lot. A girl put on her boots and took the bus to the sports centre but she left her trainers on the bus. She wanted to play volleyball with her friends so she played without her socks on.

Vocabulary Extra

Travel and transport
1
2 helicopter   **3** boat   **4** ship   **5** lorry
6 police car   **7** ambulance   **8** motorbike   **9** taxi
10 underground

2a
2 j   **3** g   **4** b   **5** d   **6** h   **7** a   **8** i   **9** e   **10** f

2b
2 miss   **3** park   **4** sail   **5** catch

3
2 came, come   **3** found, found   **4** flew, flown
5 got, got   **6** heard, heard   **7** left, left
8 met, met   **9** rode, ridden

Unit 13
Listening Part 3

1
1 B   **2** B   **3** C   **4** B   **5** A

Kyra:	There's no school next week, Josh. What are you going to do?
Josh:	Hey, Kyra. I'm going to buy some new clothes for snowboarding.
Kyra:	Oh, are you planning to go snowboarding soon?
Josh:	Yes, Dad isn't free on Thursday or Friday so we're going on Saturday. I can't wait!
Kyra:	Lucky you!
Josh:	Yes, I love it.
Kyra:	I've never gone snowboarding. Is it expensive?
Josh:	Well, I got an excellent pair of boots for ninety pounds and I bought a snowboard that wasn't new, so it was only eighty pounds. And a ticket to go on our local ski mountain is forty pounds a day. So it isn't cheap!
Kyra:	And do you get very tired when you snowboard?
Josh:	Yes, because the day is so long! Dad likes us to get there for nine o'clock so we can ski for an hour before the crowds come at ten. That means we leave home at eight.
Kyra:	Are you out all day?
Josh:	Yes, we are. Why don't you come? You'll have an amazing time.
Kyra:	Oh no! It isn't safe. I might break a leg or something and that would be terrible.

Vocabulary

Adverbs
1
2 My brother can play chess well.
3 My little sister runs quickly.
4 My friends are going to win the competition easily / are easily going to win the competition.
5 I'll carry the cake carefully.
6 We played cards happily / We happily played cards.

Jobs
2
2 journalist   **3** photographer   **4** vet   **5** nurse
6 coach   **7** mechanic

Reading Part 3

1
1 B   **2** C   **3** A   **4** C   **5** A

Grammar

Present perfect with *for* and *since*
1
for: a long time, months
since: last week, my sister's birthday, September

2
2 Our teacher has been ill for three days.
3 I haven't danced since your birthday party.
4 My uncle and aunt have had their car for three months.
5 My best friend hasn't called me since last week.

3
2 How long has your teacher worked at your school?
3 How long have you had your pencil case?
4 How long have you lived in your house?
5 How long has your best friend been at your school?

Sample answers:
2 My teacher has worked at my school for four years.
3 I've had my pencil case since my birthday.
4 I've lived in my house for a long time.
5 My best friend has been at my school since 2010.

may / might
4
2 might go   **3** might call   **4** may see
5 might not be   **6** may not like   **7** might have

5
2 My sister might be late.
3 My friends might not snowboard at the weekend.
4 You may have a broken hand.
5 We might buy a new laptop.

Writing Part 6

1
Invite Gabby to do the course with you; Tell Gabby why you want to do the course; Say when the course begins

2 *Sample answer:*
Hi Gabby,
I'm going to do a photography course. Would you like to join me? I love taking photos but I want to learn how to take better ones. The course starts next Monday.
Write back soon!

Vocabulary Extra

Work and leisure
1a
artist **12**	coach **2**	dentist **4**
journalist **10**	mechanic **6**	nurse **5**
photographer **11**	pilot **1**	receptionist **7**
shop assistant **9**	vet **3**	waiter **8**

1b
listening to music **c**   painting **a**   taking photographs **b**
skateboarding **e**

2
2 e **3** h **4** f **5** d **6** b **7** a **8** c

3a
2 terribly **3** well **4** safely **5** quietly
6 fast **7** noisily

3b
2 well **3** fast **4** terribly **5** safely

Unit 14
Listening Part 5

1
1 C **2** A **3** H **4** B **5** F

Boy:	Hi, Annabelle! What are you reading?
Annabelle:	It's a postcard from my uncle. He's a pilot and he often writes to me when he flies to new places.
Boy:	Does your aunt go with him?
Annabelle:	No, she doesn't. She doesn't like flying, but she sometimes calls me to see how I am.
Boy:	Really? Has your cousin emailed you this week?
Annabelle:	No, he never sends emails. He prefers to write his news on his blog.
Boy:	Oh, cool! Doesn't your brother have his own webpage, too?
Annabelle:	Yes, but he never writes anything there. He usually just sends messages on his phone.
Boy:	Oh yes, I remember your last birthday. We were writing a letter in our French class when you got a message from him. The teacher was really angry.
Annabelle:	Did I say that my grandmother has just sent me card with a funny cartoon on it about texting? I don't know where she gets them from.
Boy:	Awesome!
Annabelle:	Do you know, my mum's phone is broken at the moment. She has to leave us messages on bits of paper instead.

Vocabulary

Communication verbs
1a
2 shout **3** discuss **4** argue **5** chat **6** explain
7 describe **8** persuade

1b
2 argue **3** explain **4** shout **5** describe
6 persuade **7** chat **8** discuss

-ed / *-ing* **adjectives**
2
2 bored → boring
3 worry → worried
4 interesting → interested
5 exciting → excited
6 boring → bored

Reading Part 4

1
1 B **2** A **3** B **4** C **5** A **6** C

Grammar

The passive
1
2 was started **3** was called **4** was used **5** were made
6 is looked **7** were shared **8** are shared **9** are followed

2
2 were painted **3** was called **4** was known **5** is used
6 are given **7** are called **8** is shown **9** was built

3
2 Irish is spoken in Ireland.
3 The first bike was ridden in 1817.
4 Footballs are made of leather.
5 The first email was sent in 1971.
6 Samsung phones are made in South Korea.

Present perfect with *just* / *already* / *yet*
4
2 've / (have) just missed **3** have just gone **4** 've / (have) just had
5 's / (has) just sent **6** 's / (has) just broken

5
2 yet **3** yet **4** already **5** yet **6** already

6
2 A man has just got off the bus.
3 Six people have already sat down in the cinema.
4 Two girls have just arrived.
5 They haven't closed the door yet.

Writing Part 5

1
1 have **2** by **3** than **4** In **5** was **6** any/much

Vocabulary Extra

Communication verbs and adjectives
1
answer **9**	argue **6**	ask **8**	chat **10**	cry **5**
describe **7**	discuss **2**	repeat **1**	shout **4**	suggest **3**

2
2 funny **3** kind **4** noisy **5** clever
6 friendly **7** quiet **8** brave

3
2 interested **3** amazing **4** exciting **5** tired **6** boring

4
2 in **3** at **4** for **5** in **6** from

Acknowledgements

The author and publishers would like to thank the following contributor:

Text design and layout

Wild Apple Design Ltd